PRAISE FOR
THE TELL

"An enjoyable read, particularly for non-specialists; researchers who aspire to write for a popular audience can learn from the author's confident and informative writing style."
—*CHOICE*

"[W]ritten in a style that could have appeared in an article in the *New York Times Magazine* . . . *The Tell* is both entertaining and fascinating, full of interesting information about human beings and their behavior."
—*PsycCRITIQUES*

"Those curious to learn about the powers of observation and the unconscious mind should definitely put this book on their to-read list."
—*Quick Book Reviews*

"Fascinating. . . . *The Tell* succeeds as an engaging tour through current work in the science of behavior by a young psychologist who has the makings of a leading contributor to his field."
—*Shelf Awareness*

"Entertaining . . . in the Malcolm Gladwell-ian tradition."
—*Greater Good: The Science of a Meaningful Life*

"With a punchy style and a flare for digging into our minds, Hertenstein delivers an important message for the modern era."
—*Tulsa Book Review*

"Lively and engaging. . . . Hertenstein offers much material to ponder and suggests that we embrace the power of these tools for helping us predict behavior."
—*Publishers Weekly*

"Highly recommended."
—*Style Magazine*

"After reading his book you might well look upon the world in a different way."
—*The Daily Mail*

THE TELL

TH**E**
TELL

The Little Clues That Reveal
Big Truths About Who We Are

MATTHEW HERTENSTEIN

BASIC BOOKS
A Member of the Perseus Books Group
New York

Hardcover first published in 2013
Paperback published in 2015 by Basic Books,
A Member of the Perseus Books Group

Books published by Basic Books are available at special discounts for
bulk purchases in the United States by corporations, institutions,
and other organizations. For more information, please contact the
Special Markets Department at the Perseus Books Group,
2300 Chestnut Street, Suite 200, Philadelphia, PA 19103,
or call (800) 810-4145, ext. 5000,
or e-mail special.markets@perseusbooks.com.

Book design by Cynthia Young

The Library of Congress has cataloged the hardcover edition as follows:
Hertenstein, Matthew J.
The tell : the little clues that reveal big truths about who we are
/ Matthew Hertenstein.
pages cm
Includes bibliographical references and index.
ISBN 978-0-465-03165-8 (hardback)—ISBN 978-0-465-06988-0 (e-book)
1. Human behavior.   2. Body language.
3. Forecasting—Psychological aspects.   I. Title.

BF199.H47 2013
153.6'9—dc23
2013017834

ISBN 978-0-465-03659-2 (paperback)

10 9 8 7 6 5 4 3 2 1

To Margo

CONTENTS

INTRODUCTION

Every day is fraught with questions, some trivial, others monumental: Where should I go for dinner tonight? Who should I vote for to lead my city, state, and country? Is the person I want to ask out on a date interested in men or women? How will I choose my future spouse? How bright is the person I'm interviewing for a job? Is the person I see in an alley likely to assault me or help me if I trip and fall? Did my spouse just work late last night, or am I being deceived? Is my infant going to develop autism?

Unfortunately, we must often answer these questions without all the information we'd like. Our interactions with others are sometimes ephemeral, like the path of a leaf falling to the ground. As a result, we base our decisions on brief, often barely perceptible glimpses of behavior that occur in a snap of the fingers.

At its very heart, *The Tell* is about the power of prediction based on observations of brief samples of others' behavior. Anyone familiar with the game of poker, whether at the novice or professional level, knows the concept of the "tell," a mannerism that can yield clues about an opponent's cards. Does he hold a flush or a dog hand? Ask professional poker players to evaluate another player's hand, and more often than not, they can give you an accurate assessment—based simply on how an opponent stares, the speed with which he lays down cards, or how quickly he is breathing.

Learning to read other people's tells—to pick up on nonverbal clues that reveal something about them—isn't just a strategy for playing cards, as high as the stakes may be. Small clues, like those that can give away a person's poker hand, can also indicate a number of important outcomes—and not the easy stuff, like whether a guy with a scowl and a clenched fist is about to punch you in the face. Here we're talking about hard predictions—like the outcomes of national elections, the profits of Fortune 500 companies, the likelihood of marital success or failure, and the chances of a child developing autism—all made counterintuitively based on the tells people reveal unwittingly. If you want to know who's going to win the next political election, you should probably ask a roomful of kids. If you want to know whether that company you're thinking of investing in is going to make good money, you'll find the answer written on its CEO's face. If you want to know whether the salesperson you are interviewing will succeed, pay attention not to what she says to you but rather to what she shows you. You'll form some of these impressions nearly instantaneously, whereas you'll make others with deliberation. Either way, a person's tells reveal more about what's behind the curtain than we might realize.

The idea that our brains can make reliably good predictions across many spheres of life runs counter to the recent spate of books that highlight our minds' fallibility. In *Stumbling on Happiness*, for example, Dan Gilbert teaches that we're inept at predicting what will make us happy in life; in *Predictably Irrational*, Dan Ariely lets us know just how regularly we get things wrong. Books of this ilk have sold like gangbusters in the last decade, so it might seem risky to write a book focusing not on where we fall short but on where we succeed—or at least where we're capable of succeeding. Nevertheless, that is the message of *The Tell*.

The key to making accurate predictions, of course, is knowing what tells to look for. In some cases, you may already know, although you may not realize it. You interpret tells, for example, when inferring someone's sexual orientation. In other cases, you may think you know what to look for, but you really don't. This is often the case when we're evaluating others' personalities. And, finally, I'll discuss other cases in which researchers have devised ingenious methods for making good predictions about subjects as wide-ranging as what sort of adult a shy child will become or who your next congressperson will be.

This isn't palm reading or fortune-telling. Instead, by helping you develop and hone your own powers of observation, and by equipping you with findings based on rigorous research in the behavioral and brain sciences, I will show you how to increase your predictive capacities. I hope that after finishing this book, no reader will ever ask for someone's phone number, talk to children, interview a job candidate, enter a boardroom meeting, or vote for candidates in the same way again. This isn't a self-help book promising you a future of entirely accurate predictions. But, by the time we're done, you'll at least be able to see your interactions with others in a much more nuanced and sophisticated way. Perhaps Sherlock Holmes said it best: "I have trained myself to notice what I see."

I hope you'll consider the impressive perceptual and predictive capacities of our minds. Of course, the little clues I discuss in this book don't tell us everything there is to know about other individuals; rather they give us hints about specific, major aspects of who we are. I hope that you will wrestle intellectually with the studies and stories I discuss, as I mean to present none as irrefutable; I aim to begin a dialogue—whether between you and a friend or within the confines of your own mind. If I accomplish that, I will have succeeded in some measure.

Origins of *The Tell*

At this point many authors like to describe how they became interested in the topic of their book. In keeping with that practice, I shall describe a few seminal experiences in my own life that laid the foundation for this writing. But guess what. My story isn't true; nor is any other author's. If the field of psychology has taught us one thing, it's that we confabulate our own reasons for our actions. I *think* I know the origins of this book, but in reality, what follows is my mind's best attempt to construct a causal narrative for why I chose to write it. The same thing can be said for any of our choices in life; we have confidence that we know our reasons for doing something, but we really don't understand our motivations for sure.

With this caveat in mind, I trace the beginnings of this book back to a party I went to years ago when I first arrived in California for graduate school. When I told another guest I was there to study psychology, she quipped, "Matt, why do you want to dedicate yourself to psychology when the entire field is just common sense?" Her remark gnawed at my inse-curities; an awful lot of psychology does seem to be common sense. For example, did you know that children whose parents read to them early in life grow up to be better readers? Or that the greater our social network, the happier we are generally? Even if you didn't, I imagine you aren't surprised to learn that these things are true.

A while later, I shared an apartment with a friend who was studying the neural underpinnings of vision in flies for his PhD in biology. Although he never claimed his research was more important than mine, I always felt somewhat inferior: I was studying a discipline that was, according to some, on the fringe of science. These experiences and others gave me a condition Freud might have described as physics envy. Many consider physics the most privileged science, with rich historical roots, primary laws that make it cohere, and a practicality that enables us to apply its laws to make accurate predictions. I longed for my field to be more like physics and other "real" sciences.

Then I had my first physical encounter with a human brain. Although largely a lump of fat, the brain is more powerful than virtually any computer, capable of both making the precise predictions of physics and also becoming upset at the suggestion that one's lifework is just common sense. How does this piece of matter, this organ, do all that? And, given that prediction is a sine qua non of any science, how can the study of the ways the brain makes those predictions not be a worthy science?

Those experiences form the backdrop for *The Tell*, but the immediate catalyst for the book was the birth of my son Isaac. As a research psychologist whose expertise lies in development and nonverbal communication, I observed almost his every move, analyzing his behavior over the course of his early years. My inclination for analysis enriches my experience of him, but it also sometimes detracts from being "in the moment" with him—a challenge I describe later in the book. Nevertheless, watching him grow has only stoked my interest in prediction. What kind of young man will he become?

Our brains—comprised of 170 billion cells—are capable of making some very surprising predictions about others. I hope that the findings and stories I discuss will surprise you, rather than confirm any suspicions that psychology is commonsensical, and that instead you'll see it as an awe-inspiring science with much to teach us about our futures, others' futures, and ourselves.

And in case you do find yourself in a conversation like I did at that grad school party in which someone suggests psychology is merely common sense, I've taken the liberty of highlighting three of the more "partyworthy" and counterintuitive findings in the book at the end of every chapter.

In the Beginning

1

PRIMITIVE PREDICTIONS

"Prediction is very difficult, especially about the future."
—NIELS BOHR

On December 23, 2004, twenty-nine-year-old Sergeant Henry A. Watt of the US Marine Corps woke to a beautiful sunny day at Base Camp Al-Assad, an Iraqi airbase controlled by the US armed forces. He would go to bed that night a different man.

Watt had served in Iraq for about seven months, leading numerous convoys across the dry Iraqi desert into and out of enemy territory. It was a dangerous job, but Watt and his fellow marines understood the vital function they served.

On this day, Watt's battalion had been assigned to lead a convoy to Al-Qa'im, a town near the Syrian border, to deliver medicine, weapons, and fuel to troops stationed there. Watt rode in a Humvee at the head of the convoy for the five-hour journey. They arrived at their destination around noon, delivered the supplies, and then began the trek back to the base. On the outskirts of Al-Qa'im, Watt spotted an early 1990s Chevy Caprice, painted orange and white, parked on the shoulder.

There was nothing unusual about a car parked beside the road, but Watt became nervous when he locked eyes with the man sitting in the driver's seat. He was in his mid-fifties with a bushy mustache, graying hair, and long vertical folds in his cheeks; his eyes appeared glassy, his cheek muscles clenched. "He looked as though he had pure adrenaline coursing through his veins and had an 'Oh shit' look written on his face," recalls Watt. "I had never seen anything like it in my life."

Sergeant Watt immediately contacted his superior. "There's a bomb in the Caprice I just drove by. We need to stop the convoy!"

"Don't worry about it," his superior said.

Watt was furious. If he was right, soldiers would likely be injured and even killed.

A few minutes later, Watt heard pandemonium on his radio. "It's a bomb!!! It's a f*&^%#$ bomb."

According to Watt, eight combat engineers were maimed because his commander had disregarded his words of warning. To this day, he replays the image of the bomber's face in his mind and wonders how, if heeded, his prediction might have altered fate. Most of us will never have to make a life-and-death prediction based on another person's tells like Sergeant Watt did that day. Still, "prediction is indispensable to our lives," writes Nate Silver in *The Signal and the Noise.* "Every time we choose a route to work, decide whether to go on a second date, or set money aside for a rainy day, we are making a forecast about how the future will proceed—and how our plans will affect the odds for a favorable outcome." The good news is that we humans have an uncanny ability to accurately predict a variety of outcomes based on fleeting nonverbal cues, much like Watt did. The famous physicist Niels Bohr was right: it is tough to make predictions. But it's certainly possible to make good predictions, as we'll discuss in this book.

Caveman Prediction

Pick up a thesaurus, and you'll find an impressive number of synonyms for the word "prediction": foreshadow, foretell, foresee, forecast, prognosticate, envision, and so on down the page. The sheer volume of terms suggests that prediction and its various nuances are fundamental to the human experience. Forecasting future events—whether it's an upcoming flood or the next eclipse—has long fascinated human beings.

The means of foretelling events across the centuries are almost as diverse and plentiful as the words we have to describe prediction. In *The Future of Everything*, David Orrell lists some of these methods:

- Aeromancy: atmospheric conditions
- Astrology: stars and planets
- Bibliomancy: passages of sacred texts
- Cartomancy: tarot cards
- Ceraunoscopy: lightning and thunder
- Chiromancy: palm reading
- Cleromancy: rolling dice/drawing lots
- Crystallomancy: crystal balls
- Haruspicy: animal entrails
- Hippomancy: neighing of horses
- Mathematical models: astronomy, biology, economics
- Moleosophy: moles on the body
- Numerology: numbers
- Oneiromancy: dreams
- Ornithomancy: flight of birds
- Phrenology: shape of head
- Pyromancy: smoke and fire
- Tasseomancy: tea leaves or coffee grounds

I don't know anyone who relies on the neighing of horses or the aroma of coffee grounds to make predictions anymore, but you and I both know plenty of people who rely upon other means, such as the alignment of the stars or tarot cards, to foresee outcomes. And scientists have used mathematical models to forecast a host of phenomena, from the coordinates of celestial bodies to the position of electrons spinning around an atom. Thanks to the early insights of classical philosophers, especially Pythagoras, Plato, and Aristotle, as well as modern-day science and statistics, we can test most of the methods listed above. Predictions derived from quantum theory in physics have proved incredibly accurate, whereas astrology, palm reading, and dreams have not fared well under scrutiny. One reason I love science is that it allows us to test predictions systematically—let the chips fall where they may.

Foibles of the Mind

As I mentioned in the introduction, a slew of articles and books published in the last decade popularize discussion of where our judgments and predictions go awry. Furthermore, pick up just about any cognitive, social, or introductory psychology textbook used by college students across the country, and you'll find a long list of our foibles when it comes to making decisions and predictions. Here are just a few:

- Actor-observer effect
- Anchoring heuristic
- Availability heuristic
- Base rate fallacy
- Belief perseverance
- Change blindness
- Confirmatory bias
- Conjunction fallacy
- False-consensus effect
- Functional fixedness
- Fundamental attribution error
- Halo effect
- Hindsight bias
- Illusion of control
- Illusory correlation
- In-group bias
- Inattentional blindness
- Insufficient justification effect
- Just-world phenomenon
- Loss aversion
- Memory bias
- Mere-exposure effect
- Misinformation effect
- Omission bias
- Optimistic bias
- Peak-end rule
- Planning fallacy
- Primacy effect

- Proactive interference
- Recency effect
- Representativeness heuristic
- Retroactive interference
- Self-fulfilling prophecy
- Self-reference effect
- Self-serving bias
- Source amnesia
- Sunk-cost fallacy

These biases of the mind and others lead to a whole host of botched predictions in our lives. Consider these:

HAPPINESS: We think we know what makes us happy, but often we don't. For instance, many predict that having children will be a source of happiness, but the data show otherwise. If you ask mothers how happy they are engaging in different activities during the day, taking care of their children rates lower than socializing, relaxing, eating, exercising, watching TV, and preparing food. Married couples are near the zenith of their satisfaction together before they have kids; almost immediately upon having children, they become significantly less happy. The trend continues until the kids leave home, when, thankfully, marital happiness increases. So, we may *think* that we're having kids to make ourselves happy, but it just isn't so. We're having kids for other reasons.

THE PLANNING FALLACY: We are miserable at predicting how quickly we can accomplish something or how much money a project will cost. Take the renovation of a kitchen. One study showed that Americans thought turning their dark and dreary kitchens into the bright and cheery ones you see on HGTV would cost $18,658. But, on average, the project actually cost $38,769. In another study, researchers asked college students to estimate how many days they would need to finish their senior theses, giving their most realistic, optimistic, and pessimistic predictions. In their realistic predictions, they estimated needing about thirty-four days, but they actually took about fifty-six days. Only a few students finished by their most optimistic predictions. Moreover, less than half the students finished by their most pessimistic predictions, the number of days they'd need "if everything went as poorly as it possibly could." Plainly stated, we are awful at predicting how expensive projects will be or how long they'll take to complete. Just ask the people who planned the Big Dig in Boston: they originally estimated the project would cost $2.6 billion, but the bill actually ended up being $14.8 billion. The economic cost of war is difficult to predict as well. Case in point: installing a new government in Iraq was estimated to cost $40 billion to $60 billion; it actually cost over $600 billion.

ECONOMICS: Predicting the ups and downs in stock prices is a multibillion-dollar industry; countless magazines, newsletters, television shows, and online articles attempt to foretell which direction specific stocks will take. Jim Cramer, the loud and provocative host of *Mad Money* on cable television, predicts which stocks are good and bad bets on every show. He has two degrees from Harvard University as well as years of practical experience as a stock analyst. You'd think a person with his credentials and experience, coupled with the fact that a major television network chose him to host such a show, would be able to predict the movement of stocks with greater accuracy than pure chance, right? It turns out that, by and large, the stocks he selects perform like the rest of the stock market. Despite his analytical acumen, Cramer's predictive skills are merely average. And he is in good company, as the vast majority of people whose job it is to beat market averages simply do not. In fact, one recent study showed that professional prognosticators correctly predict the direction of stocks only about 47 percent of the time. As I learned in high school when reading economist Burton Malkiel's influential *A Random Walk Down Wall Street,* "A blindfolded chimpanzee throwing darts at the *Wall Street Journal* can select a portfolio that performs as well as those managed by the experts."

POLITICS: On a scale of one to ten, with one representing complete disinterest in politics and ten the fervor of a political junkie, I would rate myself about a six. I enjoy reading about politics and watch the Sunday morning talk shows peopled by the usual onslaught of pundits speculating about who will win the next election. Most of these pundits would rank a ten on my scale, devouring new political information as voraciously as a dog given raw meat. One would expect their political prowess—ostensibly the reason they've been invited to write their columns or appear on news programs—to confer some sort of predictive accuracy. In reality, however, most self-proclaimed political prognosticators are no better than chance at predicting the outcomes of elections. They may as well flip a coin to help them decide.

My impression—and it really is just an impression, as I haven't taken a systematic poll—is that the general public, and perhaps even some students of psychology, believe the mind is largely flawed and unable to make predictions with accuracy. And given the evidence, it's a fair assessment—except when it's not.

The Predictive Mind

Scientists are increasingly coming to the conclusion that the mind is a "prediction machine." Our brains don't merely register the world as we engage in it; rather, they predict, both consciously and unconsciously, what's going to transpire before events unfold. As Jeff Hawkins writes in *On Intelligence*, "Prediction is not just one of the things your brain does. It is the *primary function* of the neocortex, and the foundation of intelligence."

On a daily basis, encounters with numerous people, different visual scenes, and a wide variety of experiences bombard our psyches. From all of this noise, our brains work to identify patterns. If *x* happens, *y* is likely to follow. Most of the time, these associations occur completely below our mental radar, as handling them consciously would overload our minds. Nonetheless, our brains are constantly computing the likelihood of events unfolding in a certain way based on our past experiences.

The origins of our predictive brains lie in our evolutionary heritage. The ability to make accurate predictions about others based on small samples of behavior is advantageous for passing on one's genes. For example, being able to detect swiftly whether someone is likely to attack me or cheat me is very adaptive from an evolutionary perspective, as is quickly assessing the personalities of those around us. Natural selection in part explains why we're so good at making predictions about people. Operating over multiple generations, this process has provided us with a finely tuned and sensitive brain capable of sussing people out even from the subtlest tells. And although we are only beginning to understand the neural mechanisms of the predictive brain, we are well under way.

But the credit for our predictive capacities does not reside solely in our evolutionary heritage. We also owe a lot to our remarkable ability to learn across our lifetimes, a capacity itself based in our evolution, of course. Our infant brains are approximately one-fourth to one-third the size of our adult brains. By maturity, our brains weigh about three pounds and contain approximately 86 billion neurons, each one of which connects with hundreds and thousands of others. Day by day, little by little, interaction by interaction, our brains respond to the environments we inhabit, continually updating themselves with new information, constantly making new associations between environmental events, all of which ultimately results in changes within the brain. Developmental psychologists sometimes refer to this type of learning as "Bayesian learning," referring to the eighteenth-century theologian, philosopher, and mathematician Thomas Bayes. Our predictions are never perfect, but our brains are always calculating the probability of future events transpiring.

Virtually all of us are sophisticated statistical whizzes making millions of calculations over our lives; we just don't know it.

Remaining Humble

I'm obliged to discuss three important caveats. First, as any local meteorologist will attest, it's important to maintain humility in your predictions and avoid forecasting the future on a single-case basis. When projecting the path of a given thunderstorm, a meteorologist is making a public proclamation. We often become frustrated with meteorologists when they're wrong, which happens more often the farther out a given prediction is made in time. We often fail to remember, however, that their predictions are probabilistic.

The job of science is to study empirical generalizations—how things usually are—not certainties. Nearly all sciences make probabilistic predictions. Some are highly accurate, such as quantum theory, which can accurately predict specific properties of electrons "to within about one part in 10^{10}." Other sciences, like meteorology, seismology, medicine, and population genetics, are less accurate. In the behavioral sciences, virtually all relationships between variables are probabilistically associated. Given this, I implore the reader to be cautious when making a prediction about a specific case or example in his or her life based on tells, be it about another's personality, possible deception, or any other inference.

Likewise, it's important to remember that just because you know a person who contradicts a specific statistical trend, that doesn't render the statistical trend invalid. In my introductory psychology class, I tell students about the consistent statistical relation between longevity and conscientiousness. You know who these highly conscientious people are: they're reliable; they plan ahead, cross their t's and dot their i's, and focus on the task at hand. It turns out that, on average, such people live significantly longer than their disorganized, careless, and late counterparts. Almost inevitably, a dubious student raises his hand: "I know someone who lived until he was ninety-five years old, and he was the least conscientious person I've ever met." Or another student says, "I know someone who died when she was forty-five years old, and she was an incredibly conscientious person."

Exceptions like this are not unusual; indeed, psychology is sometimes discredited because "there are always exceptions." These same people would never question the scientific status of medicine, since everyone knows that a certain type of treatment might work for some people but not for others. Numerous scientific disciplines accept the fact that the relationship between variables is probabilistic.

The last caveat I'll leave you with is often overlooked, especially by some journalists who report scientific findings: correlation does not imply causation. Simply put, it's a logical fallacy to assume that just because two variables correlate means that one causes the other. Let's take the finding I described above about conscientious people being likelier to live longer than those who are not very conscientious. These two variables reliably correlate, and if you know the value of one variable, you can predict the likely value of the other. So, if we know that people are highly conscientious, it's a decent bet that they will live longer than folks who are very low in conscientiousness. However, it's impossible to say anything about whether conscientiousness actually *causes* differences in longevity. It may, but it's very possible that other variables—like the fact that conscientious people have better health habits—are playing a causal role.

Many studies I discuss in *The Tell* involve researchers systematically observing the world as it is and identifying reliable links between variables. This allows us to make predictions, but we need to exercise caution when trying to determine which variables are causal. I could remind you of this point throughout the entire book, but because, as Shakespeare reminds us, "brevity is the soul of wit," I'll try to say it only once here.

As mentioned, entire fields of science make predictions based on correlational data. Perhaps the most famous scientist to focus on prediction rather than explanation was Isaac Newton. In his *Principia Mathematica*, he worked out one of the most important predictive models ever devised: when masses are attracted to each other. When Newton published his theory of gravity, his critics faulted him for not describing the mechanism that attracted two objects together and focusing instead on predicting when they would be pulled together. Newton resisted calls to explain his theory by stating, "Hypotheses non fingo," or "I do not feign [propose] hypotheses." Newton refused to provide a causal explanation, content with the predictive power of his insights. Thanks to Albert Einstein and his general theory of relativity, we eventually worked out the mechanism of gravity; the lesson here is that sometimes in the evolution of science, it's important to understand first how variables correlate and to make predictions based on these associations.

With these points in mind, let us begin at the beginning: childhood.

2

THE GENES IN ALL OF US

"We can work with our givens, but we cannot totally escape them. We carry to our graves the essence of the zygote that was first us."

—MARY PIPHER

Before I had a child of my own, I found it difficult to understand how a couple having a baby could find the event so special when it has happened approximately 108 billion times in human history. After my wife gave birth, however, I finally understood the magic of the occasion.

Isaac was born shortly after 9 p.m. one evening and released from the hospital a few days later after recuperating from jaundice. We spent the ensuing weeks in much the same way as most who have a newborn in the home—sleeping only intermittently, reading books on how to care for our infant, and changing poop-filled diapers. Like most new parents, my wife and I were amazed that we had created such a beautiful human being (cliché, I know, but statements like this become cliché because they're often true).

Before Isaac's birth, I promised myself that for the first few weeks of his life I would enjoy him like any other dad and resist the temptation to "experiment" on him. Eventually, however, my curiosity got the better of me, and I began to look at him from the perspective of not only a father but as an expert in development.

Isaac's first few months felt like a marriage of my personal and professional lives. I would stroke both of his palms, for example, and watch his mouth open, eyes close, and neck bend forward in a reflexive response to my touch. When we laid him down on his back, he would almost immediately demonstrate a reflex that caused him to assume a "fencer" position, extending his right leg and both arms simultaneously, as though jousting with a mighty sword in hand. Sheer joy filled those first few months on both a personal and a professional level.

Delight and elation soon turned into concern, followed by alarm. Over the first year and a half of Isaac's life, he developed unusually in a number of ways. He rarely—if ever—gazed into our eyes when we interacted with him. Whereas most kids smiled brightly when tickled or playing peekaboo, his expressions remained muted and joyless. He barely babbled during that first year. Babbling might seem a pointless behavior, but it provides the foundation for language. By his first birthday, Isaac seldom pointed to objects around him to share them with us, as a child that age normally does. He did not crawl until he was about fourteen months old, about twice the age of typically developing kids. Sometimes, he rocked back and forth repetitively, seemingly in his own world.

Isaac's development caused anxiety like I had never experienced; I suspected that he might fall on the autism spectrum, a group of neurodevelopmental disorders characterized by problems in social communication and interaction, as well as by inflexible and repetitive behaviors. The degree of severity varies widely, so children with autism spectrum disorders (ASD) may appear very different from one another, with some of them functioning at relatively high levels and others suffering from severe impairments. Today, 1 in every 110 children falls on the autism spectrum, with a likelihood four times higher in boys than girls. Research has shown ASD to be largely genetic. If one identical twin has autism, the other twin will have the condition 60 to 90 percent of the time. In contrast, if a fraternal twin has autism, the other twin will have it only 0 to 10 percent of the time. Clearly, genes play a pivotal, though not exclusive, role in the development of ASD.

I worried about the genetic hand Isaac may have been dealt and what that portended for his future. Would he joke and laugh with us while playing childhood games? Would he have the social skills to play team sports like soccer or baseball? Would he have close friends? Would he be capable of finding a job? Would we be caring for our child for the rest of our lives? These questions and many others plagued me. I couldn't help but imagine all of the possible outcomes for him, none of them particularly good.

I don't want to overstate the anxiety I felt, as I also experienced many moments of joy with my son, but the fact that some of my research and teaching centered on infants made it impossible for me to stop analyzing his development, compounding my worry. By the time Isaac was born, observing infants analytically had become ingrained in me.

When I expressed concern to my friends and Isaac's physicians that he was showing some red flags for autism, they often said, "Wait and see. He's so young." I didn't like hearing this at the time, but it made sense, considering that most children don't ultimately get diagnosed until age four, and sometimes even later. The problem is that waiting to diagnose a child until age four or five may significantly reduce the effectiveness of subsequent treatment.

A dynamic interaction between genes and the environment shapes specific neural pathways, building the brain over time from the bottom up. Thus, the environmental interventions that take place in a child's life literally change the neural connections that a brain makes; much as Michelangelo sculpted *David* and the *Pietà*, the environment molds the brain. Moreover, we know that brain plasticity—the degree to which experience can shape the brain —decreases with age. So intervening early and often, as opposed to "waiting to see," is key to an attempt to change the developmental course of a child's life.

A growing body of evidence demonstrates the power of early intervention in treating potential autism. "What you ultimately might be doing," according to one expert, "is preventing a certain proportion of autism from ever emerging. . . . I'm not saying you're curing these kids, but you may be changing their developmental trajectory enough by intervening early enough that they never go on to meet criteria for the disorder. And you can't do that if you keep waiting for the full disorder to emerge."

This approach is akin to conducting computed tomography (CT) scans on people to determine if they are suffering from heart disease prior to their having a potentially life-ending heart attack. We don't wait for a person to have a heart attack; we try to catch the condition in its earliest stages and prevent its progression by modifying diet and exercise. Of course, just as we wouldn't be able to save all people from heart attacks, it's unlikely that we'll be able to completely prevent the onset of autism, but it's worth trying.

The good news is that researchers have begun to identify early and reliable markers that predict the diagnosis of autism earlier than age four, when most children are diagnosed. The bad news is that none of these "baby tells" are biological, so a simple blood test or brain scan can't tell us which children will fall on the autism spectrum. If only it were this easy. Instead, a host of behavioral tells, or nonverbal cues, which happen briefly but intermittently throughout the first year and a half of life, enable us to reliably predict who will develop autism and who will not.

The way researchers uncovered these warning behaviors is an excellent lesson in how good science is done. At first, they relied on case studies in the literature as well as parental histories and reports, methods that suffer from numerous pitfalls (e.g., finding that a particular behavior predicts autism for one child doesn't necessarily mean that you will find the same behavior predicting autism for another child). Finally, in the early 1990s, a team of researchers in France analyzed home movies of children who eventually developed ASD. These retrospective studies represented the first direct evidence of the behavioral markers they were looking for. But this method also had its problems, as parents don't always video-record their children in a variety of settings performing a variety of tasks.

What was really needed were studies in which researchers could assess many different developmental domains—cognitive, social, physical—in infants before they developed ASD. But there was one major problem: only 5 in 10,000 children received ASD diagnoses in the 1990s. Researchers would have to bring a staggering number of kids into the lab to find enough who would eventually develop ASD. However, teams in the United States, England, Sweden, and Israel employed a very clever design to work around this issue. They identified children with ASD and studied their younger siblings, a group at twenty times greater risk for developing the condition. This allowed investigators to conduct prospective studies comparing high-risk infants to low-risk infants from families without a history of autism, which was crucial to understanding which behavioral cues actually predict ASD.

The table on page 18 includes a list of the major domains of development in which delays or atypical progress are harbingers for an ASD diagnosis.

When I talk to others about the diversity of symptoms that actually predict autism, they are usually surprised. People sometimes consider autism a purely communicative disorder, but ASD affects multiple areas of children's lives. I witnessed this in Isaac, when his smiling behavior, his language, and many aspects of his motor development—sitting up, crawling, and walking—were delayed by months. Also, he often wouldn't respond to the call of his name.

Pediatric specialists confirmed my concerns as legitimate red flags, and a brain scan showed some abnormalities, suggesting something might be awry. As Isaac was only six to nine months old, the doctors did not diagnose him with autism, as that's not formally possible until the age of two to three years. Still, we provided aggressive early intervention for him in the hopes of rewiring his brain and changing his developmental trajectory. We spent hundreds of hours with Isaac implementing empirically supported behavioral therapies to help him.

I'm forever grateful to the researchers whose work I relied on to help me identify Isaac's potential ASD. Today, he is a healthy boy who shows no symptoms of autism. Did the therapy really wire his brain differently than it would have wired itself had we done nothing? I'll never know the answer definitively. As a scientist, I know that a case study gives one little, if any, ability to infer causation. However, when it came to my son, I thought it was better to provide potentially life-altering intervention as early as possible rather than to wait and see. I suspect that most other parents would have done the same thing if they knew which early signs predicted autism.

I Was Just Born That Way

Can we predict other developmental outcomes with predominantly genetic origins from behavior early in life?

I began to ponder this question during the summer after I graduated from college in Iowa. As I would be heading to graduate school on the

Early Signs of Autism

Social-Communication (lack of/atypical...)	Play	Language and Thinking (lack of/atypical/delayed...)	Sensory and Motor
Eye gaze and sharing attention with others	Reduced imitation of adults' actions with objects	Cognitive development	Atypical visual tracking
Positive emotion (presence of more negative emotion)	Excessive exploration of objects and toys	Babbling	Visual fixation
Smiling with others	Repetitive actions with objects and toys	Language comprehension	Unusual inspection of objects
Social interest and shared enjoyment		Language production, (e.g., odd first words or unusually repetitive word use)	Under- and/or overreaction to stimulation (e.g., sounds)
Orientation to a person when name is called		Unusual voice tone	Decreased activity levels
Pointing to objects		Loss of early words	Delayed motor skills
Emotional engagement and connectedness			Repetitive and atypical motor behaviors
			Atypical postures

West Coast to study child development, I thought it prudent to spend the summer observing children in a naturalistic setting, as I knew I'd spend most of my graduate education inside a laboratory. (I was right.)

I landed a job at a camp in Illinois, about twenty miles from my parents' Wisconsin home. Located in the middle of a forest on 150 acres, the camp aimed to promote leadership and life skills in campers who ranged in age from early elementary through junior high school grades.

One particular child made an impression on me like few others. When I first met William, I stuck out my right hand, introduced myself, and asked him his name. (I like to shake hands with kids because I think it's beneficial for them to learn how to interact with adults if they don't already know.) William, who had just finished kindergarten, physically recoiled.

As every child reacts differently when meeting a new person, I didn't give his response much thought at first. But the consistency of his behavior was striking. On numerous occasions over the summer, he was extremely timid and reticent, especially when encouraged to explore a new activity. I introduced a game called "Flinch" to the kids in his group. This simple game requires the kids to stand in a circle with one person—me to start—in the middle. The person in the middle tosses a ball to the people in the circle, and it is their job to catch it, but they must resist moving their hands up to catch the ball—i.e., flinching—if the person in the center feigns a toss to them.

After some coaxing, William joined the circle. At first, I softly tossed the ball to a few children, and they caught the ball each time. I then faked a toss to a few kids; about three-fourths of them flinched, and the rest successfully resisted the temptation. When I faked a toss to William, he cried and fell to the ground. William had a long day.

William did not fall on the autism spectrum, but he was one of the most restrained and anxious children I had ever observed to that point. Some kids approached new games and other novel activities with verve, but William approached them with extreme caution—if he approached them at all.

What contributes to the variability in children's reactions to unfamiliar and unexpected events? Was it the genes William inherited from his parents, or the way they raised him, or perhaps a combination of the two? I began to wonder what William had been like as an infant. Did he chronically cry and become upset, or was he like most infants who cry less after the first two months of life? Finally, I wondered what life was going to be like for William. Would he grow up happy and fulfilled, or was he destined to live an anxiety-ridden existence?

At the end of the summer, I packed my few belongings and headed to graduate school. There, I tested numerous infants in the laboratory, and immediately I noticed stark differences in how they behaved. When we applied equipment to infants to measure their heart rates, some kicked and arched their backs, screaming at the top of their lungs. Others were incredibly docile, cooperative, and calm.

During that first year, I immersed myself in the work of Jerome Kagan at Harvard University; for much of his long career, he had been studying high-strung children like William and some of the more spastic infants I encountered in the lab. One of his main foci has been following children who show high degrees of behavioral inhibition, that is, kids who exhibit vigilance, wariness, and anxiety in the face of new situations, new people, or new objects. Researchers attribute this behavioral orientation, like autism, largely to genetic factors.

Kagan's pioneering research shows the sometimes long-term effects of behavioral inhibition early in life. His and other research finally answered many of the questions I had about William.

One of Kagan's most famous studies focused on full-term Caucasian infants in the Boston area, many of whom he and his team followed until their mid- to late teens. Imagine that investigators have invited you and your sixteen-week-old baby to Kagan's lab, just as they have about five hundred other infants and parents. At the experimenter's request, you place your child in a comfortable baby seat with a video camera aimed directly at his body. A forty-five-minute battery of tests ensues in which the experimenter presents many different, odd, and novel stimuli: he or she plays recorded sentences and nonsense sounds in the baby's ears, shakes mobiles full of colorful dangling objects back and forth in front of his face, and places a pungent smelling cotton swab below his nostrils. Kagan and his colleagues were interested in motor behaviors such as back arching and limb movements, as well as emotional displays such as crying and smiling. Essentially, Kagan orchestrated a situation in which numerous infant tells would be on display for systematic examination.

About one in every five babies, according to Kagan, "extend their arms and legs in momentary spasticity, display bursts of vigorous limb activity, and, on occasion, arch their backs to the presentation of the stimulus events. Further . . . these infants fret or cry." Kagan called these infants "high-reactives." Two in every five infants, in contrast, were cool as cucumbers; they didn't cry or move much in response to the stimuli. Kagan called these infants "low-reactives." The remainder of the sample fell somewhere between these two groups in terms of their behavior.

Kagan invited many of these same infants to his lab repeatedly when they were toddlers, children, adolescents, and young adults. Like others who study behavioral inhibition, Kagan found remarkable stability in the behavioral and physiological profiles of the children going into adulthood. So a four-month-old's behavior in a simple lab procedure predicts his subsequent development through childhood and into adulthood; we can predict which individuals will become the Williams of the world from their behavior in infancy.

In his book *Galen's Prophecy*, Kagan recounts the experience of a child named Laura, a high-reactive baby and later an inhibited child. Laura's parent brought her as a four-month-old into Kagan's lab for the forty-five-minute series of tests. From the outset, Laura squirmed and thrashed her legs. When the experimenter dangled the mobiles in front of her face, she soon began to arch her back and cry intensely. Kagan had to bring the session to a halt because Laura was too distressed to finish. When Laura visited Kagan's lab again at nine months old, she cried when her mother unveiled a toy dinosaur before finally turning away from it and shrinking back in a chair. At fourteen months, Laura cried when placed on the floor in the warm-up period before the tests began, something less than 5 percent of the kids in the study did. Her distress only seemed to increase during her visit; she cried and fretted when a stranger came into the room and when the experimenters applied heart-rate monitors and a blood pressure cuff. She refused to insert her hands into cups full of liquid and would not allow the experimenter to put liquid into her mouth. When Laura was twenty-one months old, the trend continued. She ran to her mother when a stranger entered the room and did the same thing later when a clown entered, crying and saying, "No, no, no."

Low-reactive infants were significantly more likely to be sociable with the experimenters and approach the laboratory tasks enthusiastically. Kagan describes a subject named Anna who, in contrast to Laura, showed little motor movement and distress at four months of age. As a toddler and young child, Anna was fearless; she enthusiastically placed her hands into cups of liquid, happily allowed the experimenters to place heart-rate monitors and blood pressure cuffs on her, and eagerly approached strangers, clowns, and toys.

The behavioral trends differentiating high- and low-reactives continued into adolescence. When experimenters interviewed the fifteen-year-old adolescents, high-reactives smiled infrequently and were tense, whereas low-reactives commonly smiled and were relaxed, just as when they were infants. Kagan and his team also assessed how "sanguine" and "dour" the adolescents were. The adolescents who had been high-reactive infants, compared to their counterparts, thought of themselves as serious people who thought too much before deciding what to do. They wished they were more relaxed and didn't consider themselves as easygoing as the low-reactives. High-reactives also reported serious worry in response to unfamiliar situations relative to low-reactives.

Kagan describes one fifteen-year-old adolescent boy who had been diagnosed with social anxiety disorder. When he came to the lab as a four-month-old, like other high-reactives he arched his back and maintained a sullen expression throughout the tests. Later, in childhood, he would shriek at the top of his lungs when a stranger entered the room or when the experimenter tried to place equipment on him. According to Kagan, the boy felt "panicky" in crowds and thus spent a lot of time alone in his bedroom playing video games. As a teen, the boy missed numerous days of high school because of his anxiety. "This boy's longitudinal record," says Kagan, "invites the conclusion that his high-reactive temperament made a substantial contribution to his current mood and personality profile."

The Physiology of Temperament

Are there physiological differences between high- and low-reactive children? The answer is unequivocally yes. Kagan and others have uncovered a multitude of physiological correlates that differentiate them. When the infants in Kagan's studies were eleven and fifteen years old, more than five times as many high-reactives as low-reactives showed more right-frontal electroencephalogram activation, associated with negative emotionality and the stress response. The cardiovascular systems of high- and low-reactives also differ, the former showing increased sympathetic nervous system activation (i.e., fight-or-flight response). Finally, adults who were high-reactive infants go on to develop a thicker right ventromedial prefrontal cortex, whereas low-reactive infants develop a thicker left orbitofrontal cortex. Just think: the tells elicited by an infant in a simple forty-five-minute procedure can predict her brain circuitry eighteen years later.

These physiological differences led Kagan and his colleagues to examine one brain structure that influences these biological correlates: the amygdala. Located within the base of the temporal lobe of the brain, the amygdala—the name derives from the Greek word for "almond" and describes the shape of the structure—helps us detect and respond to alarming stimuli in the environment. In a landmark study published in *Science*, Kagan and his colleagues followed up with individuals who were then in their early twenties, thirteen of whom were categorized as inhibited as young children and nine as uninhibited. Kagan placed his subjects into a functional magnetic resonance imaging, or fMRI, machine, which measures the activity of the brain. He first showed the subjects pictures of several people's faces to obtain a baseline measure of activity in the brain. He then showed them another set of faces, some of which had appeared in the first set and some of which had not.

Were the amygdalae of the adults who had been inhibited as toddlers more reactive to unfamiliar faces compared to those of the adults who had been uninhibited as children? I would have loved to be sitting next to Kagan when he learned the results of this study. For decades, he had found indirect evidence that the amygdala held the key to the difference between timid and bold children. Now, for the first time, he had direct support; the amygdalae of adults who had been timid when young were significantly more responsive to novel faces than those of their counterparts. "Our findings," remarked one of Kagan's colleagues, "both support the theory that differences in temperament are related to differences in amygdala function, something earlier technology could not prove, and show that the footprint of temperamental differences observed when people are younger persist and can be measured when they get older."

Shy and cautious kids develop amygdalae similar to overly sensitive car alarms; they respond at full volume to the slightest perturbation. Kagan and his colleagues think that unfamiliar events, especially those that are unexpected, activate the amygdala and other brain structures, creating a heightened internal state in high-reactive children. That high-reactives experience this more strongly than low-reactives helps explain the former's subsequent cautiousness and anxiety in unfamiliar situations. At present, this is a provisional explanation, but it's the best guess as to what's happening in the brains of high-reactives.

Just as genetics does not necessarily doom a child to developing autism, Kagan's data show us that biology is not destiny when it comes to inhibition, a point parents would do well to keep in mind if they have a high-reactive child. Due to heredity, children have neural presets in the brain, but the brain shows incredible plasticity. Not all high-reactives remained shy at eleven or fifteen years of age in Kagan's studies. By these ages, kids can control their displays and behaviors toward others. Some of the cautious behavior observed in preadolescence and adolescence among the high-reactive infants had dissipated; biology did not impair their ability to cope with strangers and unfamiliar situations. However, high-reactives rarely turned into the bubbly, effervescent children that low-reactives were more likely to become. Just as some people lack the cognitive machinery to become theoretical physicists, no matter how hard they might try, most high-reactives lack the biological underpinnings to become outgoing and spontaneous with low physiological arousal. Likewise, low-reactives rarely became reticent introverts and physiologically reactive. By age eleven, according to Kagan, fewer than 5 percent of the children in the high- and low-reactive groups had "switched" behavioral and physiological profiles; it's highly unlikely that a high-reactive infant will turn into a laid-back kid or a low-reactive infant will become a bundle of nerves. Both groups tended to maintain their respective behavioral profiles or drift toward the middle.

If our biological predispositions are malleable, what environmental inputs might influence the biological bias of high-reactives? Kagan proposes several possibilities.

- Mothers who gently encourage their high-reactive infants and toddlers to explore their environments, rather than trying to protect them from unfamiliar situations tend to have less timid children later on.
- Excessive parental criticism may generate high amounts of anxiety in high-reactive children, thereby exacerbating their already anxious nature.

- Parental role models likely influence the expression of biology. If a high-reactive infant grows up observing an anxiety-ridden mother or father, she may perceive her own anxiety and cautiousness as inherited and play the part. In contrast, a high-reactive who observes an assertive parent may come to believe that she too is bold and behave accordingly.
- Kagan believes that the broader environment in which a high-reactive is raised may influence her subsequent development. An extremely shy child among a sea of bold children leads to a contrast effect, both for the child and parents. The dissimilarity may itself exacerbate shyness.

The early detection of autism and Kagan's research on early temperament have at least two things to teach us.

First, it's possible to make some fairly accurate predictions about what people will be like based on relatively fleeting behaviors in infancy. In the case of autism, these behaviors happen intermittently in the first year or so of life and beyond, whereas Kagan's work shows that infant behavior, demonstrated within a single forty-five-minute laboratory procedure, contains some predictability. Chances are that investigators would have classified William as a high-reactive infant had he participated in one of Kagan's studies. He'll likely remain a cautious person to some degree throughout his life. Next time you interact with a socially anxious person in the workplace or elsewhere, keep in mind that he was quite possibly born with a physiological profile that pushed him in this direction.

Second, both autism and temperament research indicates that genes play a significant role in who we become, but they don't determine who we are. As one psychologist once remarked, "Heredity deals the cards; environment plays the hand." The brain is much more malleable than once thought, and intervening to prevent the onset of autism or socializing an anxious child to handle the world more adaptively may have a powerful effect on how an individual turns out. I'll never know if my son would have been on the autistic spectrum had I not intervened, but what's the harm in trying to prevent it? It's incumbent on caregivers and educators to realize the power of their influence to reshape the brains of children.

Party-Worthy Findings

1. **Prediction of autism:** Even though children do not usually receive an autism diagnosis until they are about four years old, we can observe the tells of autism in the first year and a half of life.

2. **Prevention of autism:** There's growing evidence that early environmental interventions may actually prevent the onset of autism. Early intervention may rewire the brain to alter the course of potential ASD.

3. **Stability of temperament:** From a single forty-five-minute lab procedure in infancy, researchers can predict who will likely be the most cautious and anxious among us.

3

STRANGE SITUATIONS:
GROWING UP IN A THIN-SLICED WORLD

"What is learned in the cradle lasts to the grave."
—FRENCH PROVERB

M y town has a wonderful fenced-in playground with several slides, swings, teeter-totters, and swinging bridges. Over the last couple of years, I've taken my son there to play numerous times. My wife thinks I go because it makes him happy, but I'm there just as much for myself. There's nothing like watching children swirl around on a tire swing at blazing speeds until they're laughing in hysterics.

Some of the most interesting interactions I observe transpire between the children and their parents. One visit I saw a three-year-old child who was deathly afraid to leave his mother's side. This boy wanted nothing to do with exploring and clung to his mom's knee for comfort throughout their visit. Some time later, another child of similar age came to the park with his mom. Although cautious on the equipment, this little boy was more than willing to run far away from his mother, making eye contact with her only occasionally. He showed no signs of distress when she left to use the restroom, asking me to watch him momentarily. Her absence seemed of little consequence.

Both boys were emotionally connected to their parents, but their styles were very different. Developmental psychologists have been interested in these differences for decades, as well as in how young children become attached to their caregivers in the first place. Can we predict the behavioral styles of the boys described above? What causes differences in how children become emotionally tied to their caregivers? Will the first boy eventually develop an anxiety disorder while the second takes life in stride? Will the second boy have the self-confidence to become class president, while the first stays in the social shadows? Questions like these have occupied developmental psychologists' attention for decades, and their findings have shed light on the predictive power of childhood tells.

Supplanting Old Theories with a New One

For much of the twentieth century, the dominant view in psychology was that infants formed emotional attachments to their caregivers because mothers provided nourishment. Theorists from the psychoanalytic camp held that mothers provide oral gratification during breast feeding and therefore become associated with reduction of the hunger drive. Learning theorists, such as B. F. Skinner, explained the child's tie to her mother by arguing that mothers become associated with the food they provide. For both camps, provision of food to the infants resulted in subsequent attachment.

Yet, there was a problem: the data did not support these explanations. Nobel Prize–winning biologist Konrad Lorenz accidentally discovered that baby geese, shortly upon hatching, follow the first object—animate or otherwise—they see moving in their environment, irrespective of whether or not that object provides them with food. Another set of ingenious studies conducted by Harry Harlow and his colleagues at the University of Wisconsin showed that monkeys reared in isolation from their mothers became attached to objects that provided them with the physical touch they craved instead of food.

Pulling from Lorenz, Harlow, and others, English psychologist John Bowlby advanced a theory that radically changed our conception of the child's tie to her caregiver. Bowlby's "attachment theory" proposed that all infant humans and other ground-dwelling primates possess a biologically based "attachment behavioral system" that evolved through natural selection to promote survival. By genetically prewiring into our brains the impulse to keep our caregivers close by, this system maximizes our survival in potentially dangerous or stressful situations.

We've all witnessed the activation of this system in the child who cries and crawls to her mother when she is left at day care or an infant who coos, gurgles, and smiles to coax a caregiver closer. Unlike many other animals that flee to a burrow or den for protection, young primates depend on their caregivers for protection from starvation, predation, exposure to the elements, and other dangers, so the attachment behavioral system kept our Pleistocene ancestors safe.

To Be Secure or Insecure? That Is the Question

While formulating his theory, Bowlby placed an advertisement in the *London Times* seeking a researcher to help study early childhood and personality development. Mary Salter Ainsworth answered; she, her collaborators, and students would go on to conduct some of the most important research in psychology allowing us to predict so many fascinating life outcomes based on the nonverbal tells of infants.

In her most well-known study, Ainsworth and her colleagues observed twenty-six infants and their mothers interacting in their homes every three weeks during the infants' first year of life. She noted how infants emitted attachment behaviors like crying and crawling and how their mothers responded to these signals. At the end of the year, Ainsworth invited the babies and their mothers to her laboratory and had them participate in a procedure called the "strange situation," now one of the most famous controlled laboratory paradigms in psychology.

The procedure, which lasts approximately twenty minutes, comprises eight episodes, all of which take place in an unfamiliar toy-filled room at a researcher's lab. In the strange situation, Ainsworth asked a mother to enter and leave the room a couple of times, once leaving the infant with an experimenter and another time leaving the infant alone. The procedure was meant to be stressful enough to activate the child's attachment behavioral system, akin to going to the doctor's office or being dropped off at day care for the first time. Of interest was how the infants reacted when mom left and returned to the room.

Ainsworth identified three primary categories based on the degree to which the strange situation activated her subjects' attachment behavioral system (e.g., eliciting crying, crawling, outstretched arms) and the degree to which the infants explored their environment. Mary Main and her colleagues added a fourth classification about two decades later.

I had the good fortune to take a class taught by Mary Main in my first year of graduate school. As one of Ainsworth's former graduate students, Main is one of the world's leading authorities on attachment as well as one of the most kindhearted and sophisticated thinkers you will ever meet. As part of this course, she showed us several video recordings of strange situations; watching how differently these one-year-old children reacted when their mothers left and returned to the room was eye opening.

Secure Attachment	Insecure Attachment
Secure	Avoidant
	Ambivalent-resistant
	Disorganized-disoriented

I observed films of kids who fell into four different categories, as listed in the table above. The first category I describe includes infants considered to be "securely attached" in the strange situation, whereas those in the last three categories I describe fall under the umbrella of "insecure attachment" styles.

The four categories are as follows:

SECURE ATTACHMENT: I remember one child in the strange situation who cried intensely when his mother walked out of the room, leaving him alone with the stranger. When she returned, he crawled quickly to her, stretched his arms toward her, and clung to her body, while she confidently caressed the child on the back. Touch is the ultimate signal of safety and security, just as Harlow taught us with his monkeys. After his mother had soothed him, the boy happily cruised over to the toys in the room and began exploring his environment.

The majority of US children are deemed "secure" in the strange situation, like this boy: he showed signs of missing his mother when separated and was glad to see her upon reunion but was subsequently able to explore his environment. Children with secure histories have caregivers who are sensitive and responsive to their emotional cues. These parents respond promptly when their infants cry, provide appropriate stimulation during interactions, and are generally available and warm.

INSECURE AVOIDANT ATTACHMENT: Another boy I observed in the strange situation didn't seem to care when his mother left; he continued to play with the toys, barely detecting her departure from the room. Upon her return, he ignored her and continued playing as though nothing had happened. Children like this boy, who show little concern for the parent's departure and avoid the parent upon reunion, are deemed "avoidant." These children often have attachment figures who are insensitive or unresponsive to their baby's emotional signals; they tend not to respond to the infant's cries, to overstimulate the infant, and to reject physical contact.

INSECURE AMBIVALENT-RESISTANT ATTACHMENT: One child I observed outstretched her arms for the mother to pick her up upon reunion; yet when the mother did so, the infant began to slap her mother's face with one hand and tug on her hair with the other. She was clearly angry and couldn't settle down enough to explore the environment. Children like this are categorized as "ambivalent-resistant." They show distress both when the mother leaves the room and when she returns, and they are often inconsolable and sometimes angry toward their parent. Unlike securely attached children, they are unable to gather their emotions and venture out into the room again. Infants like this tend to have caregivers who are inconsistently responsive to their emotional signals; sometimes they'll pick up their infant's emotional signals and do something about them; sometimes they will not. From the infant's perspective, it's somewhat of a crapshoot.

DISORGANIZED-DISORIENTED ATTACHMENT: One child crawled to his mother when she entered the room, just as a securely attached child would, but then a few feet away from her, he froze like a statue. He stayed frozen on all fours for about twenty seconds in a trancelike state. Another child approached his parent upon reunion, but did so with his head turned away from her, as if to protect himself. A third child began to rock back and forth on his hands and knees for several seconds. Strikingly bizarre behaviors like these are evident in about 15 percent of kids in low-risk samples. Researchers deem these children "disorganized-disoriented." Infants who behave oddly, like these three, often don't have sensitive and emotionally responsive parents. Rather, the parents are usually frightening to or demonstrate abnormal interactions with their children.

The most egregious cases of frightening behavior occur when parents abuse children physically. On identifying their attachment status, researchers categorize the majority of abused children as disorganized-disoriented. In one study, for example, investigators categorized 82 percent of maltreated infants as disorganized-disoriented, whereas only 19 percent in a control group fell into this category.

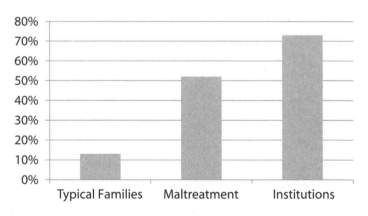

Average percentage of infants deemed disorganized-disoriented in typical families, maltreatment samples, and institutions.

Kids raised in orphanages and similar institutional settings don't fare any better; about three of every four are classified as disorganized-disoriented. Kids reared in an institution rarely have their attachment needs met; no consistent caregiver is around to be sensitive and responsive to their emotional cues. The figure above illustrates the average elevated risk for disorganized-disoriented attachment insecurity in maltreated children and those raised in institutions compared to those living in typical families. If an infant is raised in an institution or maltreating family, the odds are significantly greater that the infant will be classified as disorganized-disoriented.

Frightening and abnormal behaviors do not occur exclusively in abusive or institutional settings. Once, I was waiting in the lobby of my son's dentist's office, when a woman entered with her two children. The mother removed her infant's winter coat, and the baby boy promptly crawled over to the play area across the room. He picked up a toy and began to bang it on the floor; in response, the mother jumped up from her seat, walked quickly to the infant, pulled him up abruptly by the wrist, and removed the toy. As she did this, she made a strange sound three or four times—"psstt, psstt, psstt"—only inches away from his ears. The child was visibly alarmed. After this incident, the baby played for awhile quite happily, but when he tripped and fell, the mother responded by giggling and remaining in her seat. The baby just looked at her. Several studies suggest the outcome of the mother's unusual behavior: when parental emotional communication with infants is consistently abnormal, like the mother's above, infants are significantly more likely to be deemed disorganized-disoriented.

Researchers theorize that unlike infants in the first three categories, infants deemed disorganized-disoriented do not have a coherent strategy to deal with the stress they endure in life. Children classified as secure and ambivalent-resistant go to the mother during times of stress in the strange situation. Children deemed avoidant play with their toys when mom leaves them alone. In all cases, the children employ adaptive strategies that help them cope with the events at hand. It's as if, in the children's minds, they are saying to themselves, Okay, I'm really scared and anxious, but I can deal with this. In contrast, theorists think there is a breakdown in the behavioral strategies of children classified as disorganized-disoriented. For these kids, their caregivers are simultaneously the source of comfort (like other kids) and of fear (unlike other kids). The paradox causes them to shut down in times of stress, akin to a running car engine locking up if it runs out of oil.

What Can We Predict from Differences in Attachment?

These studies reveal a larger, long-range issue: the strange situation represents one of the most predictive snapshots of infant tells ever devised.

A mountain of research shows that secure attachment signifies a host of beneficial consequences compared to the alternative attachment styles. Children deemed secure are significantly more self-reliant and confident in life. I see this when I observe my wife's classroom (she teaches first grade). Some kids independently do their work, occasionally asking the teacher for help appropriately; others constantly seek the teacher's help, even when it's unnecessary. Secure attachments engender self-confidence; these children know that they can influence their world and achieve their goals through their efforts. Children deemed insecure have a history in which their efforts have often fallen on deaf ears, preventing them from developing the confidence to achieve in the world.

The emotional lives of children also differ as a function of their attachment history. Again, it only takes a few hours in any elementary school classroom to see differences in how kids display their emotions. When I volunteer in my son's kindergarten class, the teacher asks that I take three kids at a time into a room and read them a story. Afterward, each of the students sits at a computer to take a comprehension quiz on the book. Those who pass receive as a reward a bead for a special necklace given to them by the teacher at the beginning of the year to track progress; those who fail must watch as others obtain their beads. (I always find this uncomfortable.) Some take their failure in stride and comment that they'll try to pass the quiz the next time. Others, however, become very upset and angry; one child once picked up the computer keyboard and slammed it on the table. Kids who behave angrily and aggressively like this are significantly more likely to be deemed avoidant or disorganized-disoriented, perhaps as a response to chronic rejection from, odd emotional communication with, or frightening behaviors on the part of the caregiver.

Even more revealing are the kids' reactions to a child who has just failed the quiz. Some of the kids are indifferent to the failing child, but others show a heartening degree of empathy. One student named John reached over to a girl who had just failed and patted her on the shoulder, remarking, "Don't worry. You can get a bead next time. I know you can do it." Children like John are more likely to be securely attached.

In one of my favorite studies examining emotions and peer interaction (albeit one I find disheartening), researchers at the University of Minnesota assessed infants' attachment in the strange situation. When these same kids were preschoolers, the researchers invited them, two of the same gender at a time, to play in a room together. They videotaped the preschoolers and later had expert judges examine the tapes to determine who among the children were the victimizers and the victims. Victimizers were those kids who verbally or physically assaulted their peers. In one interaction, a child deemed avoidant began calling another child "bugger nose," "bugger face," and "hey poop." After a few minutes of verbally antagonizing his victim, the victimizer began taking the victim's toys and throwing them. Other victimizers went further, punching their victims or physically assaulting them in other ways.

The researchers had identified all of the victimizers in these interactions as avoidant in the strange situation a few years earlier, whereas they had classified none of the victims as secure in the strange situation; victims were always children they had deemed avoidant or ambivalent-resistant. Next time you see a child badgering another kid on a preschool playground, it's a good bet that the bully is avoidantly attached and the victim is insecurely attached.

Children deemed secure are more socially competent as well. Throughout childhood and into adulthood, those with secure histories more actively participate in peer groups, have more and closer relationships, maneuver more adeptly in a variety of social situations, demonstrate more leadership qualities, and are less isolated than their insecure counterparts. The data are clear: if you want to maximize the likelihood that a child will lead a socially competent life, provide him or her with a secure attachment in infancy.

The predictive power of infant attachment extends beyond the emotional life of children. A team led by Jay Belsky made a prediction grounded in evolutionary theory: because individuals with histories of insecure attachment suspect that they may not live long enough to have offspring, given the inconsistent or rejecting parental care they receive, girls' reproductive systems may develop earlier to improve their reproductive odds. As Belsky stated in a *Time* magazine interview, "An evolutionary biology perspective says, 'look, the thing that nature most cares about—with respect to all living things, humans included—is dispersing genes in future generations[.]' Thus, under those conditions in which the future appears precarious, where I might not even survive long enough to breed tomorrow, then I should mature earlier so I can mate earlier before that precarious future might get me."

To test their hypothesis, Belsky and his colleagues followed girls from birth to age fifteen. Researchers assessed the attachment status of the girls as infants in the strange situation; then starting when the subjects were around ten years old, nurses and physicians assessed their pubertal development, including growth of breasts and pubic hair. As predicted, girls with insecure attachment histories began and finished puberty earlier and had their first menstrual cycle earlier. Insecure girls' bodies were prepared to have offspring—at least biologically—before those of their secure counterparts.

Girls who go through puberty early are more sexually active than their late-blooming counterparts. Therefore, not only are teens judged insecure as infants more biologically ready for children, but their behavior increases the likelihood of reproductive "success." Early-maturing girls are also at risk for a number of other issues, including substance abuse, social isolation, and psychiatric problems. Of course genes and other factors likely play a role in pubertal development, but the idea that one's attachment relationship "predicts and perhaps programs the timing of pubertal development in humans" is extraordinary.

Attachment and Psychopathology

When I discuss these findings with my students, they are often surprised that tells in infancy can predict these outcomes. But I almost always have at least one student who is underwhelmed by the findings because they don't predict anything about psychopathology. The student often wants to know if one's attachment history has anything to say about the potential for developing mental disorders such as depression or anxiety disorders.

The answer is yes and no. There are a number of potential pathways for developing psychopathology. Moreover, few, if any, psychiatric disorders have a specific cause that is both necessary and sufficient. Thus, it's unlikely that one's attachment status alone would cause a form of mental disorder.

Studies show that having a secure attachment does not immunize one from psychopathology, but it does reduce the probability of developing a disorder. Think about being securely attached as akin to having an air bag available if you crash your car; for life's collisions, the air bag significantly reduces your chances of getting injured, but it doesn't guarantee that you won't be.

Individuals classified as avoidant or ambivalent-resistant as infants are at a greater risk for developing psychopathology later. Infants deemed ambivalent-resistant, for example, are more likely to exhibit anxiety disorders in late adolescence, while infants classified as avoidant are more likely to be aggressive and develop externalizing problems, such as hitting peers, behaving disobediently, and arguing with others.

I don't want to overstate the link between these attachment styles and psychopathology. The majority of these individuals don't have a mental disorder. But the disorganized attachment style is a "strong predictor of later disturbance." According to one leading researcher, the link between this attachment style and psychiatric symptoms "is far stronger than for any other measure from the infancy period." Infants deemed disorganized-disoriented are more likely to develop externalizing problems such as those exhibited by children with attention deficit/hyperactivity disorder, oppositional defiant disorder, and conduct disorder.

The truly alarming link is between the disorganized-disoriented attachment classification and later dissociative experiences. Dissociation, which falls into three broad categories, occurs when we have disruptions in cognitive processing. The first, memory, occurs when you have just done something but have no recollection of it. The second, absorption, occurs when you become so completely involved in an activity that you lose all sense of your environment. The last, depersonalization, occurs when you behave a certain way, but it's as if you are watching yourself; you feel somehow disconnected from your feelings and body. Dissociative symptoms run the continuum from minor disruptions in memory (e.g., driving to work from your home and, upon arriving, having no recollection whatsoever of the entire drive) to full-blown disorders such as dissociative identity disorder, where one person manifests multiple personalities with each unaware of the others.

In perhaps one of the most impressive predictions possible arising out of infant attachment classification based on the strange situation, researchers have consistently linked a history of infant disorganized attachment to dissociative symptoms from middle childhood to nineteen years of age, even when statistically controlling for whether or not the children were physically abused. Importantly, one's infant attachment status becomes more—not less—predictive of dissociative symptoms over time. Hands down, the best early predictor we have of dissociative disorders is the disorganized-disoriented classification in the strange situation.

You might argue that a baby would not encounter the strange situation experience in "real life." This is a valid point, but as one researcher remarked, the strange situation "may be artificial, but so is a treadmill test for the heart. That's a physical stress test—this is an emotional stress test. They're both artificial, but they're both diagnostic too."

The Road from Insecurity to Security

If we know that insensitive parenting correlates to insecure attachments in infancy, wouldn't it make sense to train caregivers in how to respond to their infants' emotional signals? Thankfully, researchers have developed a number of successful programs designed to do just that. In one study, the researcher randomly assigned temperamentally irritable infants to a treatment condition or a control condition. In the former, an experimenter came to infants' homes three times when they were between six and nine months of age, each visit lasting about two hours. The experimenter trained the parents to better perceive the infants' emotional signals, interpret the signals correctly, and implement appropriate responses. For example, the experimenters helped parents recognize infant fussiness and instructed them in how best to respond and soothe a baby. This sort of behavior is natural for many parents, but not all.

When assessed at nine months of age, the infants in the intervention group were more sociable, explored their environments more, and cried less compared to infants whose mothers received no intervention. Experimenters then assessed the infants in the strange situation at age one, three months after the intervention ended. The researchers categorized a whopping 78 percent of the infants whose parents received no intervention training as insecurely attached (i.e., avoidant, ambivalent-resistant, or disorganized), leaving only 22 percent securely attached. Contrast these statistics with the group of infants whose parents received the training: a majority, 62 percent, were securely attached. Just think: a simple six-hour intervention for a child can tip the scale of security in her favor.

Adults and Attachment

Let's switch gears for a moment to discuss attachment in adulthood. Imagine that a researcher has invited you to participate in a study in which she asks you questions about your family. She asks you to describe the relationship you had with each of your parents as far back as you can remember. The interviewer then asks you to provide five adjectives to describe your relationship with your father and five to describe your relationship with your mother. She then asks you to provide concrete memories to support each adjective. Numerous other questions about your childhood experiences with your parents follow, such as, To which parent did you feel closest? What did you do when you were upset? Did you feel rejected as a child? Were your parents ever threatening toward you? Have you lost a parent? What is your current relationship with your parents?

How would you answer these questions? Would it take a lot of time for you to construct your answers, or would they come rapid-fire? Would you be able to list five adjectives describing your relationship with your mother? Your father? Could you provide examples of experiences that would support the adjectives?

In the mid-1980s, Mary Main and her colleagues designed a semi-structured interview called the Adult Attachment Interview (AAI) asking questions like those above. The interview aims to assess how people understand and remember their attachment experiences. Researchers worldwide have given over 10,000 people the AAI, which allows them to assess individual differences in adult attachment, much like Ainsworth's strange situation allows us to assess infant attachment. If someone administered the AAI to you, a verbatim transcription of the conversation would include every speech error and hesitation. Then a highly trained coder would assess the coherence of your responses. The more internally consistent, clear, and relevant the answers are to the questions at hand—regardless of whether the memories are positive or negative—the more coherent the coder judges the speech. In other words, it's not *what* you remember but *how* you understand and think about your recollections.

Based on how people describe their attachment experiences in the AAI, researchers place them into four primary adult attachment classifications (see the table on page 40).

Secure Attachment	Insecure Attachment
Secure-autonomous	Insecure-dismissing
	Insecure-preoccupied
	Unresolved/disorganized

SECURE-AUTONOMOUS: These adults are able to reflect on positive and negative (even traumatic) memories completely but not excessively. Their speech is coherent, consistent, and relevant to the questions posed. These individuals tend to report that their attachment experiences have influenced their lives.

When asked to supply one of the five adjectives to describe the relationship between her and her mother, a speaker deemed secure-autonomous might say,

> Troublesome. Well, she was troublesome for me when I was young, no question. She yelled a lot of the time, I remember that, and she also— she could spank really hard, and she got angry a lot. But like I said, my father left when I was four, and she was trying to make enough of an income to support us, and trying hard to keep us on the straight and narrow at the same time that she was away such long hours. I didn't like it, what she did—like one time she slapped me in the face over something my sister had done, but she never apologized. I hated the yelling when my report card wasn't up to par. Yes, troublesome, or maybe I should have said it was a troubled relationship. But while I wish it had been different, it wasn't.

This interviewee provided a well-reasoned explanation to support the adjective of her choice. She stayed on topic and was neither excessively loquacious nor unduly brief. Even though describing a less-than-optimal experience, she did so in a coherent and rational manner.

INSECURE-DISMISSING: These adults tend to describe themselves as independent and strong, with little, if any, dependence on others in childhood or currently. They often report either no memory of childhood events or argue that rejection from their parents has actually made them stronger. They may also describe their parents in glowing terms but be unable to support such statements. They tend to have significantly briefer interviews as their responses are often terse.

A person deemed insecure-dismissing might say the following to support the adjective "troublesome":

Sobbed through her aunt's funeral. Embarrassing. Couldn't wait to get away from her. Next question?

This person's response brusquely dismissed the attachment relationship she had with her mother. She derogated her mother and tried to turn attention away from this question by moving forward with the interview.

INSECURE-PREOCCUPIED: These adults focus intensely on their attachment relationships, both past and present, and are unable to discuss them coherently. They are often indecisive; a speaker may say, "Great mother. Well, not really, actually pretty awful. No, I mean actually, a really good mother, except when she . . . " Their interviews are often long and filled with irrelevant details, digressions, and expressions of current anger toward their attachment figures.

Here is an excerpt of what a person deemed insecure-preoccupied might say to support the adjective "troublesome":

That was an understatement. It was yell, yell, yell—"Why didn't you this, why didn't you that?" Well, Mom, it was because you were just at me all the time, like last week you start yelling at the only grandkid you've got when we had you over to dinner. And angry? She's angry at me, she's angry at her latest husband—that's the latest in a series—now she's angry at her neighbor about a tree that's supposed to be blocking her view, and so on and so on. She's more than troublesome; she stirs up little things, like I was saying last week at dinner, and . . . [Continues]

Here, the interviewer requested that the subject discuss her childhood relationship; yet, she answered by discussing their current relationship. In addition, her focus was relatively inflexible, centering persistently on the mother's pervasive impact on her life.

UNRESOLVED/DISORGANIZED: Adults classified as "unresolved/disorganized" show lapses in their thoughts and language when recounting past loss or abuse in their lives. For example, some speakers recall and seem to believe, even if momentarily, that a deceased person is both alive and dead at the same time. One might comment, "It was almost better when she died, because then she could get on with being dead and I could get on with raising my family." Speakers may also remark, "She died because I forgot to think of her," demonstrating a lapse of reasoning and a misunderstanding of causality; in this case the speaker blames her thoughts for killing the loved one.

Other speakers may begin to eulogize a loved one.

She was young, she was lovely, and she was torn from us by that most dreaded of diseases, tuberculosis. And then, I remember, time and time again, the sounds of the weeping, the smell of flowers, the mother torn from where she lay weeping upon her daughter's coffin . . .

Overall, people who are unable to speak coherently about their attachment relationships and instead demonstrate lapses in their thoughts and speech are likely to fall into the unresolved/disorganized category.

What Does the AAI Predict?

I have always been fascinated by the degree to which my description of my attachment relationships with my mom and dad would connect to my own son's attachment. If I took the AAI as an adult, would it predict anything about my son's behavior in the strange situation?

Main and her colleagues interviewed men and women to grapple with this question. Five years prior, researchers had observed the subjects' children in the strange situation with their mothers and fathers separately. Adults who could talk coherently about their attachment experiences (i.e., were categorized as secure-autonomous) in the AAI were likely to have children deemed secure in the strange situation five years before. In contrast, adults not deemed autonomous-secure in the AAI were significantly more likely to have children judged insecure in the strange situation. Others drawing upon samples in other cultures have corroborated these findings.

Researchers have also given the AAI to pregnant mothers whose infants they subsequently observed in the strange situation. As expected, the views on attachment expressed by the pregnant mother predicted whether her infant would be securely or insecurely attached. Among pregnant mothers deemed secure-autonomous in the AAI in one study, 83 percent of their infants fell into the secure category, and only 17 percent were insecure in the strange situation. Among pregnant mothers deemed unresolved-disorganized, only one-third of their infants fell into the secure category, while two-thirds were insecure in the strange situation. Among those in the latter group, researchers classified fourteen of the sixteen children as disorganized, showing odd and sometimes bizarre behaviors in the strange situation. How remarkable that we can predict an infant's attachment to her mother before she is even born!

Pregnant mothers' AAI classifications ⟶ **Future children's strange situation classification**

Pregnant mothers' AAI classifications (secure versus insecure) predict their infants' behavior in the strange situation later in time (secure versus insecure).

But how? The explanation largely resides in how sensitive and responsive the parents are to their infants. Adults judged secure-autonomous are more sensitive and responsive to their infants' emotional signals relative to their insecure counterparts. Parents deemed unresolved/disorganized in the AAI show more frightening behaviors to their infants, as well as other atypical emotional communication. Thus, the parents' actual behavior toward the child and the parents' state of mind regarding their own attachment experiences predict infant attachment in the strange situation.

Does a person's attachment status in the strange situation predict how he will discuss his attachment relationships two decades later in the AAI?

Children's strange situation classifications ⟶ **Adult AAI classifications**

Infants' strange situation classifications (secure versus insecure) predict their AAI classifications years later (secure versus insecure).

At least four studies show significant links between infant strange situation behavior and eventual AAI attachment status. For most low-risk and nonclinical samples, infants deemed secure in the strange situation speak coherently about their attachment relationships in adulthood. Infants judged insecure are significantly more likely to fall into the insecure category in the AAI years later. Main and her colleagues reported that *not one* of the twenty-six infants in her sample deemed insecure in the strange situation received secure-autonomous classification in the AAI at nineteen years old. Of course circumstances derail some individuals from the track of security in infancy, leading them to become insecure in adulthood; trauma, such as the death of an attachment figure or a chronic and debilitating health issue, can have adverse effects on one's attachment style. However, barring major life trauma, our attachment styles are generally stable from infancy into adulthood.

This is good news for infants who are securely attached to their caregivers; they can count on consistent and responsive care, which predicts a multitude of positive outcomes. It's bad news for insecurely attached infants, especially those deemed disorganized-disoriented. Unless their circumstances change significantly, they will likely remain insecurely attached and suffer less-than-optimal outcomes.

On first blush, it appears that if you experienced abuse or rejection from your caregiver, your (likely) insecure attachment will continue throughout your life, and you may even pass it on to your child. After all, you cannot change the negative experiences you may have had with attachment figures during childhood. However, there is hope. It's not *what* happened to you that matters the most. Instead, it's *how* you mentally understand and discuss your relationships with caregivers that's really important. "In theory, then," writes Mary Main and her colleagues, "an adult with all attachment figures deceased and no close relationships available could still be secure-autonomous and raise secure offspring." Individuals with difficult and even abusive upbringings can be deemed secure-autonomous in the AAI if they learn how to reason about and discuss their attachment experiences coherently and value attachment relationships in their adult lives. Learning how to reprocess experiences and come to terms with the past is key.

Whether you observe kids at a playground, at school, or in your own home, realize that not only the genes they are born with but also the interactions they have with their caregivers influence their orientation to life and the people around them. Thanks to the efforts of numerous behavioral researchers, we're able to predict much about who we will become later in life by examining early tells. In turn, how we conceptualize our own attachment relationships influences how we raise our own children.

Party-Worthy Findings

1. **Early puberty:** Girls identified as insecurely attached in infancy go through puberty earlier than their secure counterparts.

2. **Prediction of psychopathology:** Infants deemed disorganized-disoriented as infants are more likely than securely attached children to develop a form of psychopathology years later.

3. **Prediction of attachment:** Pregnant mothers' attachment status in the AAI predicts their unborn children's attachment behavior over a year later.

II.

How We Size Up Others

4

WHO ARE YOU ANYWAY?

"It is only shallow people who do not judge by appearances. The true mystery of the world is the visible, not the invisible."

—OSCAR WILDE

On a beautiful autumn day, I walked down Telegraph Avenue in Berkeley, California—the street that probably best represents the city's "let it all hang out" reputation. While negotiating the throng of street vendors hawking tie-dyed T-shirts, bongs, and hemp clothing, I came across a man and woman offering "face readings." Intrigued, I proceeded to observe their setup as inconspicuously as possible. Two customers plopped down $5 bills and eagerly sat in anticipation of their "readings." The clairvoyant couple carefully examined the customers' visage, occasionally prodding them in order to assess their facial structures. The parties exchanged few words during the one-to-two minute examinations. At the end, the clairvoyants articulately described to the customers what kind of people they were, how their spiritual lives were progressing, and what joys and trials they would face in the coming weeks and months.

The customers listened intently and nodded their heads, seemingly satis-fied with the readings.

Although dumbstruck by the spectacle, I soon realized that we do something similar in our own lives every day: we size people up based on first impressions. Virtually all of us feel compelled to assess others' character based on the tells we perceive during the first moments of our interaction with them. Is the person I just interviewed for the managerial job competent, intelligent, and reliable? Was that person interested in me romantically or just being friendly? Do I trust the jeweler selling me an expensive gem? Were my in-laws sincerely happy to see me? Is the sales clerk I just met the type of person I'd want to ask out on a date? Regard-less of whether we are accurate, we give these assessments the good old college try.

The study of how physical appearance relates to character has a check-ered history. The scientific investigation of physiognomy, or the study of how appearance reveals personality, dates back to the Greeks. Aristotle wrote that by looking at someone's face, "we shall then be able to infer character from features." Since then, physiognomy has waxed and waned in legitimacy, rising to a well-respected practice in the days of Charles Darwin and falling into the realm of pseudoscience shortly thereafter. In recent decades its validity has seen a resurgence among scientists, who now use state-of-the-art methods to explore the links between our exteri-ors and our inner workings.

We make snap judgments about personality from people's faces and other tells in fractions of a second, usually showing remarkable consensus in judgment. If you and I see the same face, we're both likely to perceive it as honest and trustworthy to about the same degree. The real question is whether we can *correctly* predict someone's personality traits and future behavior from facial characteristics or behavioral cues. Some of the latest scientific discoveries suggest that the resounding answer is yes, at least in some areas of life. Our faces and actions reveal who we are in numerous ways, providing clues about our personalities, our intelligence, and even our proclivities toward altruism and aggression.

At the same time, people can sometimes completely misjudge others— occasionally with serious consequences. Judicial courts, for example, are more likely to exonerate baby-faced people than mature-looking individ-uals for crimes they are charged with. There is even evidence indicating that juries are more likely to impose the death penalty for criminals with certain facial characteristics.

A Photographic Personality

In the summer of 2008, I spent a week island hopping in the Galapagos, imagining what it must have been like almost 175 years earlier for the islands' most famous visitor, Charles Darwin. The English naturalist was there for only five weeks on his famous voyage aboard the HMS *Beagle*, and yet the data he collected would help form the foundation of his theory of natural selection.

But history very nearly took a different turn. The captain of the HMS *Beagle* was a devotee of Swiss poet Johann Lavater, whose book on physiognomy had widespread influence in the Victorian society of Darwin's day. Lavater argued that

> an exact relationship exists between the soul and the body, between the internal and the external of man, that the infinite variety of the souls or the internal nature of man creates an infinite variety in his body or externality. . . . If such differences exist then they must be recognizable; they must also be the basis for an exact science.

The captain of the *Beagle* nearly passed over Darwin for the naturalist position because he thought the young man's nose portended sluggishness, like that of a sloth that spends its days lounging in the treetops. Darwin wrote about the captain in his autobiography, "He was an ardent disciple of Lavater, & was convinced that he could judge a man's character by the outline of his features; & he doubted whether anyone with my nose could possess sufficient energy & determination for the voyage. But I think he was afterwards well-satisfied that my nose had spoken falsely."

We have come a long way since Lavater, relying not just on appearance but also examining how small fragments of behavior influence our impressions of others. Whether we're observing someone from across the room at the library or assessing how kind and positive a person is from an incidental action, we're constantly trying to figure out others' personalities. A seminal study done at the University of Michigan in the 1960s showed that we can get a pretty good read on people from observing them briefly, even if we don't interact with them. Others have followed up on this research.

Investigators in Germany videotaped subjects walking into a room, sitting down at a table, reading a weather report, and then exiting a room. The researchers then showed these ninety-second video clips to a different group of subjects, asking them to assess the videotaped targets' personalities. Subjects who viewed the video clips gauged the targets' personalities in much the same way as the targets perceived themselves, especially in terms of self-reported levels of conscientiousness and extraversion. Subjects generally identify the latter trait most accurately in other studies.

Photos also reveal clues about who we are. In the era of social media, our photographs surface all over the Internet, appearing everywhere from Instagram to dating websites, where people use them to decide whom they want to go out with. In the work sphere, employers are increasingly evaluating potential and current employees by checking out their Facebook photos to decide their employment fate.

In one study at the University of Texas, Austin, researchers photographed more than one hundred students twice. For the first image, researchers photographed the students' entire bodies, allowing them to pose any way they wished (i.e., spontaneous photos). For the second, the students stood with their arms at their sides, assumed an expressionless face, and looked directly into the camera (i.e., standardized photos).

The researchers asked the students to assess their own personalities but also included character evaluations from friends and family who knew them well. They then averaged these ratings, creating a personality profile for each student. Subsequently, the researchers showed the spontaneous and standardized photos of the students to observers, asking them to rate the subjects' personalities based on appearance.

As the table on the following page shows, observers accurately gauged the students' levels of extraversion, self-esteem, and religiosity from the standardized photos. The spontaneous photos revealed even more of their personality traits: observers accurately assessed extraversion, agreeableness, openness to experience, likability, self-esteem, loneliness, and religiosity. Although the findings were not as robust when researchers assessed the accuracy of individual observers versus the entire group, the results were generally the same. People who had never laid eyes on the targets

	Standardized Photos	Spontaneous Photos
Extraversion	++++	++++
Agreeableness	—	++
Conscientiousness	—	—
Emotional stability	—	—
Openness	—	++++
Likability	—	+++
Self-esteem	+++	+++
Loneliness	—	++
Religiosity	++	+++
Political orientation	—	—

The "+" signs indicate the degree of correlation between aggregated observers' ratings and the personalities of the students who appeared in the photos. The more plus signs in each cell, the more accurate the observers' assessments of the students' actual personalities. Blank cells were not statistically significant.

until glimpsing the photographs assessed them in much the same way as people who knew them well.

So, what cues did people actually use to assess students' personalities, and what cues should they have used? On page 54, I've indicated the cues that observers relied on and those that were actually valid indicators of personality among the spontaneous photos. Extraverts stood energetically, were relaxed, smiled with their arms unfolded, and looked healthy, stylish, and neat in appearance. Introverts, on the other hand, had a tenser, more tired stance, smiled less, folded their arms, and looked less healthy and messier. Conscientious people dressed more plainly, but observers failed to pick up on this. Subjects more open to new experiences tended to look away from the camera, appeared less healthy and neat, and wore more distinctive clothing.

When Judging...	Observers Relied on...	When They Should Have Relied on
Extraversion	Healthy appearance Neat appearance Smiling Energetic stance Relaxed stance	*Healthy appearance* *Neat appearance* *Smiling* *Energetic stance* *Relaxed stance* Stylish appearance Arms unfolded
Agreeableness	Healthy appearance Smiling Energetic stance Relaxed stance	 *Smiling* *Relaxed stance*
Conscientiousness	Healthy appearance Neat appearance Smiling Energetic stance Ordinary appearance	
Openness to experience	Distinctive appearance Smiling Energetic stance Relaxed stance Sickly appearance Messy appearance Looking away from camera	*Distinctive appearance*
Self-esteem	Healthy appearance Stylish appearance Neat appearance Smiling Arms behind back Energetic stance Relaxed stance	*Healthy appearance* *Smiling* *Arms behind back* *Energetic stance*
Loneliness	Sickly appearance Messy appearance Little Smiling Tired stance Tense stance	*Sickly appearance* *Messy appearance* *Tired stance* *Tense stance*

Bold italicized cues were both valid and relied on by observers.

These findings may be a conservative estimate of how well we can assess personality from appearance. All of the photos in this study were of undergraduate students enrolled in an introductory psychology course. Though there is nothing wrong with this sample, the findings may be limited as most university students tend to dress relatively similarly—T-shirts, jeans, sweatpants, and so forth—compared to the rest of society. Observers may be able to judge more accurately people whose appearances vary more in relation to typical college students.

This study has another implication that shouldn't surprise you: we can systematically manipulate our appearance in photos to accord with how we wish others to perceive us. Say you want to send the signal that you are conscientious and outgoing with high self-esteem. Post photos of yourself in which you're smiling, standing in a relaxed, energetic stance, folding your arms behind your back, and looking healthy, stylish, and neat. If you wish to come across as the shy, introverted type, display photos of yourself looking disheveled, not smiling much, and standing tensely. A photo of you in a church, mosque, or synagogue directory, on the company website, or on your Facebook page may reveal who you are to people before they ever meet you—something to keep in mind before your next potential employer or romantic partner takes a peek at it.

Even when we examine only head shots of expressionless individuals—devoid of clothing, jewelry, and bodily posture—we still accurately judge personality to some degree. We need view a photograph for only fifty milliseconds to detect how extraverted a person is, the personality trait most accurately assessed from a photograph. Curiously, we're also adept at judging how extraverted chimpanzees are from pictures of their expressionless faces. Who knew?

Although we should never "judge a book by its cover," the fact of the matter is that we evaluate people by their looks all the time and do it quite well in some cases. We'll never achieve 100 percent accuracy, but it appears there is a kernel of truth to our first impressions of others.

Clues to Cognition

We sometimes assess people's intelligence—either consciously or unconsciously—from our interactions with them. Perhaps a handyperson just showed up to your house to wire your new basement light, and you wonder how competent he is. Maybe you're interviewing someone for a high-level job and wonder if she has the requisite smarts for the position.

We've all been on the other side of the table as well when others are assessing us. I recall my father's employer interviewing me as an eighteen-year-old for a very generous college scholarship. I had a whopping ten minutes to impress upon a committee that I was a deserving candidate. They fired one question at me after another, and I answered to the best of my ability, attempting to demonstrate that I was intelligent, competent, and capable. I came up short that day and sometimes wondered over the years if I could have manipulated my behavior to come across as more intelligent and competent.

Is intelligence on display for everybody to see via our tells? Several researchers have investigated this question using a variety of techniques. One team videotaped people from Germany performing various standardized tasks in the laboratory. They then showed the videotapes to independent judges, whom they asked to assess the subjects' intelligence. It turns out that one of these laboratory tasks was a particularly good predictor: reading newspaper headlines and subtitles aloud. From just three minutes of watching and listening, judges could accurately predict the participants' intelligence. So, if you want to get a bead on someone's mental horsepower, simply have her read a copy of the New York Times aloud.

Nonverbal cues are also diagnostic of intelligence. On a daily basis, the people we encounter, whether in a casual interaction or a formal job interview, "interview" us. Researchers at Northeastern University videotaped several conversations between two unacquainted college students asked to get to know each other during the meeting. The researchers then obtained the students' IQ scores, grade point averages (GPAs), and SAT test scores, all of which correlated positively with one another.

The researchers selected the second minute of each conversation and showed these one-minute clips to a set of judges, some of whom watched them with sound, some without sound. A third group merely read transcripts of the conversations. Investigators gave the judges the averages and ranges of the students' IQs, GPAs, and SAT scores to use as a reference, then asked them to assess each score specifically for each student. Regardless of whether the videos contained sound, subjects could accurately assess the test scores. However, they were unable to predict those scores when reading only the transcripts, which suggests that the students' nonverbal behaviors, not the content of their speech, drove the findings.

Most of us hope to come across as bright when we interview for jobs, apply for scholarships, and meet our future in-laws, right? I know I wanted to when I interviewed for that college scholarship. Three cues not only drive people's *perceptions* of intelligence but provide clues to our *actual* mental chops: eye gaze, vocal qualities, and level of attractiveness.

People who look others in the eyes, especially when speaking, appear to be, and actually are, more intelligent than their gaze-averting counterparts. Some evidence indicates that those who speak clearly, quickly, and loudly (although not too loudly) are more intellectually astute. Finally, the perceived attractiveness of individuals is predictive of intelligence, but only for subjects with "faces in the lower half of the attractiveness distribution," that is, for low levels of attractiveness. Of course, these findings are based on averages; plenty of attractive, eye-gazing, and fast-talking people are dim, while plenty of unattractive, gaze-averting, and slow-talking people are indeed bright.

We're quite capable of fooling others into thinking that we're more intelligent than we really are simply by "appearing smart." The good news is that if you make a conscious decision to look bright the next time you want to display your cognitive chops, you will probably succeed, assuming you only need to make a brief impression on your audience. The bad news is that other people can readily fool you into thinking they are bright when they may not be.

Seeing Goodness In(side) Others

Equally relevant to our lives is the ability to predict who is friend and who is foe. Consider Paul Rusesabagina.

I attended college at a small liberal arts institution in the middle of cornfields, reading Plato and having intellectual discussions with my friends into the late hours of the night. The setting was idyllic, and I was enjoying college life. Then something happened in April of my first year that disturbed millions of people around the world, including me: the Rwandan genocides. For about one hundred days, Rwandan Hutus massacred hundreds of thousands of Tutsis while most of the world sat

Paul Rusesabagina in an interview.

back and watched. By the end of the bloodshed, more than 800,000 people had died.

In the face of such brutality and slaughter, one man demonstrated incredible bravery and selflessness. Paul Rusesabagina, the manager of a high-end hotel in Rwanda, sheltered more than 1,000 people during the massacres to save them from almost certain death, despite the risk to his own life. People have called Rusesabagina "the Oskar Schindler of Africa." In 2005, he came to my current university to tell his story. During his visit he remarked, "There was no other solution, and there was nothing else to be done. I had to listen to my own conscience, and what my conscience dictated is what I have done."

Let's face it: most of us will never need—thankfully—to behave like Paul Rusesabagina, jeopardizing our own welfare to help others. However, we do have opportunities on a daily basis to do good, even if it means making small sacrifices. A teacher may spend extra time helping a young student learn how to read after school, even though he will miss time at home with his own children. A woman may donate money to a local family whose house has just burned down, despite the fact that she is having difficulties making her own ends meet. In such cases, people behave prosocially—giving, helping, and sharing to assist others, sometimes expecting nothing in return.

We all know people who are quick to lend a helping hand and others who aren't. The question is whether we can identify prosociality from tells, even before a person has the opportunity to demonstrate them.

Although the data are still rolling in, the answer seems to be yes, at least in a lab setting. One group of researchers in Germany and the Netherlands videotaped subjects sitting behind a desk and simply asked them to look into the camera and introduce themselves. Subsequently, the subjects played a simple, well-validated game commonly used to assess levels of prosociality. Subjects were given €60 (about US$94) and told that they could distribute the money to another anonymous person; the recipient would never know the donor's identity and would have no power to veto the offer. The subjects could give €30, €20, €10, or €0 to the recipient and keep the rest of the money for themselves.

The researchers then recruited a different set of subjects and explained the logic of the game. They showed these subjects twenty-second video clips of the first group introducing themselves with the sound turned off, then asked them to predict whether people gave €30, €20, €10, or €0 to the recipient. Though the subjects couldn't predict the exact amount given, the vast majority could readily distinguish between the scrooges who gave nothing and their benevolent counterparts who gave something. Only about 9 percent of the subjects could not distinguish between the skinflints and the charitable subjects. Although we need to remember that this was a tightly controlled lab study, the average Joe and Jane may very well be able to identify the prosocial individuals among us from scraps of nonverbal behavior.

A remarkable study took these findings even further. A group of researchers led by Aleksandr Kogan showed judges films of one person at a time listening to their romantic partners retell a time in their lives when they experienced suffering. From the twenty-second silent video clips of these interactions, outside observers rated how trustworthy, compassionate, and kind the listeners were (the judges could not see the listeners' partners). Astonishingly, Kogan and his team found that listeners judged the most trustworthy, compassionate, and kind were significantly more likely than other listeners to possess a specific gene variant that helped them take advantage of oxytocin. This neuropeptide, as well as the specific gene variant more common among highly empathic listeners, has been identified in numerous studies as facilitating prosocial behaviors like trust and giving to others.

Obviously, "people can't see genes," said Kogan, "so there has to be something going on that is signaling these genetic differences to the strangers." It turns out that people with the gene variant optimized for oxytocin nodded their heads, gazed, and smiled more at their partners; they also had a more open body posture than their counterparts. Judges likely detected these tells in the clips. As the study authors acknowledge, genetics represents only one of the many influences on whether a person is likely to have a prosocial disposition. Nonetheless, I sometimes wonder if the Paul Rusesabaginas of the world are more likely to carry this specific gene variant. Perhaps such gene variants contributed to that inner voice he talked about: "I had to listen to my own conscience, and what my conscience dictated is what I have done." Given that the studies discussed above are correlational, it's difficult to tell, but they are provocative. The next time you have a serious conversation with a romantic partner, consider how trustworthy, compassionate, and kind he or she appears to be; your assessment may very well synch with that person's biological makeup.

Aggression

We're also capable of predicting the other side of the coin: aggression. The livelihood of one of my friends depends daily on this ability. He is a private detective, and part of his job requires him to knock on people's doors and serve them official court papers.

Over the course of his career, he has served papers to more than 30,000 people, informing them that a spouse wants a divorce or that they must show up to court for criminal sentencing. Though most recipients take it in stride when handed the dreaded information, some do not. One three-hundred-pound man in his fifties opened the door of his home, puffed up his chest, clenched his jaw muscles, leaned into my friend's face, and began screaming, "Get the fuck out of here, now! I said, get the fuck off my property!" The man then came after him like a bulldozer. But my friend knew what was going to happen before the man even opened his mouth; he had served papers for so many years that he quickly read the situation

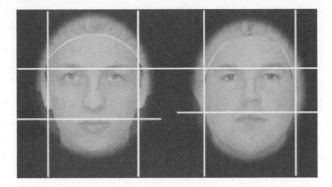

These faces differ in their width-to-height ratios.

before it unfolded and readied himself for imminent danger. He escaped unscathed.

Before we dive into what predicts behavioral aggression, take a look at the faces above for a second or two. Between these two men, who is most likely to become aggressive if provoked? If you answered that the man on the right is likely the more aggressive of the two, you probably already know where I'm going with this.

Justin Carré and his colleagues showed judges thirty-seven pictures of men's faces like those above (without the superimposed lines) and asked them to rate on a scale of one to seven, "How aggressive would this person be if provoked?" Prior to asking this question, the researchers assessed how aggressive the targets in the photos actually were using a well-validated laboratory procedure. The judges could accurately assess how aggressive the men in the photos were merely by observing their photographs. Moreover, the judges could accurately predict the men's aggression whether they saw their pictures for two seconds or a mere thirty-nine milliseconds.

From observing the photos in the figure, you've probably already figured out which cue the judges likely employed to help make their predictions: the structural dimensions of the men's faces. Specifically, the judges' assessments correlated to the ratio between the men's facial width and height, a measure independent of body size and thought to be linked to genetics and testosterone levels. Wide-faced men were deemed more aggressive. Interestingly, these facial ratios have no relation to aggressive behavior in women.

To rule out other possible facial cues, Carré and his team manipulated numerous features on the thirty-seven faces, making them blurry or cropping them in various ways, but as long as judges could observe the facial width-to-height ratios, they could accurately predict the men's aggressive tendencies.

The link between wide faces and aggression supports my private detective friend's anecdotal evidence that it's rare for a narrow-faced male to come after him; he once told me that men who violently confront him almost always have "beefy" faces. Of course, take this with a grain of cautionary salt; plenty of beefy-faced men are giant teddy bears, and some slim-faced men are violent. Remember that these are merely averages.

Researchers have uncovered a number of other fascinating links related to men's facial width-to-height ratio. Consider the following:

LYING AND CHEATING: In carefully controlled studies, men with wider faces were three times more willing to lie to gain an advantage over a competitor compared to slim-faced men. In another study, investigators asked participants to roll a pair of dice to determine how many times they'd be entered into a lottery to win a $50 gift card. Wide-faced men were about nine times more likely than slim-faced men to overstate their results—i.e., cheat—saying they rolled a higher number than they actually did. Indeed, the researchers found that wide-faced men perceived themselves as powerful, and this contributed to their unethical behavior. One of the study's researchers stated, "Our findings suggest that some men are simply predisposed to act unethically in order to achieve their goals."

EXPLOITATION OF OTHERS: In a different study, subjects came to the lab in pairs, where experimenters gave each £3 (about US$5). Subjects did not meet their partners and instead saw a facial photograph only. Researchers told Person A that he could keep his money or entrust it to Person B. If he chose the latter, they added £2 to the pot of money, resulting in £8 total (US$13). They then allowed Person B to split the pot fairly, resulting in £4 per subject, or unfairly, with Person B keeping £6 and Person A receiving only £2. Wide-faced males entrusted with money by Person A (male or female) were significantly less likely than slim-faced men to split the money fairly.

DEATH OF SLIM-FACED MALES AT THE HANDS OF WIDE-FACED MEN: In an intriguing study, researchers hypothesized that given wide-faced men's penchant for aggression and dominance, one might expect them to be more likely to survive direct physical fights with slim-faced men. To examine this prediction, researchers measured the width-to-height ratios of hundreds of skulls found across the United States, with over two hundred coming from murdered people. For those skulls belonging to victims of homicide, the researchers coded the cause of death as "contact violence" or "other." Contact violence meant there was evidence that the victims had been strangled, stabbed, or beaten to death, whereas the other category indicated that the victim had endured a gunshot or was poisoned or that the researchers didn't know the cause of death. Narrow-faced men were significantly more likely to die from contact violence than wide-faced men (facial ratios were not related to death for women). Even though wide-faced men are probably more likely get into physical fights, thin-faced men die more often in such altercations.

A slew of other variables correlate with the likelihood that men will behave aggressively and dominantly. Nonetheless, these studies demonstrate that the width of a man's face relative to its height is a reliable visual cue of aggressive behavior, which people home in on to accurately assess men's proclivity for violence. It's unclear if our evolutionary heritage has tweaked our perceptual systems to automatically tune into men's facial ratio, given the obvious adaptive advantage of being able to do so, or if we somehow learn the association over the course of our lives. It's probably a combination of the two.

The Guiltless (Looking) and the Guilty (Looking) Among Us

To this point, I've discussed how most of us are surprisingly adept at inferring various qualities of people—personality, intelligence, goodness, and aggression—from their appearance and behavior. But sometimes our conscious and unconscious perceptions of others are wrong, occasionally with serious consequences.

People perceive some men—think Zac Efron, Justin Bieber, Tom Bosley, or Babe Ruth—as relatively warm and not very dominant. Research shows that this is sometimes the case because their facial features resemble

The typical features of a baby's face: large eyes, a round face, a big forehead, and a diminutive chin.

those of babies: they have large eyes, rounded faces, a higher forehead, and a small chin. According to Leslie Zebrowitz at Brandeis University, the leading expert on baby faces, people overgeneralize their stereotypes of real babies and attribute their qualities to adults with baby faces. This leads people to perceive men and women with baby-faced features as "more naive, submissive, physically weak, warm, and honest." Some studies confirm these stereotypes; others do not. Here, I want to address the potential consequences of these perceptions and the kinds of predictions we can make from them.

Consider the following thought experiment: you and a same-sex friend with virtually identical work experience have just applied for two entry-level jobs at a local bank. You both submit your resumes and include your photos with them because you think that this may help you land one of the jobs. Both of you are relatively attractive and are about the same age, but you have a baby face, whereas your friend's face appears more mature. The two positions available are for a loan counselor and a loan officer. The bank president tells the committee making the decision that the loan counselor position requires a warm individual who can understand the needs of clients, yet will occasionally submit to the decisions of the loan officer. The loan officer position requires leadership qualities such as dominance, financial shrewdness, and low warmth. After all, the loan officer must deny an applicant for a loan occasionally; business is business.

Assuming for a moment that you are the only two applicants and you're both equally qualified for either job, guess who will likely be offered which position. According to the study on which this thought experiment is based, you will get the loan counselor position, and your more mature-looking friend will become the new loan officer. Also, in this study, men were preferred over women for the loan officer position, even when they had equal qualifications. Interestingly, the study indicates that having a baby face would have impeded a man's ability to land the loan officer position as much as being a woman.

Other work shows that women with baby faces are more likely to work in the "helping professions," such as nursing and teaching, compared to their mature-faced counterparts. There's even evidence that baby-faced men do not rise to the highest ranks of the military as often as mature-faced men. It's impossible to say with any degree of confidence whether such findings reflect discrimination, or if there truly are behavioral differences between baby-faced and mature-faced individuals.

Having a baby face does have a powerful upside though. If you ever find yourself in small-claims court trying to recover money from a baby-faced individual who has intentionally wronged you, odds are you will lose, according to one study. In over five hundred cases, researchers carefully coded the degree to which male and female plaintiffs and defendants had baby faces in Boston courtrooms, along with a host of other relevant variables. Here, I'll focus on the approximately three hundred cases that involved defendants accused of intentionally harming plaintiffs or withholding payment from them. The researchers predicted that judges would misattribute childlike characteristics, such as honesty, to baby-faced defendants, thereby finding them guilty less often than mature-faced individuals.

The findings were downright unsettling: when defendants denied wrongdoing, Boston judges found the vast majority of the most mature-faced among them—92 percent—guilty, whereas they deemed less than half—45 percent—of the most baby-faced defendants guilty. These astonishing results held even when investigators took into account the attractiveness and age of the litigants, as well as the evidence presented. "The effect of the defendants' babyfaceness," wrote one of the researchers, "was comparable in magnitude to the effect of evidence to support their case." When defendants admitted wrongdoing, judges ordered more mature-faced culprits to pay plaintiffs significantly more money—but only if the plaintiff had a baby face. It's almost as if the judges wanted to make sure dominant, mature-faced offenders paid baby-faced plaintiffs well.

Whether you're a defendant or a plaintiff in small-claims court, the odds certainly are in your favor if you have a baby face.

Predicting who is going to win a small-claims court case is one thing, but accurately predicting who will go to jail or die for an alleged crime is quite another. Here is another case in which our inaccurate perceptions can have potentially devastating consequences for both individuals and society as a whole.

Warning: The following may disturb you.

Researchers at the University of Colorado examined the criminal histories and facial features of convicted male felons in Florida. After controlling for the severity of the crime and criminal history, they found that judges sentenced whites and African Americans to equal prison terms. Florida has taken explicit steps to ensure race-blind sentencing. The researchers then showed head shots of the criminals to subjects and asked them to assess "the degree to which each face had features that are typical of African Americans." The researchers refer to these features as "Afrocentric features."

Their findings are incredibly unsettling: regardless of race, the perceived Afrocentric facial features of the inmates—broad nose, full lips, and dark skin—predicted the length of their sentence, even when researchers controlled for criminal history and the severity of crime. That is, if two people of the same racial category with the same history of crime committed the same offense, the one possessing more pronounced Afrocentric facial features went to jail for longer than the person without these features. Despite the fact that the judges were capable of maintaining racial neutrality in sentencing, they appeared unable to do so when it came to facial features.

Other researchers examined perceived Afrocentric features of African Americans convicted of murder in Philadelphia. Controlling for a host of factors, such as the severity of the crime, the courts condemned the defendants with more stereotypical Afrocentric features to death more frequently, but *only* if the murder victim was white; 24 percent of the men with the least stereotypical Afrocentric features received death sentences, as opposed to 58 percent of the men with the most stereotypical features. That is more than double.

Some think that when people are considering the culpability of offenders, they associate Afrocentric facial features with stereotypic traits such as danger and blameworthiness. This faulty linkage of traits to facial features results in judges and juries erroneously taking facial features into account rather than ignoring them. Face discrimination is just as serious as any other type. The problem is that people do not even realize they're committing this injustice. Having a face with stereotypical Afrocentric features may literally mean the end of your life if you're a convicted murderer in some states.

I highly doubt we're capable, as the clairvoyants I observed on the street claimed, of forecasting people's futures, but tells enable us to make some surprisingly accurate predictions about others' personalities and intelligence, as well as their altruistic and aggressive proclivities. Sometimes, however, facial features with no link to actual personality or behavior dupe us. How we perceive others, then, is serious business.

Party-Worthy Findings

1. **Prediction of intelligence:** A silent one-minute video of a person interacting with another accurately reveals his or her IQ, GPA, and SAT scores.

2. **Prediction of genes:** Peoples' ratings of trustworthiness, compassion, and kindness of people listening to others during twenty-second silent video clips predict the type of genes they have.

3. **Linkage of severity of prison sentences with stereotypical facial features:** Both whites and blacks with more stereotypical Afrocentric facial features receive longer sentences compared to those who do not have these facial features.

5

THE TARGETS OF OUR ATTRACTION

"I must be giving off one of those vibes again. That's what we do . . . we give off vibrations and then we pick up the vibrations from our gaydar . . . so I've heard."

—ELLEN DEGENERES

Growing up, I became acquainted with a kid named Joe who would eventually become a close friend. We went to movies, played sports, and spent time at each other's homes. As I became closer with Joe, some people began asking me, "Does Joe like girls?" I shrugged it off. Friends of mine labeled him "gay" and began teasing me about the amount of time Joe and I spent together. I ignored it when my friends made these "accusations." Eventually Joe and I grew apart naturally, making other friends and occupying different social niches. I learned later from someone else that he was indeed gay.

What tells did my family and friends see in their brief interactions with Joe that I missed during the countless hours he and I spent together? One can make a pretty good guess about another person's sexual orientation by reading the "Damn straight I'm gay!" button on his or her bag, but can people accurately and consistently infer sexual orientation—gay or straight—when such obvious cues are unavailable? Although one's age, gender, and ethnicity are often evident, one's sexual orientation may not be readily apparent. To me, Joe's sexual orientation was "invisible in plain sight."

People sometimes refer to the ability to infer if a person is gay, based on indirect cues such as the way one looks, talks, and walks, as "gaydar" ("gay" + "radar"). If there is, in fact, such a thing as gaydar, then "straight-dar" must necessarily exist as well. We must acknowledge that discerning sexual orientation is not so much about identifying people with a same-sex preference as it is about inferring sexual orientation for all people.

When I've discussed this topic over the years with friends, family, and colleagues, their reactions have varied markedly. Many people ask, "Is gaydar actually real?" Others say, "Duh! Everyone knows that gaydar exists." Some think gaydar is an ability held exclusively by people with a same-sex preference, while others think that everyone has the capacity to discern a straight person from a gay one. In most discussions I've had about gaydar and straightdar, people usually want to know what cues to look for to distinguish people who are straight from those who are gay. People who think they have gaydar often refer to it as a sort of sixth sense; they're not sure how to describe it, but they know it's real. As you'll see, however, science has largely demystified gaydar.

Science and Sexual Orientation

Over the years, I've also encountered people who believe scientists should not study gaydar, either because science merely confirms what we already supposedly know (even though people disagree on the validity of the phenomenon) or because it's unimportant. Some also think gaydar is resistant to scientific analysis. The latter group commonly argues that we can't possibly measure another's sexual orientation objectively or that language imperfectly captures the multidimensional nature of sexual orientation. In addition, they sometimes contend that we can't possibly translate lab results into real-world phenomena.

I'm sympathetic to some of these critiques. It's simplistic to think that sexual identification is categorical (i.e., one is straight, gay, or bisexual). In reality, sexual identification and behavior belong to multiple dimensions, but the studies I'm going to discuss tend to categorize sexual orientations nonetheless. I acknowledge such limitations when it comes to the scientific analysis of inferring sexual orientation, but I still think there's value in attempting to better understand the phenomena of interest, even if they are complex in nature.

The perception of sexual orientation is a real issue in our lives and makes a difference in the world, just as money, ethnicity, and learning style do. We can study all of these empirically, albeit with limitations. Noticing potential mates for potential reproductive success is part of the bedrock that constitutes evolutionary biology broadly and sexual selection specifically. Top-rate researchers have published many of the studies that form the basis for this chapter in the very best journals in the field. Moreover, I remain unconvinced that "having gaydar" makes someone homophobic. As op-ed contributors to the *New York Times* recently wrote, "Adults with normal perceptual abilities can differentiate the faces of men and women, and of black and white people, but such abilities do not make us sexist or racist."

The Perception of Sexual Orientation and Society

Throughout modern history, the belief that people are capable of inferring sexual orientation has had incredibly deleterious consequences. In the McCarthy era, President Dwight D. Eisenhower issued Executive Order 10450 three months after his inauguration in 1953, making dismissal of gay people from all government jobs official US policy. In *The Other Side of Silence,* John Loughery details how the US government historically thought gay people posed a threat to national security. "With the Soviets on the lookout for new agents," writes Loughery, "the 'lack of emotional stability' that homosexuals were known for, as well as the 'weakness of their moral fiber,' made them obvious targets or suspects." Given this threat, government employees were on the lookout for telltale signs of these "sexual deviants" who might succumb to Soviet influence. Ironically, this "purge of the perverts," as some called it, resulted in more dismissals from the government than the total number of those accused or found guilty of sympathy with the Soviet cause. Such absurd policies are unconscionable.

The US government's assumptions about the validity of gaydar have not always been consistent. Whereas US policy during McCarthyism rested on the belief that behavior could tip people off to others' sexual orientation, the government has also implemented policies that deny the legitimacy of this view. One of the most infamous examples was the military's Don't Ask, Don't Tell policy in place from 1993 through 2011, which disallowed the military to inquire about a person's sexual orientation and prohibited gay people from disclosing their sexual preferences. The policy assumed "that sexual orientation is evident only when there is a conscious decision to reveal it." In 10 U. S. C. § 654, the government held that the presence of gay people "in the armed forces would create an unacceptable risk to the armed forces' high standards of morale, good order and discipline, and unit cohesion that are the essence of military capability." Again, such a policy strikes me as ridiculous. And a recent study actually shows no adverse consequences from the repeal of Don't Ask, Don't Tell.

Although the underlying assumption of this policy was that one's sexual orientation is undetectable unless voluntarily revealed, many soldiers lived in fear that their identity would be detected. And that fear was legitimate, as the US military discharged more than 13,000 members for being gay. "I constantly was always thinking 'life would be better if I was not here,'" said Marcus Prince, a soldier in the Oklahoma Army National Guard. The repeal of Don't Ask, Don't Tell in 2011 changed that, and Prince later came out on the Web as a result: "I'm not hiding who I am anymore," he said.

Gaydar and straightdar play a role in other societal institutions. One of the most notable is professional sports—more specifically, male team sports such as baseball, basketball, and football. To my knowledge no professional athlete in baseball or football has come out while in uniform for fear of the possible repercussions to their relations with teammates, management, and fans. Still, people often "accuse" players, as well as soldiers, athletes, politicians, and others within larger institutions, of being gay based in part on their appearance and nonverbal signals.

The Perception of People and Sexual Orientation

The implications of gaydar and straightdar extend beyond such societal institutions as the military and professional athletics. We consciously and unconsciously size up the people we encounter on a daily basis based on how they look and act. We may treat people of one race or age differently than we would people of a different race or age purely due to our own interpretation of these categories. These initial perceptions frame our subsequent interactions and can drive how we behave toward others. For instance, an elderly man recently asked me if I knew where the restroom was in an office building. Instead of merely giving him the directions, I opted to escort him to the restroom because I suspected he might become confused. If the man asking me had been in his fifties or sixties, I would not have thought twice about telling him where to go and letting him find his own way, but he looked like he was in his eighties. This is a relatively benign example, but like it or not, humans do not perceive and treat others equally, no matter how much we think we do or wish we did.

Our perceptions of sexual orientation have profound and sometimes dire consequences. Gay people are the US minority group most targeted by hate crimes—at a rate 2.5 times that of African Americans and about 4.5 times that of Muslims. And the trend is growing.

Negative evaluations of people with a same-sex preference show up in the lab as well. Researchers at the University of Toronto examined people's perceptions of others who were gay and straight as a function of their ethnicity. They showed study subjects numerous head shots of men taken from Internet dating sites but gave no information about their sexual orientation. The pictures fell into four categories:

1. Straight white men
2. Gay white men
3. Straight black men
4. Gay black men

After showing each picture, the researchers asked subjects, "To the average Canadian, how likable would this person seem?"

Straight white men were significantly more likable than straight black men. The results are even more interesting when we consider how sexual orientation interacted with ethnicity. Subjects perceived straight whites as significantly more likeable than gay whites. They showed the exact opposite pattern with black targets: they perceived gay black men as more likeable than straight black men. Remember that the researchers did not tell these study subjects that the men in the photos varied in sexual orientation, and none of the subjects reported thinking that some of the men were gay. These findings fascinate me because they demonstrate that our unconscious perceptions of sexual orientation actually interact with consciously perceived variables—race, in this case—to influence our impressions of others.

If We Can Tell, How Accurate Are We?

Although the University of Toronto study suggests that our perceptions of others' sexual orientation can influence us unconsciously, detecting sexual orientation is often a conscious process, if for no other reason than that we want to identify a viable mate. Estimates vary, but about 3 percent of men and 1 to 2 percent of women report being gay. Approximately 85 to 90 percent of the population reports desiring only partners of the opposite sex, and the rest are interested in partners of both sexes to varying degrees. No matter what our sexual orientation, it makes little sense to expend time and energy on potential mates who will show no interest in us. One self-identified lesbian described gaydar as "an essential survival strategy." One straight woman remarked in the *San Francisco Chronicle,* "Women *had* to develop gaydar to prevent hours of heartbreak and dashed hopes. Life is too short and the dating scene is too hard; best to know whether you've got at least an outside shot."

Can we accurately infer sexual orientation? How much exposure to a person do we need to do so? And what tells lead to such a judgment?

Several researchers have examined the accuracy of gaydar. In one study, they separately invited almost one hundred men and women who self-identified as gay or straight into the lab—four groups in all—and video- and audio-recorded interviews with each subject for about twenty minutes. After the interviews, the researchers created five different stimuli from their recordings to show different subjects:

- First, they selected a tiny fraction—only six to ten seconds worth—of the twenty-minute interview.
- Second, they removed sound from the clips and exaggerated the visual contrast, thereby reducing observable detail in the photos and emphasizing interviewees' movements—gesture and posture—rather than their appearance.
- Third, they created audio-only clips from the interviews.

- Fourth, they photographed each of the interviewees standing up.
- And, finally, they prepared written transcripts of the clips for subsequent subjects to read.

Subjects accurately perceived the sexual orientation of interviewees based on their overall behavior in the brief clips, their movements, their speech, and their photograph alone. This study, among others, shows that it takes mere seconds for naive judges to detect sexual orientation. In fact, they correctly judged the interviewees' sexual orientation 81 percent of the time from the six- to ten-second clips. As the authors reported, "Raters tended to be very accurate in assessing sexual orientation." Importantly, subjects were unable to determine the interviewees' sexual orientation by reading the written transcripts, indicating that they made their determinations based on tells from body language and speech quality.

Many people with a same-sex preference have told me that they think they are more skilled at detecting gay people than their straight counterparts. One gay man told me, "I've never been wrong!"

Do gay people have superior gaydar? After all, they may be more motivated to identify viable partners, and they are likely more familiar with gay people's behavior. "We have learned antennae," one lesbian told me, "to detect others like us."

It turns out that the data are mixed; some studies find that gay people are more accurate, and others find no difference. If gay people can detect the tells of sexual orientation more accurately than straight people, the difference is likely small.

Concealment of Sexual Orientation?

In an earlier chapter, I told you about a camp I worked at in northern Illinois. The camp provided a wonderful place for most of the children to learn about nature, sing camp songs, and play games in the hot and humid weather. The experience wasn't so good for one boy named John, however. Though he had done nothing to provoke them, other campers were relentlessly cruel to him throughout the entire summer. Why? Because of his "girly" behaviors, according to the campers. John looked and behaved in exaggerated stereotypical feminine fashion—he walked, talked, and behaved differently from the rest of the boys. I saw him try to act in a more "gender-typical" manner to reduce the other children's taunts, but this didn't change their behavior toward him.

Some adults also make efforts to conceal their sexual orientation to some degree. Many have told me that they must remain vigilant for situations in which it might be unsafe to reveal that they are gay. In one interview I conducted for this book, a man named James told me how he had consciously tried to conceal his sexual preference before coming out. Growing up in a devoutly Christian home in the Midwest and fearing that others would discover his sexual orientation, James learned how to disguise it. "After all," he told me, "I had to have a place to live." James walked in a masculine fashion—shoulders back and chest out. He straightened his wrists and curbed his hand gesturing. He deepened his voice. For years, he monitored the cues he might be emitting. According to James, he felt relief when he came out to his family and friends in high school because he no longer had to exert the mental and physical energy to try to deceive others.

Were John's and James's efforts to conceal their sexual orientation in vain? Is it possible to do so successfully? (Whether they should feel the need to do so, of course, is a very different issue.)

A stereotypically feminine gay man might adopt a more "manly" way of walking and talking and dress differently in an attempt to appear straight. Yet, people simply cannot modify some anatomical features, such as facial structure or body configuration, at least not by natural means. Since the face often reveals a host of information, such as gender, age, and ethnicity, does it also provide clues about sexual orientation?

To find out, male and female subjects looked at photographs of men who self-identified as gay or straight. Some images included men's hair and face, whereas others showed only specific facial features, such as the hair, eyes, or mouth. Three relevant findings deserve mention. First, subjects accurately identified the men's sexual orientation from the photographs of their entire faces. Second, no specific component of the face was necessary to discern sexual orientation; when researchers removed specific components such as the hair, mouth, and eyes, subjects could still accurately identify the sexual orientation of the people in the photos. Finally, multiple features of the face—hair, mouth, and eyes—signal sexual orientation, not just one. Interestingly, judgments based on hairstyle—a controllable feature—drive accuracy more than judgments based on the mouth and eyes.

Such studies suggest that at least some people—both gay and straight—would be hard pressed to conceal their sexual preference. Humans' facial structures and features signal sexual orientation independently of the makeup we wear, the style of our hair, how we walk, and the vocal intonation we use. Other work indicates that body shape is also diagnostic of sexual orientation for some people, especially women. We will circle back to this a little later.

Policies like Don't Ask, Don't Tell rest on the premise that people can successfully conceal their sexual orientation; thus, no discrimination is possible unless gays and lesbians intentionally signal who they are. Such policies are not only unjust but futile often times.

The Tells of Sexual Orientation

Aerosmith's song "Dude Looks Like a Lady" depicts one man's stereotypical feminine nature. Even though it has nothing to do with sexual orientation, the song does describe something that may be happening when it comes to homing in on someone's sexual orientation: people identified as gay, both correctly and incorrectly, often have physical features and behaviors deemed atypical of their biological sex. That is, others sometimes judge as gay men perceived to have feminine qualities and women perceived to have masculine qualities.

On average—and "average" is a key word to remember—women and men differ across a number of physical and behavioral attributes. Some obvious examples include the following: (1) women are shorter and less physically strong than men; (2) women's bodies are shaped differently than men's, with the former more often having an hourglass figure compared to men's more tubular form; (3) women's voices and vocal patterns differ from men's; (4) women walk differently than men; and (5) men's and women's faces differ in structure and features. In relation to men's faces, women's faces are smoother and lighter in color, thanks to the lack of facial hair. Their eyebrows are narrower and arched, and they have larger eyes and fuller lips. Women also have rounder faces with smaller, less angular jawbones and higher eyebrows. There will always be exceptions to these empirical generalizations, but more often than not, they hold true. I'll call these empirical generalizations "sex typical."

Researchers think the degree to which some people's features are sex atypical may largely drive the ability to distinguish gay from straight individuals. The term "sex atypical" refers to traits that others perceive as atypical of a person's biological sex. If my face were not angular with small eyes but rounder with arched eyebrows and larger eyes, it would be sex atypical. Men on average do not have faces with these features, but women do.

So, what physical and behavioral traits help us distinguish between people who are straight and people who are gay? Obviously, some, like height and strength, are out of the running. But research suggests that others indicate sexual orientation, at least for some people. Take faces. Gay men have faces that people perceive as more feminine compared to straight men, and lesbians have faces that people perceive as more masculine compared to straight women. The more sex atypical someone's face is, the more likely others are to be able to assess his or her sexual orientation.

Sex-atypical body shape, walking style, and vocal qualities lead to accurate inferences of sexual orientation as well. People are more likely to accurately judge men perceived to have an hourglass figure as gay and women perceived to have a tubular figure as lesbians. Body type is diagnostic of sexual orientation for both sexes to some degree, but more so for women. Self-identified "butch" women tend to have bodies resembling men's tubular shape, whereas self-identified "femme" lesbians tend to have the hourglass-shaped body characteristic of heterosexual women.

Research has also linked walking style to sexual orientation. Females judged to be lesbians walk more like typical men, with a swagger, whereas males judged to be gay walk more like typical females, with a sway. This effect is most powerfully diagnostic for male sexual orientation. That said, plenty of men who are gay walk like straight men (i.e., sex typically) and vice versa.

Of course, not all people who are gay have sex-atypical physical traits. Although the voice is diagnostic of sexual orientation to some degree, plenty of people with a same-sex preference talk in a sex-typical fashion. This leads to errors in inferring sexual orientation "mostly in the direction of misidentifying gay people as straight." As one leading researcher stated, "Many gay men have 'straight-sounding' voices, but not many straight people have 'gay-sounding' voices."

This last point is worth emphasizing and expanding. Rock Hudson and Marlene Dietrich were paragons of masculinity and femininity, respectively; they looked and behaved like most people of their sex, even though Hudson, it was later discovered, was gay, and Dietrich famously had relationships with both men and women. Likewise, plenty of straight people are sex atypical in some ways; that is, they look and behave in ways more typical of the opposite sex. Therefore, even though having sex-atypical features is diagnostic of sexual orientation to some degree, basing judgments solely on this criterion can lead to mistakes. This teaches us that while humans are adept at inferring the sexual orientation of others based on brief interactions, *we are undoubtedly wrong sometimes.*

The Nature and Nurture of Inferring Sexual Orientation

What are the origins of gaydar and straightdar? We can take two approaches to address this question. One involves examining the origins of the sexual orientation of the observed individual, and the other involves examining the perceptual origins of the observer.

Some researchers hold that the origins of the cues that hint at sexual orientation are unknown. The fact that a man swings his hips more than most men tells us nothing about the biological origins of this trait. He may be consciously or unconsciously imitating the other sex or other people who are gay. Or perhaps the behavior expresses an aspect of his genetic makeup. From this perspective, the findings regarding the efficacy of gaydar inform us little about the biological origins of sexual orientation. Others, however, think such cues elucidate the origins of sexual orientation. Given the complexity of these issues, I refer the reader to a provocative book by Simon LeVay titled *Gay, Straight, and the Reason Why: The Science of Sexual Orientation.*

To what degree have we evolved to detect others' sexual orientation and to what degree have we learned to do so? The answer to this question is unresolved and undoubtedly complex. The evidence gathered thus far is consistent with biological explanations, but, as we'll see, environmental factors almost certainly also play a role.

The most compelling evidence of a biological foundation for the detection of sexual orientation comes from a series of studies conducted at the University of Toronto and Tufts University. In one study, researchers asked heterosexual women not taking contraceptive medication to sit down at a computer that displayed eighty pictures of different men's faces one at a time. The women pressed one key if they thought a man was gay and another if they thought he was straight. Unbeknownst to the subjects, half the men in the pictures self-reported as gay and the others as straight. After the women had pressed eighty keys, researchers asked them when they had had their last menses and how long their fertility cycle typically lasted. The figure below depicts the general pattern of findings obtained.

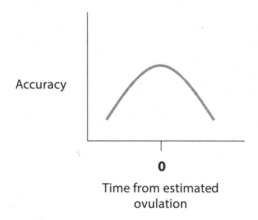

0

Time from estimated
ovulation

The women were more accurate at inferring men's sexual orientation the closer in time they were to ovulating.

Astonishingly, the closer women were to the peak of their ovulatory cycle—the time of the month when they were most likely to conceive—the more accurately they detected the sexual orientation of the men in the photos. The researchers suggested that women may be more sensitive to male sexual orientation during peak ovulation because being able to identify a potential mate is important in maximizing the likelihood of conception.

You might be skeptical that the females were more sensitive specifically to male sexual orientation during peak ovulation; it's possible, after all, that they picked up on nonverbal cues generally related to sexual orientation. To test this alternative explanation, the researchers conducted an identical study, but with one difference: female subjects examined photos of women who self-identified as lesbian or straight.

The subjects could accurately distinguish between the straight and lesbian females in the photos, but their ability to do so did not correlate with their ovulatory cycles. These data support the hypothesis that women's ovulatory cycles are linked to identification of male sexual orientation because of its association with reproduction. This hypothesis gained further support from a follow-up study in which women experimentally primed to think about romance and mating were more accurate than control subjects in discerning male, but not female, sexual orientation. During the time of the month when a woman is most likely to conceive, she is most capable of identifying the guy who might provide the other 50 percent of the genes for her offspring.

The rapidity of our perceptual systems in distinguishing between gay and straight people also supports the biological underpinnings of the phenomenon. After seeing men's and women's faces flashed on a screen for merely one-twentieth of a second, people can detect their sexual orientation at above-chance levels. Clearly, our perceptual systems are finely and efficiently attuned to detect and interpret the subtle signals of sexual orientation.

The ability to detect sexual preference appears to be universal, which is, again, consistent with an evolutionary explanation of the phenomenon. In one study, men and women from Japan, Spain, and the United States could accurately assess men's sexual orientation. However, some differences between subjects from these countries suggest that our evolutionary history is not the whole story. American observers more quickly and accurately discerned sexual orientation than those from Japan and Spain. Moreover, the pattern of observers' errors differed depending on their country of origin. People from Japan—where homosexuality is least accepted among the three countries—were significantly more likely than Americans and Spaniards to miscategorize gay men as straight. This finding, along with other data, indicates that cultural factors almost certainly play a role in the perception of sexual orientation.

It is important to note that most of the studies I've discussed in this chapter have limitations. For starters, they were performed in the laboratory. How much these findings correlate with real-world phenomena is anyone's guess. I have a hunch that the lab studies may actually underestimate our species' ability to perceive sexual orientation. Such studies often strip away extraneous information that could provide clues to sexual orientation, but in the real world, these clues are often available.

Also, most of the studies rely on people who self-identify as gay or straight in a public way; most often, these individuals have either responded to an advertisement to participate in a lab study or posted their photos on dating websites. Thus, the findings may apply only to those people who are public about their sexual orientation.

Finally, sexual orientation is a multidimensional phenomenon that deals with thinking, identification, and behavior. As such, we can index sexual orientation in any number of ways, and we should keep that in mind when evaluating this work. Relatedly, it's worthwhile noting that the studies I've discussed look at people who are gay or straight. Few examine people who are bisexual, so it's difficult to say how others along the sexual orientation spectrums are represented.

I opened this chapter with a quip from Ellen Degeneres: "I must be giving off one of those vibes again. That's what we do . . . we give off vibrations and then we pick up the vibrations from our gaydar . . . so I've heard." Some are understandably incredulous of the concept of gaydar. But the data seem to indicate that we are capable of inferring people's sexual orientation. Just as you'll occasionally be wrong when guessing others' ethnicity by looking at them, however, you'll undoubtedly be wrong sometimes when assessing their sexual orientation too.

Party-Worthy Findings

1. **Facial structure:** Facial structure alone, independent of hair and jewelry, is enough for others to predict sexual orientation at above-chance levels.

2. **Ovulation and detection of sexual orientation:** The closer women are to the peak of their ovulatory cycle—the most likely time of the month to conceive—the more accurately they detect the sexual orientation of men.

3. **Blink-of-the-eye prediction of sexual orientation:** When men's and women's faces are flashed on a screen for merely one-twentieth of a second, people can detect their sexual orientation at above-chance levels.

III.

Love and Lies

6

FROM DATING TO MATING

"Who ever loved that loved not at first sight?"
—SHAKESPEARE

Millions of people are looking for a romantic partner. Some will develop a relationship with someone they've had a long time to get acquainted with. Many will have to decide whether to ask another person out on a date based on little more than a few minutes' worth of information. Should I invite the guy I just met in the grocery store out to dinner? Should I accept if I'm asked? The answers to these questions could determine a person's future.

Thanks to eons of evolution, our brains come preprogrammed with specific preferences in prospective companions. In a nutshell, evolutionary theory suggests that the primary function of members of every species is to pass their genes on to the next generation. Therefore, it is vital that we choose our mates with care. We don't view potential candidates impartially; rather we have preferences for specific mates. Why? Because these predilections lead to maximum reproductive success. In essence, we are dating in a modern world with Stone Age minds.

The gender differences we observe in sexual behavior and preferences stem from the challenges faced by our Pleistocene ancestors. According to evolutionary theory, reproduction is incredibly costly to women in terms of energy and effort. Not only do they carry an infant for nine months before birth, enduring morning sickness, discomfort, and relative immobility during pregnancy, but they also remain the primary caregiver for a number of years, breast-feeding and nurturing offspring throughout childhood. Because of this, women could not procure the required calories and nutrition for their children, who took years to venture out on their own. On the evolutionary savannah, choosing a lazy, abusive, or unskilled mate would jeopardize a woman's reproductive success, as he would be less likely to provide the necessary resources for her and her child. If she chose an industrious, skilled mate who successfully provided essential assets, both she and her baby would be more likely to flourish. These selection pressures, operating over thousands of years, have programmed women's brains to desire mates able to provide the support and resources needed to raise children successfully.

While women vary in their mate preferences, on average, the data support the evolutionary story. In a now famous study, David Buss asked more than 10,000 people on six continents and five islands what they wanted in a potential partner. Both men and women preferred long-term mates who were kind and intelligent, but women placed more than twice as much value on financial resources than men did, and this finding held across all racial groups, political systems, religious affiliations, and continents.

In a different study, researchers sought to investigate what predicted women's responses to personal ads. In line with evolutionary theory, the four most powerful predictors were men's education level, height, age, and resources. Education, height, and age all correlate positively with economic resources. One study indicates that a six-foot-tall man will earn an estimated $166,000 more than a five-foot-five man over the course of a thirty-year career.

In short, women carry the legacy of their maternal descendants' preferences because these penchants tended to lead to success in the past. Of course, characteristics associated with financial success, such as ambition, industriousness, social status, and stability are not all it takes to court a lady. Women prefer men who demonstrate love, kindness, humor, and commitment, as well as those who profess a willingness and capacity to invest in future children. As *New York Times* columnist David Brooks points out, this is why we see so many young and childless couples playing so enthusiastically with their friends' children; the men are signaling, albeit unconsciously, their delight in the prospect of fatherhood to woo their nubile dates. Women desire stick-around dads to likely cads, as they say. Finally, women favor mates with good, healthy genes. After all, why, from an evolutionary perspective, should a woman invest inordinate amounts of time and energy into offspring destined to lack the requisite genetic foundation for good health?

Just because we have inherited preferential tendencies from our ancestors, this does not mean they are "good" or that we should necessarily adhere to them today. But evolutionary theorists and their research provide us with an explanation for why many of us have some of the predilections we do.

Seeing Men

When a heterosexual woman meets a man, several readily apparent qualities may influence whether she finds him attractive romantically, such as his ethnicity and age. But from an evolutionary perspective, women are interested in other, less obvious qualities as well, including potential economic resources, social status, kindness, and health. Are women able to predict any of these qualities based on tells when they first meet a man? As we'll see, there is wisdom in what many parents have told their children: first impressions count.

Imagine you're looking at two virtually identical faces, but one is slightly more symmetrical than the other. If you're like most people, you'll deem the more symmetrical face more attractive than the other. This tendency holds true across races, ages, cultures, genders, and sexual orientations.

If you look in the mirror, you'll likely see asymmetries in your own face. As the figure on page 88 shows, my left eye is higher on my face and larger than my right eye; the two parallel lines across the photograph show how uneven they are relative to each other. Also notice that my teeth are not centered exactly beneath the middle of my nose. In contrast, many male models and actors, such as Bradley Cooper and Tom Cruise, have faces that look almost as symmetrical as a perfectly shaped football.

Your author's asymmetric face. The images are identical, other than the lines.

Don't feel bad if you are asymmetrical like me; most faces contain such misalignments.

Both men and women prefer symmetrical faces and bodies over their lopsided counterparts for two reasons: good genes and good health. During development, the cells on both the left and right sides of your body must grow and reproduce at exactly the same rate to be symmetrical. Any number of factors—including genetic anomalies and environmental stressors, such as disease or wounds—can generate asymmetries in the body. Thus, when we see someone like Bradley Cooper or Tom Cruise, we see men who have the physiological capacity to deal with all of these stresses better than others (like me). In essence, because of their genetics, Cooper and Cruise were better able to withstand challenges they faced during development that might have thrown off bodily symmetry. According to evolutionary psychology, we should prefer potential mates with greater genetic fitness and better health over those less genetically fortunate.

When I first read about this a number of years ago, I thought, surely one's perception of a man's attractiveness would not predict the quality of his genes or the level of his health, especially when we can ascertain good looks in fractions of a second. However, a fair amount of evidence supports the notion that people with attractive and symmetrical faces really are healthier than their less-than-symmetrical counterparts. Men with symmetrical faces tend to have greater emotional, psychological, and physical health outcomes. These men also have sex earlier in life and have more sexual partners; women also choose them more often as affair partners. And physically attractive men are stronger, more socially dominant, and longer-lived than less attractive men. A woman's preference for a man who will likely live longer, and therefore be around to invest in his children and grandchildren, makes evolutionary sense.

However, does the attractiveness of a man's face predict any immediate benefit to a woman concerning reproduction? A group of researchers photographed sixty-six undergraduate males' faces and asked them to provide a sperm sample. Men whom women perceived as more attractive had higher-quality sperm compared to their less attractive counterparts. What does "higher quality" mean? Basically, the sperm possessed a better shape and were better swimmers.

Among the most fascinating and best-known studies ever conducted demonstrating the power of symmetry linked this quality with smell. Researchers computed men's symmetry levels by measuring their ears, elbows, ankles, and fingers. They then asked the men to wear a T-shirt to bed for a couple nights without applying deodorant or other fragrances. Subsequently, the researchers gave the shirts to women, who rated how good they smelled. Astonishingly, the men with the most symmetrical bodies produced the best-smelling T-shirts. The preference for T-shirts worn by symmetrical men was particularly evident among women at the peak of fertility during their menstrual cycle. Symmetrical men may also possess genes for heightened immune system functioning, and we know that they have fewer respiratory illnesses. I'm not sure if it's based on science or not, but recently people in New York and Los Angeles have been putting T-shirts they've slept in into bags with a random number, then bringing them to singles' parties so others can choose whom they want to date based on the odor of the shirt.

Women may also be clueing into another facet revealed by men's faces: their testosterone levels. We've all seen Clint Eastwood's and Daniel Craig's chiseled jaws, pronounced cheekbones, and prominent brows (in addition to their fine symmetry). These rugged masculine features undoubtedly place such men at the end of the bell curve for masculinity, as testosterone is responsible for many of their facial features. The hormone leads to greater cell growth in these areas, which becomes more apparent in some men than in their baby-faced counterparts. It turns out that heterosexual women prefer masculine-looking faces like Eastwood's and Craig's. Researchers are still investigating why, but they posit that masculine faces signal greater health and resistance to disease, as well as greater dominance, another quality preferred by women.

Clearly, however, women do not always prefer men for their looks, particularly when looking for long-term partners. Remember that, all other things being equal, women across the evolutionary savannah benefitted from choosing men who could provide food, shelter, and other resources to support them and their children. According to David Buss, an "enormous" body of empirical evidence supports the contention that women across the world have evolved a powerful preference for men with resources, as mentioned above. In fact, according to one study, women looking for a marriage partner reported desiring men with an earning capacity in the seventieth percentile or greater (i.e., an earning capacity exceeding that of 70 percent of all other men). Most women do not want the average Joe when it comes to earning potential. Women also prefer men who hold high social status and educational achievement as these correlate with men's capacity to control and acquire resources.

Considering these preferences, we must wonder if certain tells don't betray men's socioeconomic status. Reflect on a couple scenarios:

In the first, consider a man in his early thirties named Nate. (I'm opting to discuss a gay man in these examples to show that often times sexual orientation is irrelevant; the same information is equally available to gay and straight people.) He enters his local fitness center and hops onto the exercise bike, as he would on any normal day. After finishing his workout, he walks over to the water fountain and strikes up a conversation with a man who seems somewhat interested in him, at least enough so to engage him in a minute of conversation. After their brief chat, Nate dresses in the locker room and thinks about the man he just met.

In the second scenario, John, a man in his mid-twenties, strikes up a brief conversation on a Sunday afternoon in a local grocery store parking lot with a casually dressed man who seems interested in him. When they are finished talking, John observes the man load his groceries into his five-year-old sedan and drive away.

Because Nate met the first man in a gym and John met the second man on a weekend run to the grocery story, they have no way of knowing how these men dress from day to day. And their interactions with the men were brief, so they couldn't really get to know them well. Do the men have white-collar or blue-collar jobs? Do they typically wear a well-tailored pin-stripe suit with a crimson symbol around their necks signaling power and status (i.e., a tie)? Are they well educated, or did they drop out of high school? Do they come from old-money families, or are they barely making ends meet?

Sociologists and psychologists define social class as encompassing ma terial wealth, occupational prestige, and educational attainment. Social class differentiates us in a number of fundamental ways, often influencing, for instance, the neighborhoods we live in, the schools we send our kids to, our health, our religious beliefs, and even the type of music we enjoy. Further, social class actually affects our thoughts about the world, our emotional reactions to events in our lives, and our behaviors. Those from lower-class backgrounds feel less in control of their lives but more accurately perceive other people's emotions compared to their upper-class counterparts. Given that people of similar social class have somewhat similar worldviews, on average, individuals often seek potential mates who occupy the same social class.

Nate and John can never be sure about the wealth, occupational status, or educational achievement of the men they met based on such brief interactions, but a cleverly designed study suggests that they are capable of discerning social class. Michael Kraus and Dacher Keltner invited about one hundred unacquainted subjects to the lab to talk to each other two at a time. Some of these subjects had well-educated parents earning large salaries, while others came from families with much more modest means. The researchers then examined one minute of the conversation between the subjects.

Their study revealed two important findings. First, subjects from high-class backgrounds were more aloof and sometimes even rude during the conversation, whereas those who came from more modest families were more polite and attentive to their conversational partners. Second, observers of these conversations could predict the individuals' educational and income backgrounds. Keep in mind that they based these predictions on merely one minute of interaction—about the same amount of time Nate and John spent with the men they met. As Kraus and Keltner wrote, "Nonverbal displays of the capacity to provide resources are likely to be important in mate selection."

Considered as a whole, men reveal information about themselves simply through their tells. Their facial attractiveness, symmetry, and masculinity hint at numerous outcomes, from their emotional and physical health to the quality of their sperm. Their behavioral cues also suggest their overall social class. Many potential mates deem this sort of information vital.

These tells are not perfectly valid for every individual, and there is more to choosing a mate than evaluating economic resources and other relatively superficial qualities. But whether you are a man or a woman interested in meeting a potential male mate, will you ever look at men the same way again?

Seeing Women

On the evolutionary savannah, both sexes sought to pass on their genes, but they faced somewhat different issues. While reproduction demanded much of women in terms of time and energy, it incurred little cost for men: they need only have sex with women a few times, perhaps less, to have a son or daughter. So while women developed preferences for healthy men who would also provide them and their offspring with the required resources and support in the long-term, men sought to maximize their reproductive success by having sex with women—ideally, many—who appeared capable of bearing and raising children. Thus, when it came to reproductive strategies, women paired wisely, whereas men paired widely.

From King Henry VIII to modern day philanderers, men have sought to spread their seed. Although evolutionary theory may shed light on their promiscuous behavior, it does not serve as an excuse, of course. Many men throughout history have made long-term commitments without straying. From an evolutionary perspective, however, why would a man commit to a woman in the first place if he need only inseminate her to pass on his genes?

It turns out, males commit for a number of reasons. First, pledging his dedication may help a man secure a potential mate, as she may withhold sex until he has done so. Second, men who are willing and able to commit for the long term have a wider pool of women from which to choose; thus they may be able to attract a more desirable mate. Third, a man who marries a woman can be more confident that any babies she has will be his, rather than another man's. From an evolutionary perspective, it makes no sense for a man to invest in another man's offspring, as they do not carry his genes. Fourth, a man's long-term presence increases the probability of his children surviving. And finally, in many cultures marriage confers status upon men, in turn enhancing the resources available to them and their families.

Whether or not heterosexual men pursue short-term or long-term mates, men around the world prefer women who are attractive, youthful, and display signs of fertility. Our male ancestors had to mate with women capable of becoming pregnant to become reproductively successful. Evolution has conditioned men to prefer and respond in predictable ways to specific female cues that signal fecundity. After all, we are descendants of men who chose women who succeeded in reproducing. Again, this line of thinking provides no answer for what men *should* prefer; rather it explains *why* men, on average, prefer the things they do.

I have several friends in their thirties, forties, and fifties who are currently seeking a long-term mate. One of them—I'll call him Bill—is a gregarious, well-educated, and energetic forty-five-year-old. Bill has never been married and has been looking for years for "the one" to settle down and have kids with. From an evolutionary perspective, what are Bill's likely female preferences? Do these reveal anything about the women he could potentially meet?

One of the most salient cues is a woman's age, which we can predict based on any number of obvious cues, like skin elasticity and hair texture. Consider men such as Dennis Kucinich, Rod Stewart, Mick Jagger, and Donald Trump. At one point, they all married women who were much younger and, most would argue, more attractive than themselves. Can you name three well-known couples in which an affluent woman of average attractiveness has married a handsome younger man with considerably less monetary cachet? My guess is that you probably can't, at least not easily. There simply are too few examples of mature and powerful women marrying debonair young beaus. From an evolutionary view, a man should prefer younger women, who are more likely to bear children, enabling him to pass his genes to future generations. If Bill is anything like most men in their mid-forties, according to the data, he almost certainly would not prefer a mate older than himself; indeed, he would willingly be with a woman as young as thirty-one.

My friend Bill could also examine a number of other signals that predict women's genetic fitness, health, and fertility. He could look at the symmetry of women's faces, since the more symmetrical her face, the better a woman will have withstood disease and other environmental insults during development. He could also observe the femininity of women's faces; more than symmetry, the femininity of a woman's face predicts how attractive people find her, and this is thought to be culturally universal. Women with feminine faces tend to have small chins, full lips, large eyes, high cheekbones, and thin jaws. Among the celebrities on the big screen, Angelina Jolie takes the cake for distinctly feminine facial qualities, with her large eyes, high cheekbones, and the fullest lips I've ever seen. (Of course, we don't know the degree to which these features are truly hers versus the work of the world's best plastic surgeons . . . more about this later.) These women also have significantly higher levels of the hormone estrogen, which research has linked to greater fertility. Thus, by inspecting a woman's facial femininity, Bill can predict something about her physiological capacities.

Bill might also assess potential mates by their weight, as it often signals women's health status and propensity for disease. Interestingly though, men's preferences for body weight differ between cultures. In societies where food is plentiful, like the United States and Europe, men prefer thin women. But in those where food is scarce and nutrition poor, men prefer heavier women.

Does a specific region of women's bodies reveal information? A ubiquitous topic in dorm rooms when I was in college was what female body part men prized most highly. There were the butt guys, the leg guys, and the breast guys. For the record, Bill, by his own admission, belongs firmly in the latter category. But there is scant evidence that breast size correlates

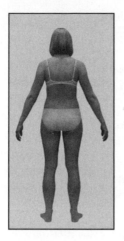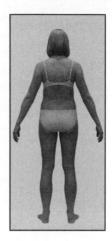

Two different waist-to-hip ratios.

with fertility, and it bears little relationship to women's ability to breast-feed. In terms of prediction, Bill would do better to examine a different region of the female body.

Examine the photos above. Which do you prefer? If you are like most, you chose the photo on the left. Why? The answer lies in the woman's midsection. If you look carefully, you'll see that the ratio of the woman's waist to her hips is greater in the right photo (0.7 and 0.8, left and right, respectively). Men worldwide prefer women with smaller waist-to-hip ratios (WHRs), that is, with narrower waists and broader hips, to females with larger WHRs. In fact, the "preferred" WHR ratio in most studies is about 0.7 or less in developed Western countries. All other things being equal, the more a woman's WHR exceeds 0.7, the less likely men are to rate her as attractive. I've computed the WHRs of some famous celebrities from yesterday and today to give you a sense of their measurements. Of course there are exceptions, but many women widely deemed beautiful have waist-to-hip ratios hovering around 0.7 or less.

Tyra Banks	0.67
Halle Berry	0.67
Gisele Bündchen	0.66
Naomi Campbell	0.71
Salma Hayek	0.68

Audrey Hepburn	0.59
Scarlett Johansson	0.69
Heidi Klum	0.71
Beyonce Knowles	0.68
Elle MacPherson	0.71
Eva Mendes	0.69
Marilyn Monroe	0.67
Kate Moss	0.66
Rihanna	0.69
Elizabeth Taylor	0.58
Uma Thurman	0.71

In one seminal study, a researcher examined how weight and WHR fluctuated among Miss America Pageant winners and Playboy models over several decades. Despite the growing emphasis on thinness over the same period, the pageant winners' and playboy models' waist-to-hip ratios remained relatively constant, at around 0.7, demonstrating a continuity in the features that Western society deems attractive.

One of my undergraduate students has participated in beauty pageants throughout most of her young life, recently winning the swimsuit contest in her state. When I asked her if women in beauty pageants pay much attention to their WHR, she replied, "Absolutely." She explained that achieving the perfect hourglass figure is, by and large, the key to winning the swimsuit contest. Further, she said that women make very conscious decisions regarding the swimsuits they wear, the specific workouts they endure, and even where they place shiny jewelry on their suits. "The goal," she said, "is to entice the judges to look at the hips and make the waist appear as thin as possible."

Thousands of women across the country endure plastic surgery to manufacture this aesthetic, transplanting fat from their waists to their bottoms to accentuate their waist-to-hip ratios. This procedure presented a unique opportunity for researchers at the University of Texas, Austin, who wanted to study the neurobiological underpinnings of the preference for low WHRs. Men looked at women's pre- and postoperative photos while a functional magnetic resonance imaging, or fMRI, machine scanned their brains. As compared to the preoperative pictures, the postop photos depicting the hourglass shapes highly activated the parts of men's brains associated with rewards.

Before puberty, men and women have similar WHRs, but after that the ratios differ dramatically, with men in the range of 0.85 to 0.95 and women in the range of 0.67 to 0.80. The WHR really measures how fat is distributed on our bodies. During puberty, men lose fat in their legs and buttocks, while women gain fat in their upper thighs and hips, due primarily to the hormone estrogen. A low WHR on a woman means that she carries her fat around her hips, whereas a high WHR indicates that she carries it around her waist.

This difference in fat distribution has significant implications for a woman's health. Women with elevated WHR are at risk for numerous illnesses, such as cancer—particularly ovarian and breast cancer—gall bladder disease, adult-onset diabetes, hypertension, and depression. These findings help explain why the World Health Organization says that female waist-to-hip ratios exceeding 0.80 are unsafe.

Men like Bill prefer a relatively low WHR because it not only signals a woman's current and future health but also tells us something about her reproductive fitness. A low WHR signals that a woman is unlikely to be pregnant at that moment and also that she possesses broad enough hips to make childbirth less taxing on her and her infant. As a woman goes through menopause, her WHR approaches that of males, providing clues about age and fertility. WHR also tells us something about women's physiology; women with lower WHRs menstruate more regularly, ovulate more frequently, and are more apt to conceive via artificial insemination and in vitro fertilization. One study showed that women with a WHR of 0.7 to 0.79 were almost twice as likely to conceive via in vitro fertilization than women with WHRs over 0.80.

Perhaps one of the most novel studies investigating why men prefer lower WHRs comes from William Lassek and Steven Gaulin. Having examined data from thousands of women, Lassek and Gaulin made a straightforward prediction: relative to mothers with high WHRs, women possessing lower WHRs would be more likely to give birth to children who could perform well on cognitive tasks. The hips and thighs have fat deposits containing long chains of fatty acids drawn on by the fetus during gestation and lactation for brain growth. If women with low WHRs have more of these fatty acids available to their offspring during pregnancy and breast feeding, the researchers reasoned, their children should be smarter. Controlling for a number of preexisting variables, they found exactly that. Of course, a myriad of variables predict cognitive outcomes in life, but as a first pass, Bill would do well to examine a woman's waist-to-hip ratio—a predictive tell—rather than her bust size to make a decent forecast about her reproductive fitness as a mate. Of course, whether Bill should consider a woman's WHR or any other physical characteristic when selecting a mate is a very different question.

Accentuating Our Evolutionary Signals

Consider what some women do to "advertise" their evolutionary prowess. One of the first cosmetic surgeries practiced was the removal of the two lowest female ribs, which gave patients narrower waists. For hundreds of years, women have artificially manipulated their waist-to-hip ratios by wearing corsets to thin the waist and pad the hips, despite the fact corsets can cause significant internal injury. Today, we still see women wearing uncomfortable undergarments to minimize their waist-to-hip ratios. The *New York Times* recently featured a photo of a woman sucking in her belly with all her might to don a *faja*, which drastically accentuated her hips. The design of today's popular hip-hugger jeans also accentuates the width of a woman's hips relative to her waist. Whereas women tried to hide their girdles in years past, today celebrities and some other women proudly profess their devotion to Spanx and other accessories that accentuate WHR. Despite the fact that ideals for body weight and breast size have continually changed over time in Western society, the desire for a thin waist and large hips seems to endure.

Western media is also partly responsible for women's desire to accentuate their WHRs. Take the iconic Barbie doll, which first appeared on the market in 1959. Consumers worldwide purchase an average of two Barbies every second, making the doll one of the top-selling toys of all time.

In 2011, Galia Slayen wrote a piece for the *Huffington Post* describing her high school project for National Eating Disorder Awareness Week. Her post caused a media explosion, landing her on almost every morning television news program. Why? Because Galia, a student at Hamilton College, built a life-size Barbie doll. If one were to extrapolate Barbie's

*Galia Slayen
standing next to the
Barbie model she
constructed.*

dimensions to a life-size human, she would be about five feet, nine inches tall and have a bust of thirty-nine inches, a waist of eighteen inches, and hips measuring thirty-three inches. She would wear a size three shoe and weigh 110 pounds. Moreover, her WHR would be 0.55. Given her proportions, Barbie would literally topple over and walk on all fours. Convincing experimental evidence shows that young girls become more dissatisfied with their body images after merely being exposed to Barbie compared to other realistically proportioned dolls.

Makeup has been around for centuries and has grown into a multibillion-dollar industry. Evolutionary theory and everyday experience suggests that many women use makeup to accentuate a variety of fertility signals, such as youth and health. Genetics may program their bodies to display the signs of decreased fertility with age. After the mid-twenties, their eyes become smaller and the sclera—the white part—becomes darker. At about the same time, their lips become thinner and less red. Cheekbones become less pronounced, and skin becomes paler, less elastic, and less smooth. Many women overcome these physical cues with the use of mascara, eyeliner, eye shadow, lip liner, lip gloss, lip plumper, blush, foundation, and a whole range of other chemical substances.

I asked Madeline, a professional in her mid-thirties and the mother of two boys, what motivated her to wear makeup. With the help of fashion magazines, she began to apply makeup at about twelve years of age. She told me that she aims for the "natural" look, so that "people don't even realize I have makeup on." She uses makeup to make her eyes appear larger, to highlight her cheekbones, and to accentuate the fullness of her lips. In addition, she mentioned that she has skin blotches that she tries to cover up so she looks "healthier and younger."

When I asked a thirty-year-old woman named Brandy about her makeup, she replied, "Wow, I could talk for hours about makeup. It's one of my passions." Brandy began applying makeup in early adolescence and is self-taught. She spent hours experimenting. Unlike Madeline, she applies her makeup conspicuously (think bright red lipstick and pronounced brow lines). Like Madeline, however, Brandy tries to maximize the size of her eyes and accentuate her cheekbones. She told me she exaggerates the line of makeup around her naturally thin lips to make them appear fuller and more luscious. She also takes great pains to apply foundation to reduce blotchiness and concealer under her eyes to look "healthier" and "fresh."

I don't want to overstate the case and suggest that all women wear makeup—we all know many who do not. Nor do I claim that most women apply makeup like Madeline and Brandy. I nevertheless found it uncanny how both women applied makeup to accentuate many of the facial cues that signal reproductive fitness and health.

Makeup is merely one tool women use to modify their tells. Many women choose the plastic surgery alternative, deciding to submit to a doctor's knife or receive hypodermic injections. Americans spend an astounding $10.1 billion on cosmetic surgery each year, with women accounting for 91 percent of the procedures performed. Breast augmentation, nose reshaping, liposuction, eyelid surgery, and tummy tucks are the five most common surgical procedures for women; the most common "minimally invasive" procedure is the injection of botulinum toxin type A to reduce wrinkles in the skin. Like makeup, these procedures modify such cues as youth, symmetry, WHR, and the feminization of the face.

While they account for only 9 percent of all cosmetic procedures, men also modify their appearance to signal their biological competency. Nose reshaping, eyelid surgery, liposuction, breast reduction, and hair transplantation are the five most common surgical procedures for men. And, as in women, injection of botulinum toxin type A is the most common "minimally invasive" procedure.

Some men are more likely to exaggerate their material wealth to signal their potential value as a mate. Most of us know "that guy." Recently divorced, he purchases a new designer watch, a fresh wardrobe, and a shiny sports car to replace his decade-old family sedan when he starts dating again. After all, he must fit the part of a desirable date when he picks up a new woman for dinner at a fine restaurant. Of course, this description is a caricature of a man, but most of us know men who like to buy "things" to impress women.

In his fascinating book *The Mating Mind,* Geoffrey Miller argues that humans evolved not only as survival machines but as courtship machines as well. As a result, men sometimes engage in conspicuous consumption— Polo shirts, BMWs, and designer suits—to demonstrate their potential resources to lure women. One study showed that men who spent more than they earned reported having significantly more sexual partners in the last five years and desired to have more sexual partners in the next five years compared to men who did not overspend. This finding held even when researchers controlled for age, education, and marital status. It seems that big spenders are more likely to seek out women than their frugal counterparts. Not surprisingly, research did not link financial consumption to females' sexual history and intentions.

Despite the power of clothes, cosmetics, surgery, and behavior to transform how we appear to others, we can differentiate between honest and dishonest signals, as evolutionary theorists call them. Honest signals reflect a person's true reproductive potential and health, whereas dishonest signals may improve one's aesthetic but have no effect on these characteristics. Thus we would consider women's waist-to-hip ratios and men's facial symmetry honest signals, since they relate to reproductive capacity. A waist-to-hip ratio artificially manipulated by extracting fat from the waist and depositing it on the hips, however, would constitute a dishonest signal. Like the NutraSweet I consume in my Diet Coke, which has "all of the taste but none of the calories," plastic surgery enhances appearance but can't influence one's genetic makeup.

The Partner Dance

Choosing a partner is one thing, but maintaining a long-term relationship is quite another. Watching people try to navigate their relationships can be quite entertaining and fascinating. For me, someone trained in behavioral observation, the world is my laboratory. I'm particularly intrigued observing couples when they are having a conflict. Over the years I've surreptitiously witnessed—as you probably have—scores of these interactions at parties, community events, family gatherings, and coffee shops. Although observing couples interrelate over points of friction can be depressing, we can learn much from such quarrels.

One day in a San Francisco coffee shop, I observed a professionally dressed couple in their thirties; he wore a black tailored suit, and she sported a navy blue blouse with black slacks. When I entered the cramped café, they were already conversing at a table. Along with some of the other customers in the shop, I quickly picked up on the couple's conflict: she thought he drove too fast and endangered her safety. She told him in very direct terms that his risk taking behind the wheel not only terrified her but indicated the reckless type of person he was. He responded by blaming her; if she didn't take so long getting ready at home, they could leave earlier, allowing more time to get to their destination. A clear facial signal of contempt accompanied her response that he was an idiot. With disdain dripping from her voice as well, she remarked that he made them run late just as often as she did. After about five minutes of this conversation, the man shut down. He picked up his *New York Times* and ignored her while she continued talking.

The behavior of this couple contrasts with that of a couple I observed one autumn day in a Princeton, New Jersey, coffee shop. The sun was shining brightly through the windows, and the fall leaves were turning outside. The couple, both in their fifties, appeared very athletic and looked as though they might have just finished exercising, judging from their casual attire of shorts and T-shirts. After entering the café, they sat down in the booth adjacent to mine and began talking about how beautiful the day was. Before long, however, the conversation turned toward a topic that was clearly dicey for the pair: how they were going to afford gifts for their family and friends for the holidays.

In no time, they moved from the topic of money for holiday gifts to money issues in general. The husband lamented that the wife overspent on her wardrobe consistently, making it more difficult to afford discretionary items such as holiday gifts. Interspersed between these comments, he smiled occasionally and acknowledged that he knew appearance was important to her. Her response was revealing. With a slight smile and a light touch to his shoulder, she said she understood his concerns and conceded that she probably spent too much on clothes.

Relationships are dynamic dances between two people. Conflict is inevitable in all relationships, whether about sex, in-laws, friends, habits, children, money, or driving. As demonstrated by the couples above, people dance very differently when discussing these areas of contention; some look like well-trained professionals, twirling effortlessly across the dance floor, while others are complete wrecks, stepping on each other's feet at every turn. Can we predict relationship success and failure by observing these interactions? If so, what tells should we look for?

John Gottman knows the answers to these questions perhaps better than anyone. He has dedicated his career to the study of relationships and marriages, and unlike some psychologists in the popular media who rely solely on anecdotal evidence to inform their opinions, Gottman is the real McCoy. He has systematically and painstakingly observed hundreds of couples, looking for revealing tells. As he remarked in one interview, "Von Frisch discovered the language of bees by going right to the hive and watching them dance. So we will discover the human dance."

Gottman and his team carefully examine the behavioral intricacies that transpire between couples on a second-by-second basis and use these observations to predict connubial bliss versus a marital miss. In a typical lab study, Gottman asks couples to discuss an area of conflict in their relationship such as money or sex. As they face one another talking, researchers videotape the couple and monitor them with equipment that keeps track of physiological responses, such as heart rate. Gottman codes their behaviors, then follows them to see whether they stay married or eventually divorce.

One of my favorite findings in psychology comes from Gottman's work. Based on the interactions of these couples, he and his colleagues can predict who will remain married and who will divorce up to 90 percent of the time. Even more impressively, perhaps, Gottman can make these predictions based solely on the first three minutes of the couple's discussion of conflict. For the vast majority of couples, the first three minutes of communication about a conflict accurately predicts how the rest of the conversation will go. Therefore, if you see a couple really tearing into each other and making negative facial displays at the beginning of a squabble, you'll likely see a similar pattern later in the conversation. In contrast, the couples who take a more positive orientation toward the conflict tend to continue using this tactic throughout.

Unlike the vast majority of marriage counselors in practice, Gottman has amassed an extensive data set that illuminates why some marriages fail and others thrive. Consider the couples I discussed from San Francisco and Princeton. According to the data, the San Francisco couple exemplifies many behavioral cues that predict divorce. The first indicator was the wife's assertion that her husband was a reckless person because of his driving—an obvious criticism of his personality. The Princeton man, on the other hand, criticized an action, his wife's penchant for buying expensive clothes. When a person singles out flaws in another's character versus specific flawed actions, the likelihood of divorce increases.

Emotional and verbal expressions of contempt are particularly corrosive to relationships. When the woman in San Francisco called her partner

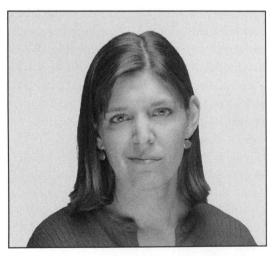

A classic facial display of contempt.

an idiot and flashed the classic lip tightening and lifting on only one side, as in the photo above, she gave away her contempt.

Defensiveness is another key ingredient in marital discord. This was readily apparent with the San Francisco couple when the man began blaming the woman for taking too long to get ready, thereby forcing him to drive fast. Instead of acknowledging her points, he counterattacked, an ominous sign for the well-being of a relationship. Conversely, the Princeton couple showed no defensiveness. After listening to her husband's criticisms regarding her expensive purchases, the woman smiled and touched his shoulder, acknowledging his complaint.

Stonewalling constitutes another revealing tell of marital discontent. When the man in San Francisco picked up his newspaper and stopped acknowledging his partner, he was clearly stonewalling. When a person's heart rate exceeds about one hundred beats per minute, he or she sometimes begins to stonewall to reduce the physiological arousal, something that happens to men more frequently than women.

One of the most important factors distinguishing couples who stay together from those who do not is the amount of positive and negative emotionality demonstrated. I enjoyed watching the Princeton couple work out their spending issue; their positivity was clear in the way they peppered the conversation with smiles, quick jokes, and a lot of empathic touching. Gottman has found that couples who stay together make about five positive statements for every negative one in the course of a conversation. Couples who do not stay married make more negative than positive statements about each other. So the golden ratio for marital bliss seems to be 5:1—five positive statements to every negative one—whereas the toxic ratio for marital dissolution is about 1:1.

One of my intellectual heroes is Francis Galton, an English dilettante who happened to be Charles Darwin's cousin. Obsessed with measuring human behavior, Galton believed that we could quantify virtually anything, from intelligence to an audience's boredom based on the number of times members yawn or fidget. In true Galtonian spirit, I've actually tallied the number of positive and negative verbal and nonverbal cues couples express during the normal course of conversation. I don't follow these couples to see if they remain intact, but the exercise is quite revealing as it predicts their future relationship success.

Showing us exactly what to look for in relationships, Gottman's research teaches us to predict something about their quality and ultimate destiny. He has shined the light of science on a complex phenomenon—couple interaction—thereby illustrating what to focus on in our own interactions and those happening around us. Moreover, he has developed a comprehensive guide to marital therapy grounded in scientific data. His program teaches couples healthy ways to confront the inevitable challenges of marriage without resorting to many of the toxic predictors he has discovered in his research.

Smiling, Frowning, and Divorce

Predicting who will divorce from dynamic interaction is one thing, but doing so from a simple photograph is quite another. Recently, I perused photos from my childhood and teen years. As I peered at one from middle school, I remembered that at the time I thought I looked really cool, but now I saw a pimple-faced, awkward, and insecure kid. In another photo taken when I was in college, I sported a dark green suit with a gaunt face and a cheesy smile. Even though I have changed a lot, I still see me in every photo. Throughout our lives an essence of who we are endures across space and time and gets recorded in photographs. Do these snapshots contain tells that predict anything about who we are today and what our destiny may be?

Determined to help answer these questions, two of my students set out with a mission: to ask senior citizens to borrow their most cherished childhood photographs. Astonishingly, within five minutes of the students' introducing themselves, many of the seniors willingly relinquished their photos on the mere promise that we would return them. We obtained numerous types of photos capturing milestones such as weddings, birthdays, baptisms, and graduations, as well as assorted candid photos taken with family and friends. Might the photographs depicting youthful smiles and frowns from decades before predict one of life's most significant events?

As we all know, about half of all marriages end in divorce, taking a significant toll on both men and women. Research links divorce to a host of negative health outcomes, including emotional disorders, heart disease, diabetes, cancer, and earlier mortality. Divorce also portends some negative childhood outcomes. One study indicated that adults whose parents divorced when they were children died five years earlier than adults raised in intact homes. Interestingly, adults whose parents died during their childhoods did not die earlier, suggesting that lack of a parent, per se, does not cause premature death.

To my surprise, not only were the snapshots we collected interesting to look at, but they predicted divorce. One set of pictures showed their subjects as children and adolescents. Those who remained with their spouses were more likely to be smiling authentically and brightly in the photographs than those who would eventually divorce. Those who smiled most contracted not only the muscles that elevate the cheek muscles but also those around the eyes, the orbicularis oculi muscles. Contracting these muscles results in a twinkle in our eyes and crow's-feet at the sides, evidence of a so-called Duchenne smile, which occurred more often in people who stayed in lasting marriages. Those who ended up divorcing tended not to contract the muscles around their eyes and had a more forced-looking smile, like you might see among airline flight attendants or a person who is tired of talking to you at a cocktail party.

This study was replicated with another in which we examined several hundred photographs in college yearbooks to see how intensely people smiled. We then asked the alumni, ranging in age from their early twenties to their late eighties, if they had divorced later in life. Those who smiled the least in their photos were five times more likely to divorce at some point in their lives relative to those who smiled the most. Have you rummaged through your old photos yet?

More recently, researchers examined photos taken in the early 1950s of baseball players who had subsequently died. They divided photos into three groups: those who did not smile, those displaying a partial (non-Duchenne) smile, and those displaying a full Duchenne smile. Statistically controlling for a number of variables such as marital status, college attendance, and so forth, investigators found that those who exhibited Duchenne smiles lived, on average, until the age of eighty. Contrast this result with the average life expectancy of the players who smiled only partially, seventy-five years, and those who did not smile at all, seventy-three years.

It appears a Duchenne smile is worth an extra five to seven years of life—or more if you're the "Say Hey Kid," Willie Mays. This San Francisco

Willie Mays (1931–).   *Eddie Mathews (1931–2001).*

Giants Hall of Famer, famous for his contagious smile, is eighty-two years old as I write. Eddie Mathews—the great baseball Hall of Famer—wasn't as fortunate, although it's impossible to say that his muted smile had anything to do with his death at sixty-nine.

Since the beginning of my career, students in my classes have humored me by posing for mug shots at the beginning of the semester. I always tell them that I need their photographs for two reasons. The first is that I want proof that they were in my class should they ever become famous. Then, after a good laugh, I tell them that the most pressing reason is that the photos help me learn their names. When I arrive to class the first time after photographing them, I can rattle off their names as I point to each of them.

But one's smiling behavior in a single photograph does not necessarily predict marital destiny, personality, or lifespan. Plenty of people who smile brightly end up divorced and die early while plenty who frown remain married and live long lives. It's always possible that a person doesn't like to smile in photographs for fear of showing his teeth or some other feature. Or a person may be having an emotionally difficult time on the day a picture is taken. Yet, on average, smiling behavior in photographs differentiates those who remain married and live long lives from those who tend not to, despite these individual differences.

How can an instantaneous facial display of emotion predict something about our lives decades later? Perhaps people who smile in their photos are simply being more compliant when the photographer says, "Cheese." It may be that this level of obedience is the glue that keeps some marriages together. The explanation with the most support, however, is that people who smile in their photographs have a more positive emotional disposition and more extensive social network. LeeAnne Harker and Dacher Keltner found that women who smiled more brightly in their college yearbook photos tended to be more organized, nurturing, compassionate, and sociable than those with less intense smiles. Another study showed that people who smiled in their Facebook photos were happier years later and had a richer social network than their frowning peers. When life throws us inevitable curveballs, those with a positive emotional disposition and strong social support tend to thrive.

Party-Worthy Findings

1. **Smelly T-shirts and sperm:** Women prefer the smell of T-shirts worn by symmetrical men compared to their lopsided counterparts. Also, men perceived as more attractive by women have higher-quality sperm compared to their less attractive counterparts.

2. **Prediction of divorce:** By examining only about three minutes of interaction between an engaged couple, researchers can predict whether they will stay married or divorce with about 90 percent accuracy. Even the degree to which we smile in photographs predicts the likelihood of divorce.

3. **Prediction of longevity from smiles:** Baseball players with Duchenne smiles lived about seven years longer than those who did not smile.

7

DETECTING DECEPTION

"Actions lie louder than words."

—CAROLYN WELLS

About a decade ago, I was giving a final exam when a student named Sue politely asked if she could use the restroom. Her expression said she really needed to go. I agreed to let her leave, making sure she was not carrying anything with her. A few minutes later, she returned, said thank you, and took her seat. But I noticed an odd, fleeting facial expression when she spoke. Something didn't seem right.

I stepped into the hall and asked a female colleague passing by if she would go into the women's bathroom and have a look around for anything unusual. I felt guilty for suspecting my student of malfeasance, but I needed to satisfy my curiosity. After a few minutes, my colleague exited the bathroom holding up a copy of my lecture slides, which she'd removed from their hiding place behind the paper seat cover inside a bathroom stall.

My guilt immediately morphed into shock. How could someone cheat and then lie to me? In reality, though, I shouldn't have been surprised. Lies bombard us every day: kids lie to their parents about their whereabouts, staff lie to their employers about their health, politicians lie to their constituents about their intentions and shortcomings, and spouses lie to their partners about their fidelity. And despite encountering so many lies, we still aren't adept at detecting when someone is deceiving us.

Natural-Born Lie Detectors We Are Not

It stands to reason that if others barrage us constantly with lies, we must be telling lies ourselves. Indeed, humans are capable of intentionally deceiving others quite early in life. In one study, researchers individually invited three-year-olds into a lab and sat them at a table. A cruel predicament ensued: behind the child, an experimenter set up a complex and interesting toy and instructed the child not to look back at it. Then the experimenter left the room for a few minutes, reminding the child not to look at the toy during her absence. It will come as no surprise to anyone who has spent time around children that the vast majority of kids—about 90 percent—peeked at the toy. Of these, 62 percent denied doing so or said nothing when the experimenter asked, "Did you peek?"

Mark Twain wasn't too far off when he wrote in his essay "On the Decay of the Art of Lying," "Everybody lies—every day; every hour; awake; asleep; in his dreams; in his joy; in his mourning." We continue to hone our deception skills throughout adulthood, telling an astonishing number of lies every day. On average, people lie at least once, if not twice, daily. A back-of-the-napkin computation indicates that the average person lies roughly 28,000 times throughout his or her life—about the same number of showers we take in a lifetime.

"And the Lord said unto Cain, Where is Abel thy brother? And he said, I know not: Am I my brother's keeper?" Our predilection for prevarication is so strong that Cain thought he could lie to God about murdering his brother.

How do we keep getting away with it? In *Lie to Me*, a recently cancelled show on Fox, the characters Dr. Cal Lightman and Ria Torres are virtually perfect human lie detectors; their firm works with law enforcement agencies such as the FBI and local police departments to solve high-stakes cases. Lightman and Torres make lie detection look effortless and nearly foolproof.

Can we know whether someone is lying to us based on behavior and physiology? Although scientists currently employ functional magnetic resonance imaging, or fMRI, technology to scan brains and other lie-detection machines to detect when someone is lying, the consensus is that physiological measures are still unreliable. The alternative is good old-fashioned analysis of tells. These clues can be revealing, but many of us miss them. It turns out that the vast majority of us are virtually no better than chance—about 54 percent accurate—at predicting whether someone has lied to us. You may as well flip a coin to help you decide.

Why Are We Dismal Lie Detectors?

There are numerous explanations for our meager abilities, but most boil down to a few reasons.

IGNORANCE IS BLISS: It's so much easier going through life taking what people say to us at face value. After all, who wants to remain constantly vigilant for the lies people tell us? Making false accusations and doubting others is counterproductive in cultivating relationships. We may not want to know if our spouse is cheating on us or if the employee who just called in sick is really playing hooky.

THE SIGNAL-TO-NOISE RATIO IS LOW: The behavioral and verbal cues that can betray the lies that our spouses, children, employees, and friends tell us are subtle. When emitted in the complex matrix of other verbal and nonverbal cues—facial displays, gestures, pauses, blushing, vocal intonation, words, head nods, posture, blinking, fidgeting, eye contact, speaking rate, and leg movements—they can be downright unnoticeable if you're not looking for them. To make matters more confusing, the clues we do pick up on may have nothing to do with deceit and everything to do with a truth teller's anxiety; when questioned by the police about a murder, a suspected liar and an honest person may give off similar signals of nervousness. Finally, there is no telltale sign of lying despite researchers' best efforts to identify one—our noses do not grow like Pinocchio's.

Pinocchio

IT'S DARWIN'S FAULT: We may be poor at detecting deceit because evolution has not selected for this ability. In evolutionary history, the cost of detecting deceit was probably so great that there was no opportunity for evolutionary pressures to select for successful lie detection. Therefore, we're not innately gifted with a talent for detecting the deceitful cues that pervade our daily lives.

IT'S YOUR PARENTS' FAULT: Parents and others often socialize us to "go along to get along" when people tell us seemingly innocuous lies. And parents frequently lie to their children to protect them from the vagaries of life. In so doing, rather than teaching their children to spot trickery, parents may paradoxically hinder their ability to do so.

WE DON'T RECEIVE FEEDBACK (MOST OF THE TIME): We're rarely given any feedback on the correctness of our hunches. I may suspect that my son lied when he told me that he didn't take a cookie out of the cookie jar, but I have no way of knowing for sure. Occasionally, there is an exception. A manager of a major fast-food restaurant once told me about an incident when an employee called in sick. Later that day, the manager was working as a volunteer at an event for a local organization where he dressed up in a superhero costume—think oversize shoes, a huge helmet, and beefy muscles like the Incredible Hulk's. The manager spent the afternoon posing for pictures and giving hugs to kids. Then he saw his "sick" employee, who was all smiles, having a great time with his kids. The pièce de résistance? The unwitting employee posed with his own boss for a picture. Before the employee stepped away, the manager held up his index finger as if to say, "Wait a minute," removed his helmet, and, with a grin, said, "You're fired."

Before we come to the last reason we're so bad at lie detection, imagine the following: You are a manager at a local bank and discover at the end of the workday that a recently hired teller named Melanie is missing $100 from her drawer. This news comes on the heels of several complaints from customers and fellow employees that she is not performing well. Because it is your job to determine where the money went, you go through all of Melanie's transactions, one by one, to determine if she made an honest accounting error somewhere. You hope you'll be able to find a blunder, but after exhausting all the possibilities, you're unable to determine where the money went. You invite Melanie to your office to ask her where the missing cash is. She flatly denies stealing it. As she talks about the incident, she fidgets a lot, especially with the pencil she picked up off of your desk during the conversation. She bites her lip slightly after she finishes a statement. Despite the fact that she appears somewhat friendly during the interaction, you observe her touching her nose and ears a lot, while tapping her foot rapidly and constantly averting her gaze to the left as if she's unwilling to look at you. Moreover, she constantly shifts her posture back and forth in her chair.

Do you believe Melanie's claim of innocence? If not, which of the following cues do you think reliably predict that she's lying?

Averting her gaze	Shifting her posture
Biting her lip	Tapping her foot rapidly
Fidgeting with the pencil	Touching her ears
Looking to the left	Touching her nose
Presenting a friendly demeanor	

This scenario brings into sharp relief the last reason why we're so poor at detecting lies: we think we know what the tells of deceit are, but much of what we believe marks dishonesty does not. None of the cues listed above reliably betray a lie.

If you thought some of the above cues indicate lying, you're in good company. Researchers asked people in fifty-eight different countries from Samoa to China what behaviors they thought were diagnostic of deception. Respondents offered more than one hundred different behaviors, with gaze aversion—looking away, like Melanie did—being the cue most commonly mentioned and deemed most powerful. The sticking point, however, is that no reliable link exists between where a person is looking and whether he or she is lying. Much of what we believe about lying is mythical and has no foundation in reality.

Police Officers Are Good Lie Detectors—Untrue

It turns out that some people are quite good at detecting lies. These people and the researchers who study them have helped us to know which cues actually predict deceit.

Among the following, which groups, if any, do you think have superior lie-detection skills? And by "superior," I mean that at least half the group's members can detect lies with 70 percent accuracy or greater.

> US Secret Service agents
> Federal polygraphers comprising CIA, FBI,
>   and other agents
> Judges
> Police
> Psychiatrists
> Students

Researchers showed a number of subjects from various occupational backgrounds videos of people either lying or telling the truth. Only one group, the US Secret Service agents, fared significantly above chance at detecting when the people in the videotapes lied; but even then, only 53 percent of these agents correctly distinguished truths from lies over

70 percent of the time. The members of the other groups guessed at about chance levels.

I was surprised to learn that most police officers, including those who investigate and even interrogate suspects, are no better than the average Joe or Jane at detecting lies. If we as a society would want anyone to have superior lie-detection abilities, it would be the police. Consider the fate of Jerry Watkins, whom a jailhouse inmate implicated in the murder of an eleven-year-old girl. After the girl had been missing for five days in 1984, her body was found in Indiana; she had been raped and stabbed repeatedly. Police considered Watkins a suspect in the case because the girl was his sister-in-law, and her family suspected he had molested her prior to the murder. But not until an inmate held in the same cell as Watkins testified that Watkins had confessed the murder to him did police charge Watkins with the killing. Due largely to the testimony of his cell mate, Watkins received a sentence of sixty years in prison.

The only problem was that Watkins didn't commit the murder. The cell mate's lie went undetected, misdirecting the investigation all the way down to Watkins's conviction for the horrific murder. After he had served thirteen long years in prison, DNA evidence proving that he had not been at the scene of the crime finally exonerated him.

I wonder how often suspects and informants successfully dupe law enforcement officials. Like virtually all murder cases, this one was complex. But that's no excuse for the fact that most people in law enforcement either receive no instruction in detecting deception or are unfortunately trained to recognize cues that have no scientific basis, or are flat-out wrong.

The Clues to Use

Before we get to the correct cues to look for, let's pause for a moment for a couple of important caveats.

First, all of the tells researchers have linked reliably to deception are merely clues, not telltale signs of dishonesty. Recognizing one sign of deceit, or even many, doesn't mean that you've definitely identified a liar. Second, despite much consensus among researchers as to which specific cues predict deception, there is some disagreement as well. I've tried to boil the clues down to those that I think have received significant support.

People telling high-stakes lies such as, "I didn't cheat on my spouse," are more likely to signal deception than people who tell white lies such as, "You look nice in that outfit." Therefore, I focus on clues that researchers have found when studying people who tell real whoppers.

Back from the commercial break.

Recall Melanie, the bank teller questioned by her boss about the missing $100. This time, let's assume she stole the money by sneaking it out of her drawer when the bank opened in the morning and concealing it under the front seat of her car. Later, her boss puts her on the spot in his office: "Did you steal the money?" Melanie has a choice: she can tell the truth or lie. Telling the truth is far easier because she knows exactly what happened. But if she wants to hoodwink her boss into thinking that she didn't take the money, she might dream up a story, perhaps telling him she thinks she inadvertently gave a customer two $100 bills instead of two $50 bills. This honest mistake would explain the $100 shortfall in Melanie's drawer.

An expert lie catcher observing Melanie would look for two types of clues. The first, "thinking clues," result from the extra mental effort that it takes to fabricate a story. If Melanie decides to lie to her boss, she must concoct the story about accidentally grabbing the incorrect bills. This additional mental work—or "cognitive effort," as researchers sometimes refer to it—beyond simply telling what actually happened potentially generates a number of behavioral clues. For example, Melanie may hesitate in answering the question as she tries to think of a plausible story. Melanie may blink less, stammer a bit when she talks, repeat some words more often than usual, and talk less overall. Her story will likely contain some discrepancies. She may come across as more distant or removed as she recounts what happened. And her conversational gestures may be less animated, reflecting the cognitive load she's experiencing.

We can find it difficult to stamp out entirely the emotions that erupt in us when we tell high-stakes lies. As a result, they provide "emotional clues" to deceit. Chances are, when telling her boss a bald-face lie, Melanie will experience emotions such as guilt or fear, which can come about not only from telling the lie itself but from trying to cover up how she really feels.

No one has studied the emotional clues to deceit more than Paul Ekman, who spent most of his career in the medical school at the University of California, San Francisco. Ekman's work actually inspired FOX's *Lie to Me* series. In 2009, *Time* magazine named the seventy-five-year-old Ekman one of the hundred most influential people for his seminal contributions in the field of emotion and for "teaching us how to recognize the subtle signs of truth."

The serendipitous origins of Ekman's interest in deceit would ultimately lead him, his colleagues, and others in the field to numerous discoveries. Early in his career he taught psychiatry students in the medical school where he was a faculty member. According to Ekman, the students expressed interest in his work demonstrating the universality of emotional displays—something Darwin had proposed about one hundred years earlier. They were especially interested in a vital real-life question that Ekman didn't know the answer to: "When a patient who had been admitted for acute depression requested a pass to return home for a day, claiming to feel much better and to no longer be thinking of suicide, how could they tell if the patient was telling the truth?"

Ekman learned that "Mary," a female patient, had lied when she requested a weekend pass to visit her family after the hospital had admitted her for depression a few weeks prior. Mary had a history of trying to take her own life, and she would do so again on this furlough. Fortunately, Ekman had videotaped the conversation in which she made the request, so he was able to review it to see what signs the staff might have missed.

Ekman and one of his colleagues watched the film, hoping to identify a sign of deceit, but they saw none; Mary appeared happy and optimistic. Then they watched the twelve-minute interview frame-by-frame, which took more than one hundred hours. They saw something critical: just before answering a doctor's question about her future plans, Mary had flashed a strong facial signal of anguish. It lasted a mere one-twelfth of a second, occupying 2 frames out of more than 17,000 in the interview. Mary resumed smiling to mask the emotion. Once Ekman knew what to look for, he found other fleeting signals of despair on Mary's face throughout the interview, even without playing the film frame by frame. With practice, he could identify the signals in real time.

Ekman didn't stop there. He knew that Mary's behavior might be unique to her and that he was looking for behavioral clues after he knew she had lied rather than before the fabrication. Ekman and his colleagues went on to study—and confirm—the links between emotional clues and deception. In some of his latest work with colleagues, Ekman can accurately predict from the face alone the presence of deception 70 percent of the time. When analyzing videotape that includes all of the known signals in the face, voice, speech, and body, Ekman can predict whether people are lying about 90 percent of the time.

So here's what the data tell us:

MICROEXPRESSIONS: When people lie, they sometimes try to conceal their emotional state. They may be fearful or guilty or experience anguish like Mary did, despite her proclamations of happiness. But sometimes the liar's emotions "leak" through facial cues, like those that passed over Mary's expression in a blink of an eye. These microexpressions last no longer than a quarter second or so. One of Ekman's colleagues analyzed the video of a famous professional baseball player during an interview with a television news magazine. When asked, "For the record, have you ever used a performance-enhancing substance?" the player said no, but then flashed a fleeting facial signal of contempt by contracting the corner of his lip on one side of his face. A few months later, the baseball great admitted to using performance-enhancing drugs. Microexpressions like Mary's and the baseball player's are barely perceptible, and research shows that most people cannot detect these expressions in real time. The good news, especially for law enforcement officers, is that Ekman has developed a short program to train people to detect microexpressions.

"RELIABLE" MUSCLES: Some muscles of the face are almost impossible to contract voluntarily; Ekman calls these the "reliable" muscles. If you observe a person expressing sadness both verbally and facially, but the inner corners of his eyebrows are not going up and in, he may not be experiencing sadness at all. He's unable to contract these muscles voluntarily despite his best efforts. Likewise, the muscle that surrounds the eyes, the same one that gives you crow's-feet, is the reliable muscle associated with joy. I recently observed numerous smiles on television when watching the

2012 Olympics in London. The vast majority of medalists on the podium smiled during the awards ceremonies. But, looking carefully I could see that the silver medalists often didn't contract the reliable muscles surrounding the eyes, whereas the gold and bronze medalists did most of the time. Silver medalists' smiles seemed controlled and occasionally blended with other negative emotions like sadness. Systematic studies in which researchers have carefully recorded smiling among Olympic medal winners bear out these observations. When you observe someone smiling at your joke but don't see the reliable muscle contracted, you can infer with some degree of confidence that the person didn't find your joke all that funny.

SQUELCHED EXPRESSIONS: One elderly woman I know—I'll call her Ethel—is incredibly sharp but has many of the aches and pains that most experience at her age (arthritis, muscle soreness, and so forth). When I see her, I often ask, "How are you feeling?" I immediately see on her face that she is not feeling well, but she quickly feigns a smile, quipping that she's feeling fine. Ekman calls Ethel's initial countenance a "squelched expression," because a person becomes aware of it and tries to clamp down on it, masking it with another expression, most often a smile. Squelched expressions are less complete than microexpressions, but they last longer, which makes them more identifiable. A person's interrupting one expression and masking it with another is a reliable clue to deception.

LOPSIDED FACIAL DISPLAYS: If a person displays an emotion with the facial muscles of one side of his face contracted more than the other, it's possible that the person is feigning the expression. The vast majority of genuine facial displays of emotion are bilateral—that is, they show up on both sides of the face equally. When fabricating an emotional display, people are more likely to do so in an unbalanced manner. Next time you tell your friend a joke, look to see if her smile is symmetrical when she laughs.

TIMING OF THE EMOTIONAL DISPLAY: If you've ever watched politicians on Sunday news programs or in debates, you'll see numerous smiles that appear fabricated because they violate the timing of typical facial displays of emotion. My favorite example involves John McCain. During his presidential bid in 2008, several people in the blogosphere commented that his smile was "weird" and "peculiar." Observations like these led *The Onion*, a satirical website, to publish the following about Joseph Chappel, McCain's speechwriter, in the run-up to the election:

> Dreading a repeat of last month's speech to a group of businesswomen in Ohio, during which McCain followed a mention of his wife with an awkward and eerie smirk, Chappel has avoided personal anecdotes for the new speech, omitted any mention of "God" or "this great nation," and cut several phrases that had the potential to draw the 72-year-old candidate's mouth open in a horrifying display of teeth and gums.

The timing of McCain's smile largely explains why observers and *The Onion* detected the oddity of his grin. Rather than contracting the muscles of his face smoothly and quickly, he sometimes did so in a delayed and jerky fashion. Most revealing, however, was the extended duration of his smiles. "Unless someone is having a peak experience, at the height of ecstasy, in a roaring rage, or at the bottom of depression," wrote Ekman, "genuine emotional expressions don't remain on the face for more than a few seconds." In addition to his atypical timing, the "dead eyes" behind his smile did nothing to mitigate its plastered-on quality. Like most of us, McCain was unable to voluntarily contract the reliable muscles surrounding his eyes.

THE RELATIONSHIP BETWEEN FACIAL DISPLAYS AND OTHER BEHAVIORS: Genuine facial displays of emotion generally unfold at the same time as other relevant behaviors, whereas fabricated expressions precede or follow other cues inappropriately. For example, you should be less inclined to believe that a person is really upset with you if he displays anger on his face after he stamps his foot on the ground.

THE EYES: Although there is some disagreement about whether people blink more when they lie, strong evidence indicates that when we prevaricate, our pupils dilate because our nervous system is aroused due to either stress or the need to think more. Obviously, tears seeping from someone's eyes reveal that he might be experiencing an intense emotion, such as sadness, distress, or even utter enjoyment. With tears, we see the literal "leaking out" of emotion. Like blinking and pupil dilation, however, tears don't tell us anything about deception per se, only that a person may be experiencing strong emotions.

THE VOICE: People who lie tend to speak in a higher-pitched voice, making them sound tenser or more distressed than people telling the truth.

They Walk Among Us

One group of people walking the planet could teach the rest of us a lot about lie detection: truth wizards. Researchers have identified these lie-detection all-stars by administering several video tests to over 15,000 people. Whereas most people correctly identify deceit only about 50 percent of the time, or at chance, these so-called truth wizards accurately detect it in excess of 80 percent of cases. To date, researchers have identified only about fifty truth wizards.

One such truth wizard is a woman who calls herself Eyes for Lies (EFL). EFL is middle-aged, has brown hair and eyes, and holds an undergraduate degree in journalism and a master's degree in science in education. She is to lie detection what Yo Yo Ma and Jimi Hendrix are to music; she is among the very best at what she does.

EFL grew up knowing she had an uncanny ability to read others. The first related memory she recalls is playing the card game "Lie," in which players detect when someone is lying or telling the truth. Her friends soon figured out that playing against her was a losing proposition. At the time, EFL attributed her decisive wins to good luck, but now she thinks the game reflected her early capacities as a human lie detector. By middle school, she was fully aware of her gift; she knew what made people tick, what they really wanted from others, and their fears and anxieties in life. One of her friends in middle school even accused her of being a witch—a charge she denied—because of her seemingly supernatural capacities.

Throughout her adult life, EFL strove to understand others and analyze their behavior. In her early thirties, she went on a "mission" to figure out why she was so good at reading people's nonverbal cues. To test her capabilities, she began providing insight and advice to others to see if events would bear her predictions out. Then, in 2004 EFL saw something that changed her life: an article on MSN.com discussing the Wizards Project. She quickly wrote to the late Maureen O'Sullivan, a researcher who helped spearhead the project. Within a week of being tested, EFL won official truth wizard status.

I asked EFL about her reaction to the news:

> When I got the test results, I actually bawled my eyes out. My reaction surprised even me! For years and years, I had friends who couldn't see what I saw. They always told me that I overanalyzed people and that I was crazy, that I thought too much, and to hear that I was truly gifted caused years of stress to come barreling out in tears. Once that passed, I was happy with the news, and it changed my life.
>
> Dr. O'Sullivan flew to my home and spent four days interviewing my family and me, and it was then that I started to learn why I saw the world differently. For the first time in my life, I could articulate "why" I was different. I saw nuances in body language, communication, facial expressions, and emotions that other people didn't—and that's why I saw the world so differently! It felt so good to finally understand it all!

Today, EFL provides training for law enforcement agencies across the country and maintains a website and blog detailing her analyses of individuals suspected of lying in publicly available interviews. She scrutinizes these interviews and predicts whether the people are lying before the truth becomes known. In some cases, she analyzes the potential truthfulness of high-profile murder suspects; in others she scrutinizes more trivial aspects of life, such as whether Britney Spears was as happy in her marriage as she claimed. As I write, she has correctly predicted whether people lied or told the truth in thirty-seven of the thirty-nine incidents she has analyzed—an impressive record by almost any standard.

Truth wizards share one common denominator: they are highly determined and motivated to find the truth in situations that call for it. Unlike most people, they have an insatiable curiosity to know the truth. They analyze the subtleties of interaction that slide right past most of us. For example, a truth wizard would contemplate all the gradations of behavior exhibited by her teenager as he told her he was at his best friend's house the previous night, whereas most people would briefly consider the comment and move on. "Our wizards are extraordinarily attuned to detecting the nuances of facial expressions, body language, and ways of talking and thinking," said Maureen O'Sullivan. "Some of them can observe a videotape for a few seconds and amazingly they can describe eight details about the person on the tape."

Are truth wizards innately gifted at detecting deceit, or do they develop the ability with dedication and practice alone? The answer is probably a combination of the two; there's little doubt that Mozart had an innate gift, but we wouldn't know his name or music unless he had dedicated himself passionately to his craft. Truth wizards are likely the same; their genes give them a foundation to read other people, but their constant analysis of others' behaviors and the feedback they seek make them lie-detection superstars.

Concluding Thoughts

Whether or not your spouse looks at you when he tells you he didn't have a clandestine affair at work has nothing to do with the truth of his statement. It also doesn't matter if he fidgets, touches his nose and ears, or shifts his posture a lot when trying to convince you. It does matter if he shows some of the tells reliably linked to lying.

Be careful though: just because you're confident you see one or two bona fide deception tells, that doesn't mean he's not telling the truth. It's important to look for a cluster of behaviors that betray a person's deceit. If you ask your spouse whether he cheated on you and he says no, but you hear his voice pitch heighten and catch a microexpression of fear coupled with a disingenuous smile (especially when smiling isn't called for in this situation), you should be more concerned. "Most liars leave a wake of clues in their path," according to EFL. Noticing multiple clues rather than relying on only one signal in isolation is fundamental. We are always revising probabilities of deceit given new information.

But even if you do notice a constellation of clues, I encourage you not to snap to judgment about the truth of others' statements. Instead, such a pattern should signal you to ask more questions.

Party-Worthy Findings

1. **Not much better than chance:** Most of us are virtually no better than chance at detecting the lies of others.

2. **Accurate analysis of tells:** When analyzing videotape that includes all of the known signals in the face, voice, speech, and body, researchers can predict whether people are lying 90 percent of the time.

3. **Truth wizards among us:** Truth wizards, a very select group of people, can detect lies with greater than 80 percent accuracy.

IV.

Making the Grade:
Education, Business, and Politics

8

THE POWER OF ENTHUSIASM

"Good teaching is one-fourth preparation and three-fourths theater."

—GAIL GODWIN

Since the beginning of my academic career, I've invited undergraduate students to my home for dinner midway through the semester. These dinners provide a great opportunity for us to get to know one another in a more relaxed atmosphere outside the classroom. During these evenings, I often ask students which classes have been their favorites, and inevitably they begin describing the professors who teach these courses. According to my students, the best teachers are those who have mastery of and passion for their fields and also communicate clearly and assess students fairly.

These conversations often make me reminisce about my own college professors. I think of Dr. Bishop, who taught developmental psychology —a "womb-to-tomb" course that covered the gamut of development across the lifespan. He meticulously prepared his lectures, each of which featured a variety of interesting techniques, including stories, illustrations, theory, and data, to adroitly communicate the pertinent information. I remember leaving class each day with my head filled with fascinating ideas, unanswered questions, and a thirst for more. In contrast, I can recall some professors with less than optimal teaching styles, who failed to fan even an intrinsic interest in the course material. I'm confident that you too can conjure up the images of your most and least cherished teachers throughout your education.

Whereas we judge the quality of a waitress with a tip or a politician with a vote, we evaluate professors at the end of their courses with anonymous student surveys. These forms vary among institutions in terms of the specific questions posed and the balance between quantitative data (i.e., ratings on scales) and qualitative data (i.e., opportunities to provide written comments). Evaluations might ask students to rate professors on a scale of one to seven in terms of how much the course contributed to their education, the professor's knowledge, preparation, availability outside class, fairness, timeliness, and the degree to which the professor stimulated their interest in the course content. In addition to soliciting information about the faculty member, surveys often ask students why they enrolled in the class and their expected grade. When the students finish answering the questions on the form, they submit it to the institution, and, typically, the faculty member receives the evaluations after submitting final grades for the course.

These evaluations, which have become ubiquitous in higher education, allow us to address fundamental questions: Are students really as perceptive as they think about judging the quality of their teachers? Does the content of courses drive students' opinions of what makes for a good teacher, or is something else more important? And, perhaps most relevant for the topic at hand, how long does it take for students to form their opinions of instructors? Studies addressing these questions are stacking up, and the answers, I think, will surprise you. So will the implications.

It Only Takes Six Seconds

How quickly do students begin to form their impressions of instructors? Consider one study in which students in fourteen different courses taught by five different instructors completed teaching evaluations. One group filled out the evaluations at the end of the first class of the semester, and another group did so at the end of the first week. At the end of the semester, all of the students filled out the same evaluations.

Students' ratings at the beginning of the term—both at the end of the first day and at the end of the first week—accurately predicted their ratings of the instructor at the end of the term. They accurately predicted how much interest the instructors showed, how well they communicated the importance of the subject and their expectations for the class, the degree to which they provided good feedback, how available they were to students, the degree to which they graded based on expectations, how much they encouraged students, and how challenging students would find the course. In other words, students form their first impressions of an instructor as early as the first day and hold these perceptions as much as four months later.

Perhaps students are truly getting an honest sense of how good an instructor is on the first day. After all, the faculty member may be accurately communicating her expectations, her interest in the material, and how much feedback she'll be giving students throughout the semester. But what if students' impressions are based not on what the instructor discusses during the first day but on her personality or nonverbal tells?

Expert knowledge, clear communication, and an enthusiastic style can lead to highly successful teaching.

In a seminal study, Nalini Ambady and Robert Rosenthal set out to determine just how quickly people can infer the "quality" of an instructor. The study was elegant in design: The researchers videotaped graduate teaching fellows at Harvard as they led undergraduate courses in the humanities, social sciences, and natural sciences. At the end of the term, students in the classes rated them on the following using a numeric scale:

"Rate the quality of the section overall."
"Rate section leader's performance overall."

The researchers averaged these ratings to derive an overall score for the instructor.

Ambady and Rosenthal then showed the videotapes to people who had never taken the courses with the instructor. These subjects rated the teachers on a number of specific nonverbal behaviors, such as confidence, likability, and enthusiasm. But rather than show the subjects the videotapes in their entirety—that is, asking them to view one hour per instructor—these researchers were more ambitious: they showed only thirty seconds of video for each instructor (ten seconds each from the beginning, middle, and end of class). Moreover, they showed the strangers the brief clips without sound.

With only thirty seconds of video, the strangers could differentiate the high- from the low-quality instructors. Instructors whom students rated as performing well and having high-quality sections struck strangers, based on their nonverbal cues, as warmer and more active, enthusiastic, optimistic, supportive, confident, likable, dominant, and competent. In a follow-up study, the researchers employed a similar methodology, but with high school teachers. Based on thirty-second clips, strangers deemed teachers rated more highly on effectiveness by their principals as warmer and more accepting, attentive, professional, optimistic, likable, and enthusiastic. Importantly, the correlations between nonverbal behavior and instructor ratings were exceedingly high, speaking to the highly predictive nature of tells for subsequent quality ratings by students (in the case of college classes) and principals (in the case of high school teachers).

In a study they dubbed "'Thinning' the Slices," Ambady and Rosenthal cut the three ten-second clips down to three two-second clips (six seconds total). Astonishingly—at least to me—strangers' ratings of the graduate instructors' nonverbal behavior during these six seconds predicted their end-of-semester scores. Specifically, instructors whom students rated as performing well and having high-quality sections appeared to the strangers to be more active, attentive, competent, confident, empathic, enthusiastic, honest, likable, optimistic, and supportive.

Counterintuitively, the predictions of judges shown the thirty-second clips to assess the nonverbal behaviors of the graduate instructors were no more accurate than those of judges shown the six-second clips. This was not the case with the strangers evaluating high school teachers, as the shorter clips did not predict performance. And, if you're wondering, judges assessing the nonverbal behavior of both the graduate instructors and the high school teachers were relatively unaffected by their attractiveness.

When I tell my faculty colleagues that mere seconds of behavior, even with no vocal cues, can predict course evaluations, they're often surprised. "What exactly happens in those precious seconds?" they ask. According to one study, good lecturers "are very expressive in their faces, hands, bodies, and voice, and they stand rather than sit and move in the classroom space. They show strong orientation toward their audience. They make continuous shifts." In other words, they inundate their audience with enthusiasm tells.

Are warm, enthusiastic teachers really more knowledgeable and better teachers than people who are reserved? Or are students' evaluations of the quality of a faculty member largely influenced by presentation style?

Dr. Ceci's "Enthusiasm Experiment"

The studies above adopted a correlational design, so one doesn't really know for sure what caused end-of-semester teaching evaluations to vary with nonverbal behavior. To ascertain this, we'd need an experiment in which the instructor manipulated his presentation style but maintained the exact same content across courses. Fortunately, a team at Cornell University conducted this exact study. Stephen Ceci, a renowned behavioral scientist, had been teaching developmental psychology for years, receiving student evaluations typical of other similar-level courses at the university. After he had been teaching the course for almost two decades, Cornell invited him to enroll in a workshop on presentation style between the fall and spring semesters.

This offered Ceci a great opportunity. In the fall, he audio-recorded himself giving well-rehearsed lectures during the semester. Then he took the workshop taught by a media consultant who focused purely on presentation style. The consultant trained the instructors to present information more enthusiastically by gesturing with their hands and varying their vocal inflection.

FALL SEMESTER   **SPRING SEMESTER**

Armed with this training, Ceci taught the identical content in the spring. He took great pains to make sure everything else about the class was the same as it had been the previous fall; he used the same book, the same lectures, the same grading policies, the same exams, the same office hours, the same syllabus, and the same slides, videos, and transparencies, and the student demographics were the same. He listened to the audio recordings he had made of his fall lectures and tried to memorize each before delivering it in the spring. He used the same detailed outlines and transparencies to ensure he talked about the exact same content. At the end of the spring semester, two naive coders listened to several randomly selected lectures from both the semesters. They found 100 percent agreement in the ideas communicated in the fall and the spring.

As you can see in the above graphs, the data were clear. Students exposed to Ceci's enthusiastic presentations were much more positive

RATINGS OF COURSE

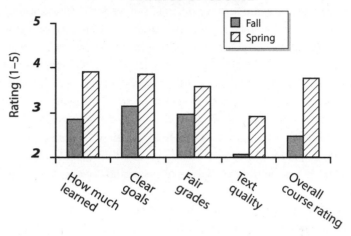

RATINGS OF INSTRUCTOR

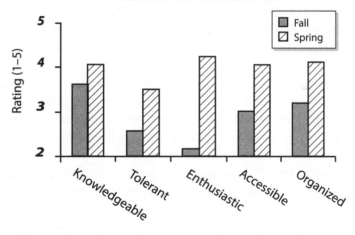

All comparisons between semesters were statistically significant (1–5 scale).

about both the instructor and the course—even though everything else was identical. They perceived him as more enthusiastic and knowledgeable, more tolerant of others' views, more accessible to students, and more organized.

In terms of the course itself, students in the fall reported that they learned about an "average" amount, whereas in the spring they reported learning "a lot." To test this perception against reality, the researchers compared students' exam scores and final grades for both semesters and found them virtually equal. Students taught by "Enthusiastic Professor Ceci" only *thought* they learned more than those instructed by "Reserved Professor Ceci." The students in the spring semester also reported that the course goals, expectations, and grading policy were more clearly stated and that the grading was more fair. They even rated the identical textbook more positively in the spring.

The evaluations asked students one final question: "Among courses that you have taken at this level, how would you rate this one?" Students in the fall rated the course somewhere between "poor" and "average," whereas students taught by Professor Ceci's enthusiastic alter ego rated the course as "good." Numerically, the rating on this question increased more than 1.5 standard deviations—not an insignificant amount. Was the enthusiastic version of Professor Ceci a better teacher than his more serious counterpart? Did the students learn more? Although not a perfect study, it should give us pause about the power of enthusiasm both in and out of the classroom.

So What?

So, why should we care about what drives students' perceptions of good teaching? These studies may appear a bit esoteric—though I hope you agree with me that they're quite surprising—but I think the implications are relevant and important. Consider three.

First, the studies tell us something about how our minds work and the importance of remaining humble. If you ask students, they will never tell you that hand gestures, voice inflection, and the like largely drive their opinions of teachers. But the studies described above suggest exactly that. We think we know what makes a good teacher—expertise in the field, clear goals, fair grading, quality course materials, organization, and accessibility—but we really don't, at least not when we're asked about it in evaluations. The evidence suggests that *how* a teacher conducts herself is at least as important, if not more so, than course content when it comes to the experience of learning.

The larger point is that so much more than we understand or acknowledge molds our perceptions of those around us. How much you've based a favorable impression of your pastor, rabbi, new romantic partner, mayor, kid's teacher, or physician on true talent and quality versus superficial characteristics is hard to ascertain. Quality and superficial characteristics are often intertwined, and we are seldom conscious of how much one impacts our overall assessment. The bottom line is that we *think* we know why we like or dislike someone, but we probably don't, at least not completely.

Second, the data have significant implications for the field of education. As a college student, I spent about five to ten minutes filling out teaching evaluations for each class. I had no idea what happened to them afterward or how they were used. I thought that perhaps faculty open to feedback might consider my comments, but beyond that, the forms might have been sucked into a black hole.

Nothing could be further from the truth, at least for faculty who still are up for professional review. These evaluations often have high-stakes consequences; they are the most widely used means by which institutions of higher education evaluate faculty teaching. In fact, tenure, promotion, and salary decisions at many institutions rest to a significant degree, and sometimes solely, on the performance of the faculty as assessed by evaluations. "If I trust one source of data on teaching performance," said one dean, "I trust the students." Poor student evaluations can turn faculty members' lives upside down; they can be denied tenure and effectively told to look for a job elsewhere. Should some institutions reconsider the weight placed on evaluations in personnel decisions, considering that only a few seconds of content-free nonverbal behavior can predict what students will say?

Other problems ensue. The gravity placed on evaluations in decisions regarding tenure and promotion gives instructors incentive to inflate students' grades. Faculty in the United States are handing out As like hotcakes: in 2008, 43 percent of grades were As, compared to only about 16 percent in the 1960s. Today's students may be mastering the course material better than their earlier counterparts, but I highly doubt it. Instructors' standards for an A are lower, on average, than they were in decades past. Of course, multiple factors likely enter into the equation of grade inflation, but one of them is almost certainly the fact that teaching evaluations play such an important role in some faculty members' academic livelihoods.

There's another danger in placing such heavy emphasis on evaluations: faculty may be consciously or unconsciously sacrificing rigor in their courses. In a recent review of the literature, an author wrote that "the research almost universally finds a negative association between rigor and learning on teaching evaluations. . . . Students seem to associate rigor with negative instructor characteristics that override positive learning relationships." American humorist Donald Marquis (1878–1937) summed this relation up succinctly: "If you make people think they're thinking, they'll love you. If you really make them think, they'll hate you."

The implications reach beyond the college classroom. Every year, school districts evaluate thousands of K–12 teachers across the United States to assess their merit. One component of whether or not my wife, who teaches first grade, receives an "effective" teacher designation is the principal's evaluation of her in the classroom. For a few hours during the semester, the principal observes her teaching style and then fills out a standardized form that is supposed to reflect the quality of her teaching. On the face of it, this seems like a reasonable way to assess teaching, but if you apply the findings I've described in this chapter, this procedure should concern you if you care about the US educational system. It's quite likely that across the country, teachers' expressivity influences administrators' evaluations at least as much as their ability to articulate information clearly and provide a content-rich experience. Of course, being expressive surely plays a role in the educational process, especially at the elementary level, but it probably shouldn't drive evaluations.

The final implication of this work focuses on the power of something called the "expressivity halo." Others perceive people who are expressive and animated in their social interactions—like the enthusiastic version of Professor Ceci—to be warmer and more sociable, dominant, motivated, and interpersonally skilled than their less expressive counterparts. This is the likely explanation for the findings in the studies of teachers described above. One professor I know who had taught only a few years stumbled on the phenomenon before going up for tenure: "I think I figured out how to raise my course evaluations, just by trial and error and taking lumps over the years. I learned to pretend to be an extrovert." When it's adaptive to harness the power of extroversion, professors can be perceptive.

The power of the expressivity halo—or the "what is expressive is good" principle—goes beyond education. I noticed this when I brought my grandmother to see two physicians. The first was in his mid-forties and appeared very competent, but if I were to rate his expressiveness during interactions with her, I'd give him about a two on a ten-point scale. For various reasons, my grandmother had to switch doctors. The new doctor was in her mid-forties as well, but she was very expressive and personable; she had a large presence in the room when she entered, smiled and nodded a lot, and gestured amply during conversation. She wasn't off-the-charts expressive—I'd give her about an eight on the same scale—but the contrast between her and the other physician was stark.

Not only did my grandmother like the expressive physician better, but she did "what the doctor ordered" more. Of course, any number of reasons could explain my grandmother's perceptions and compliance, but at least one set of studies in a health-care setting supports the expressivity of the doctors as an explanation. Researchers videotaped physical therapists interacting with patients who were at least seventy-five years old; for each practitioner, they then extracted three twenty-second clips from these interactions and showed them to a group of judges with the sound off. They also measured patients' perceptions of the health-care providers and their interactions.

Much like my grandmother, elderly patients with physical therapists who were more emotionally expressive during their interactions perceived them to be warmer and more empathic, concerned, and caring. Importantly, though, the expressivity halo went beyond mere perception; patients with expressive therapists were cognitively sharper and could perform more daily activities like dressing, walking, and going to the bathroom independently, compared to those with the least expressive therapists. Thus, by watching only one minute of silent video, judges could predict, based on their perceptions of therapists' expressivity, which patients would improve most.

Despite the power of the expressivity halo in driving how we perceive others, most people do not recognize its effects. When I ask my students over dinner which classes are their favorites, none of them ever tell me that they appreciate a particular faculty member's emotional expressivity. Rather, they comment on the course content, the professor's expertise, and how fairly the instructor grades work. Other peoples' level of outgoingness largely influences how much we like them—at least at first. The problem is that the effects of the expressivity halo are powerful and yet unrecognized.

Frankly, I think the expressivity halo is pernicious in that, although we shouldn't, we often judge people based on their expressiveness. How do we guard against doing this in both our personal and our professional lives? Perhaps as importantly, how can people leverage the consequences of the expressivity halo? I once told a colleague, who had recently received his PhD, about the findings in this chapter. About three weeks later, he half-jokingly said to me, "Matt, thanks for helping me land a job." I asked, "How on earth did I do that?" He replied that during the job talk he gave, he upped his level of expressivity significantly. He thought that his enthusiasm had engaged his audience. Whether he should attribute his success to expressivity is questionable, but he clearly took the implications of these data to heart.

Party-Worthy Findings

1. **Parallels between first- and last-day evaluations:** Students' evaluations at the end of the first day of a professor's class map to those same students' evaluations at the end of the semester.

2. **Six seconds to a quality professor:** From a six-second video of a professor teaching, strangers can predict the end-of-semester evaluations of students who had the professor the entire semester.

3. **The power of enthusiasm:** By merely behaving more enthusiastically, a professor can not only raise student evaluations of his teaching but also improve the quality of the course textbook.

9

CATCHING THE CUES OF
THE CASH COW

*"One of the hardest tasks of leadership is understanding
that you are not what you are, but what you're perceived
to be by others."*

—EDWARD L. FLOM

L et's face it, in life's grand scheme, it probably doesn't matter much if
one instructor teaches a course well or ineptly; each class represents
only a fraction of a student's overall education. The performance of a
corporation in the massive economy of the United States, however, is a
different story. Its success or failure can impact the lives of millions. If a
company grows over time, innovates new products, and creates profits, a
number of different groups benefit: stockholders make money, employees
have jobs that generate tax revenue, and customers gain access to desired
products for affordable prices.

To be a part of this economic equation, companies must vie with each
other in the marketplace to offer goods and services, generating fierce
competition. Andrew Carnegie addressed this clash of corporations:

"While the law of competition may be sometimes hard for the individual, it is best for the race, because it ensures the survival of the fittest in every department." According to Carnegie and renowned economists like John Maynard Keynes, Frederick von Hayek, and Joseph Schumpeter, the tooth-and-nail fights companies engage in are essential for them to survive and thrive in the economic milieu.

Herbert Spencer, a nineteenth-century English philosopher who came to America in 1882 and whom many prominent business leaders welcomed as a capitalist savior, likely inspired Carnegie's sentiment. A well-known scholar of his day, Spencer adapted Darwin's principles of evolution and applied them to almost every sphere of life, including economic systems and institutions. According to Spencer, capitalistic companies operate according to what he termed "survival of the fittest," a phrase often mistakenly attributed to Charles Darwin. This principle operates exactly as one would expect: companies compete, and those that are better adapted to a particular economic climate thrive, whereas the more poorly adapted fail. Though companies such as Swissair, Polaroid, Commodore, DeLorean, and Pan Am were very successful at one time, they did not change with the economic environment and eventually died out. Companies that make innovative products and smart business choices, like Walmart, General Electric, and McDonalds, grow and prosper.

CEOs, then, are charged with adapting their companies to excel in ever-turbulent economic and consumer environments over time. Many CEOs, some synonymous with the companies they lead, have become household names—think Steve Jobs, Bill Gates, Jack Welch, Michael Dell, Mark Zuckerberg, Oprah Winfrey, Martha Stewart, Donald Trump, and Warren Buffett, to name only a few. Their reputations impact their companies long after their tenures have ended. Walt Disney's family-oriented emphasis has remained synonymous with the Disney brand since his death in 1966.

Given the central role CEOs play in their companies and the godlike status they seem to have acquired in recent years, it takes an enormous amount of money to hire the best person available. CEO salaries have increased dramatically over the last few decades. In 1980, CEOs made about forty times more than the average worker; by 2010 they earned a whopping 350 times more.

So it pays—literally—to know what qualities define the business world's best CEOs. Is it charisma? Economic acumen? Knowledge of the industry? It turns out that the answer depends on whom you ask. If you do a Google search, scores of different people claim to know what qualities predict CEO success. Even the academic studies on the subject are mixed.

What Predicts CEO Success?

The ability to predict a company's success is extremely valuable; stock traders try to do it every day to make their clients (and themselves) wealthy. Neither the popular nor the academic literature can identify one specific and consistent personality trait that directly affects success, but it turns out that we can predict the accomplishments of CEOs—at least as measured by the profitability of the companies they run—from the thinnest possible slice of evidence: a photograph.

In a landmark study, Nicholas Rule and Nalini Ambady, both at Tufts University at the time, addressed a simple question: can we predict the profits of companies by examining the facial tells of the their CEOs? Rule and Ambady examined at-a-glance ratings by complete strangers who knew nothing about the CEOs' day-to-day behavior and decisions. The researchers asked subjects to examine head shots of male CEOs who ran the top and bottom twenty-five companies listed on the Fortune 500 in 2006 (fifty companies total). The subjects rated the faces on the following:

POWER: assessed by ratings of CEOs' competence, dominance, and facial maturity

WARMTH: assessed by ratings of CEOs' likeability and trustworthiness

LEADERSHIP: assessed on a seven-point scale in response to the question "How good would this person be at leading a company?"

How could strangers, who know nothing about the identities of the CEOs or the companies they run, look at the businessmen's faces and predict the success of their companies? And yet, a link surfaced: CEOs with faces perceived as powerful—competent, dominant, and mature—were significantly more likely to run profitable companies; those with less-powerful-looking faces tended to run companies at the bottom of profitability. CEOs whom subjects thought would be good at leading a company were significantly more likely to manage profitable enterprises. These findings held even when researchers statistically controlled for CEOs' attractiveness, emotional displays in the photos, and age. The CEOs' perceived warmth had no link to profits. A follow-up study showed that competence and leadership ratings, but not the other traits, also predicted profits of Fortune 1000 companies run by female CEOs. According to Rule and Ambady, "The ability to infer success from faces is applicable to both male and female CEOs."

"These findings," wrote the authors, "suggest that naive judgments may provide more accurate assessments of individuals than well-informed judgments can." In fact, most previous studies that have failed to find potential links between CEOs' characteristics and the success of their companies have relied on surveys from employees who know their bosses. The fact that people who know nothing about a CEO can predict his or her company's profits is powerful. Might it be prudent for boards of trustees who hire CEOs to take into account strangers' perceptions of candidates' faces? Obviously, this is only one piece of evidence that merits replication, but it's an empirically valid finding that's difficult to argue with.

Objective Criteria That Predict CEO Performance

A distinction is relevant at this point. With the student evaluations discussed in the previous chapter, the predicted outcome is a *subjective* criterion since it depends on people's perceptions of instructor quality. In contrast, Rule and Ambady's study on CEOs found that subjects' ratings of a variety of traits based on photographs could predict an *objective* criterion: company profitability. Here, a subjective measure, people's perceptions of power, predicted a real-world objective criterion, profits.

Are there objective means to predict objective outcomes among the CEOs' businesses? We can investigate this question from two angles. First, can we measure any objective predictor variables within the *perceivers* of the CEOs that predict the performance of companies? Second, can we measure any objective predictor variables in the *CEOs* themselves to predict the performance of their companies? Let's take each of these questions in turn.

To answer the first question, Rule, Ambady, and some of their colleagues asked subjects to examine sixty-eight photographs of CEOs (both men and women) for two seconds each, while a functional magnetic resonance imaging, or fMRI, machine scanned their brains to see which parts lit up. After completing this task in the scanner, subjects sat at a laptop computer and rated how successful they thought each CEO would be at leading a company. Finally, the researchers asked a separate group of subjects to rate the CEOs on a number of other traits, including attractiveness and emotional expressiveness. When subjects looked at faces of CEOs who ran profitable companies, the amygdalae on the left side of their brains were significantly more active, on average, than when they looked at photos of those who led less profitable companies (see below). The researchers propose that these CEOs' faces "stand out," signaling a greater degree of power and dominance than those of their less successful counterparts.

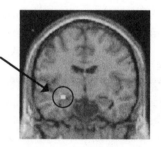

Response of the left amygdala when subjects viewed CEOs who led the most profitable companies.

Let's turn then to our second question: is there an objective measure of CEOs that will predict their success in running a company? One team at the University of Wisconsin, Milwaukee, set out to find the answer by examining the photos of fifty-five male CEOs who led Fortune 500 companies. Specifically, they examined each CEO's facial width-to-height ratio (WHR), a trait linked to aggression in men (as mentioned in Chapter 4) and to a psychological perception of power. Since CEOs don't make decisions in a vacuum, the researchers also assessed whether companies' leadership teams tended to see decisions as black-and-white, deferring to the authority of leadership, or in shades of grey, actively soliciting diverse opinions in their decision-making process.

CEOs with greater WHRs, that is wider faces, tended to run better-performing companies, but this trend only held if their leadership team was deferential and conceded to their authority. The researchers reported an anecdote about General Electric CEO Jeffrey Immelt, who had a high WHR compared to most CEOs in their sample. In the middle of the first decade of the 2000s, Immelt confronted a decision concerning the company's environmental responsibilities. The authors reported that although the leadership team at General Electric strongly disagreed with his vision on this issue, they conceded to his strategy. The authors argued that because company performance correlated to CEOs' WHRs primarily when boards were passive, CEOs actively influenced the performance of their companies. Whether the wide-faced CEOs were actually more aggressive or just perceived as such is unknown, but researchers found a statistical link between the dimensions of a leader's face and the performance of a company. (That being said, I wouldn't suggest purchasing stock based on the CEO's facial breadth.)

Pick up a picture of the head of your company. What tells do you pick up on? What is she communicating to the rest of the world, and what impact might this have on the performance of your company?

Are Leaders Born or Made (or Both)?

These studies raise an intriguing question. Are the differences in facial appearance among business leaders innate, or do the leaders come to acquire the look of leadership with increased success and other life experiences?

One hypothesis—let's call it the "face begets success" hypothesis—posits that some individuals are born with physical features that result in more leadership opportunities. From this perspective, looking successful actually fosters success. This effect can occur in any number of ways. People may treat powerful-looking people more like leaders, in much the way that adults tend to treat attractive infants more positively than less attractive babies. Also, people who look like leaders may receive more opportunities to develop their leadership skills. Thus, looks beget opportunities, yielding experiences that may cultivate leadership success.

A second hypothesis—let's call it the "success begets a face" hypothesis—implies that successful leaders' faces may change over time to "look the part." Some evidence suggests that repeated facial movements can leave their mark by wrinkling the skin and shifting the musculature. Data also suggest that the facial structures of married couples who spend an extensive amount of time together begin to resemble each other more closely as a result of facial mimicry.

Although no definitive evidence exists to tease these hypotheses apart, two studies do shed light on the issue. First, consider the above study in which CEOs with wider faces were more likely to run financially successful companies with a deferential board. Given that width-to-height ratios are relatively stable over the life span, it's almost certain that neither the facial bones nor the musculature of the CEOs changed as a result of success. Since one's facial structure is relatively fixed throughout life, this study supports the "face begets success" hypothesis.

Another piece of evidence sheds further light on this question. Researchers asked subjects to assess the facial warmth and power of managing partners at America's top one hundred law firms. Just as in their studies of CEOs, Rule and Ambady found that when examining current photos of the partners, subjects' perceptions of power, but not warmth, predicted the profitability of law firms. The researchers then asked a different group of subjects to assess the college yearbook photos of the same managing partners, taken, on average, more than thirty years before the study. In line with the results from current photos and in support of the "face begets success" hypothesis, perceptions of power in college photographs, but not warmth, predicted the profitability of law firms. The images put forth by profitable law firms could have been professionally polished and chosen specifically because they projected confidence or power. In contrast, no such possibility exists regarding the standard college yearbook photos taken thirty years prior. Nevertheless, the study authors appropriately caution that one's innate facial appearance does not determine leadership acumen; natural appearance may increase the probability of success, but life experiences undoubtedly play a role as well.

When considering the findings regarding CEO perceptions and profitability, one should consider the influence of culture and race. Although the perception of male CEO power predicts company profits in America, the same is not true for companies in Japan. For instance, Japanese, unlike Americans, do not associate leadership ability with traits like dominance and power. Also, the race of CEOs may mediate the influence of qualities like power and warmth. Due to their disproportionately high representation in the corporate world's upper echelons, Caucasian CEOs have been the predominant focus of virtually all of the studies discussed. Black CEOs who display a warmer baby face, versus a powerful face, are more likely to lead more prestigious companies and earn higher salaries, according to one study. The authors of this study argue that among black CEOs, having a warm baby face mitigates stereotypes of black males as threatening.

What Predicts Salesperson Success?

What about the performance of employees, particularly salespeople? Can tells predict their success, and if so, in what capacity?

Recently, I did something that I do only if absolutely necessary: purchase a vehicle. My wife did some homework and realized that the car I was driving had poor safety ratings for a rear impact, and since I transport my son in the back daily, I began shopping for a different vehicle. After reading a variety of reviews, we decided to purchase either a used Toyota Camry or a Honda Accord—both safe, popular, and affordable vehicles.

Over several days, I visited a number of dealerships selling Camrys and Accords. I couldn't help but notice the marked differences among the salespeople at these dealerships. One of the first salesmen I met was Tom, a tall, well-dressed man in his mid-thirties with blond hair and a thin build. Just after I parked my car, Tom approached. As soon as I got out of my car, he gripped my hand confidently, introduced himself, and asked, "What brings you here today?" I proceeded to tell him that I had identified a couple vehicles on his lot that I'd like to look at and possibly test drive. I also told him, like I do almost every salesperson I encounter on a car lot, that I had limited time and would like to use it efficiently. Tom began by asking me some relatively perceptive questions about my needs in a car, how much I wanted to spend, and so forth. I was most struck by his warm approach and supportive style of communication. He seemed genuine and came across more as a partner in the process than as just a salesman, as though it were his mission to ensure that I obtained the product I wanted. Frankly, his style impressed me.

My experience at another dealership was vastly different. I walked in, and Rob, another man in his mid-thirties with brown hair and a muscular body, promptly approached. We introduced ourselves, and I proceeded to inform him that I was on a schedule and really wanted to make my time with him count. Though Tom and Rob were similar in age, their interpersonal communication styles differed drastically. Perhaps because I told Rob that I wanted use our time efficiently, he didn't ask me any questions about what I was looking for in a car. However, once he found out that I worked at a nearby university, he couldn't stop asking me questions about the demographics of the students, what the campus was like, and what institutional strengths were evident. Though I politely answered his questions, albeit briefly, he didn't seem to consider that I really did want to spend my time with him productively. When I finally managed to redirect the conversation to the reason I was there—to look at cars—Rob appeared disinterested. When he showed me the vehicles in the lot, his routine seemed more mechanical than tailored to my specific interests in a vehicle. Despite the fact that Rob showed me what I needed to see and allowed me to drive the cars I wanted, my experience with him was lacking compared to my time with Tom.

I'd be willing to bet that Tom sells more vehicles per month than Rob. Tom's style was warmer, more enthusiastic, and more genuine than Rob's. Individuals who make their living in sales convey their motivations, emotions, and personality to customers within seconds of a first encounter. We quickly judge: Is this person competent? Can I trust him? Does he have my interests in mind? And there's little doubt that our answers to these questions, albeit oftentimes unconscious, influence the likelihood of our ultimately making a purchase.

How much does the interpersonal style of the salespeople we meet predict our buying behavior? Researchers asked upper management at a large US corporation to rate several of their sales managers as either "average" or "outstanding" based explicitly on their sales effectiveness and supervisors' evaluations. Investigators interviewed the sales managers about their educational and career histories, as well as positive and negative experiences over the course of their careers. For each subject, the researchers randomly chose three twenty-second audio clips from the interview; one clip focused on educational and career history, one on a positive career event, and the last on a negative career event. They then played these clips to eight judges individually, each of them rating the salesperson on a variety of dimensions, including task-oriented variables such as professionalism and decisiveness; interpersonal qualities such as warmth, empathy, and perceptiveness; and finally, anxiety.

The eight judges readily differentiated the average from the outstanding salespeople. Interestingly, anxiety and task-related ratings, such as perseverance and decisiveness, did not affect judges' ability to assess the caliber of each salesperson. The tells that mattered—a lot—were the salespeople's interpersonal qualities: judges rated outstanding sales managers, compared to their average colleagues, as warmer and more collaborative, supportive, understanding, enthusiastic, cooperative, empathic, and perceptive. These results reflect my experience at the car dealership: Tom demonstrated understanding and respect for my time, as I had asked, and posed perceptive questions that communicated his desire to ensure my needs were met. He was enthusiastic during the entire time I spent with him, describing the cars' features and the services provided by the dealership, and I could relate to him.

In life, we are constantly bombarded by salespeople and potentially influenced by their interpersonal styles. This makes sense, of course, given that they constitute most companies' lifeblood. As one author recently put it, "No computer network with pretty graphics can ever replace the salespeople that make our society work." These are the people on the ground, like Tom and Rob—men and women who spend their entire careers trying to persuade you to buy any number of products, be they televisions, insurance, or furniture.

We also see salespeople at work promoting products in advertising, itself a multi-billion-dollar industry. According to one estimate, businesses spent $139.5 billion on advertising in the United States in 2012 alone. Again, salespeople in these venues likely have an effect on us as consumers.

Radio and television advertisements are some of the briefest and most expensive modes of advertising; salespeople have only thirty seconds or less to persuade us to buy their products. As they have only a thin slice of time to gain our trust, success may largely rest on the nonverbal behavior they display to influence our future behavior.

If you are in charge of hiring salespeople either as a business owner or manager, I hope you're considering the implications of these studies for your own bottom line. Were I in charge of a company looking to put together a "high-yielding" sales team, I would first hire someone to design a study in which potential customers assess candidates' interpersonal nonverbal cues. The use of nonverbal behavior is vital to meeting custom-ers' needs and preferences. Effectively employing nonverbal skills helps the customer first, with the byproduct of greater sales. With such a study, a company could distinguish the potentially effective and ineffective salespeople.

The next time you have an interaction with a salesperson at a car deal-ership or jewelry store, consider how his or her appearance and behavior might influence your purchasing decisions.

Party-Worthy Findings

1. **CEO power predicts company profitability:** The perceived power of male Fortune 500 CEOs' faces predicts the profitability of their companies.

2. **Brain activity predicts company profitability:** The amygdala on the left side of our brains is more active, on average, when we look at the faces of CEOs who run profitable companies compared to those who run less profitable companies.

3. **We can predict success in sales in one minute:** Based on only sixty-second audio clips, people could differentiate average salespeople from outstanding salespeople.

10

POLITICAL PUNDITRY: ANY KID CAN DO IT

"Democracy is the theory that the common people know what they want and deserve to get it good and hard."

—H. L. MENCKEN

On Election Day 2012, I drove by scores of political signs and advertisements strategically placed by the road to the polling station near my home. My son and I walked past the numerous green camouflaged military cannons before entering the National Guard Armory, where I waited in line for a couple minutes before the volunteer waived me into the next available voting booth. I was delighted that I could bring my son inside with me.

Afterward, as we were leaving, my son asked me why I voted for one candidate over another for president. I explained the social and economic issues that were important to me. I truly felt as though my choices were rational and consistent with my values. But then I began to question the underpinnings of my choices: was my preference in candidates solely the result of conscious and rationale thought, or might I be influenced by superficial factors outside my awareness? I fear that the latter may have played at least some role in my decision making, and it probably does for others as well. But, as you'll see, superficial variables don't play a role in the way you might think.

Elections and Campaigns

Growing up I always thought of elections as part of the natural world, much like gravity, the sun, and tall sequoias, but nothing could be further from the truth. Humans are unique within the animal kingdom in how we choose our leaders. Bees choose their leaders based on reproductive capacity, and chimpanzees choose alpha males based on size and influence within the group; many human societies choose their leaders based on votes cast by millions of people. Moreover, elections are a relatively recent phenomenon, with representative democratic elections beginning only around the end of the eighteenth century, a blink of the eye ago in the course of human civilization.

Elections are the linchpin between the citizens of a country and the government that presides over them. They give elected officials the power to translate the promises they make on the campaign trail into policy. Political scientists suggest that the very act of taking off work and sometimes waiting in long lines for the privilege of voting has the unintended, yet positive, consequence of bolstering support for the government the people are electing.

I brought my son to the polling station with me for a reason. From early childhood, many Americans are socialized to value and respect the electoral process. Though I was only six years old, I can still remember my mother turning on our thirteen-inch black-and-white television to watch Ronald Reagan's first inauguration as president. State employees—that is, teachers—bestow on children the importance of a representative democracy in the classroom as well. I was reminded of this two weeks ago while organizing some boxes in my home, when I came across my eighth-grade social studies project, which featured a compendium of campaign paraphernalia from local, state, and national candidates.

Yet many of us often don't vote. In a presidential election year, only about 60 percent of the populace shows up at the polls; during a nonpresidential year, only about 40 percent of eligible voters see the inside of a voting booth.

The low level of voter turnout in the United States is not for lack of effort on the part of candidates. Most candidates running for election at the presidential, congressional, and gubernatorial levels press the pause button on their personal lives for months, if not years, and take to the campaign trail, expending inordinate amounts of time and energy. And, of course, none of this would be possible on a large scale without the engine for all of these activities: money. "There are two things that are important in politics," said William McKinley's campaign manager in the 1896 presidential race. "The first is money and I can't remember what the second one is." The amount of money spent in modern campaigns and the time spent to raise it are staggering and have only increased in recent years.

Decisions, Decisions . . .

On the campaign trail, candidates try to persuade you, the voter, that they are the best potential officeholders and that their policies will best serve their constituencies. They spend millions of dollars, put in countless hours of work (as do their volunteers), and place their lives on hold to court you all the way to the ballot box. And there you stand in the voting booth, as I did, in early November. For whom shall you vote? Why?

For decades, political science and economics—the fields that predominantly study voting behavior—have largely held that voters make rational choices in the voting booth, that they base their decisions on numerous pieces of information, such as economic conditions and candidates' policy positions, articulateness, and leadership potential. But could some people vote for candidates based on issues that have little or no substance?

More than at any other time in history, we are deluged with information about what's happening in the world, from Lady Gaga's latest fashions to the most recent disaster on the other side of the globe. Political news forms only part of the cacophony of data from myriad confusing and contradictory sources, and even this sphere is filled with innumerable talking heads spouting opinions at a dizzying pace. All of this occurs in a world where people are working longer hours, for less pay, and getting less sleep than at any other time in recent history.

So even though we have unprecedented access to vast amounts of information, US citizens are woefully uninformed about the political process and the positions of candidates running for office. Late-night talk show host Jay Leno occasionally goes out into the streets of Los Angeles and asks random people what seem to be ridiculously simple questions, such as who the vice president is now or who the American president was during the Civil War. A significant number of people do not know the answers.

Studies support Leno's entertaining, but sad, findings. I could list numerous examples, but consider only a few:

- An astounding 60 percent of Americans cannot name the three branches of government.
- Less than a third of Americans know why *Roe v. Wade* is significant.
- Only 25 percent of Americans can name more than one of the five freedoms protected by the first amendment of the US constitution (freedom of assembly, press, speech, religion, and petition for redress of grievances). Curiously, one in five people think the first amendment protects the right to own a pet.

If deciding whom to vote for depends on knowing basic civics, the United States is in a heap of trouble.

When it comes to awareness of more specific information regarding candidates' policy positions, the outlook is equally bleak. A study conducted just before the 2000 presidential election, in which George W. Bush ran against Al Gore, asked citizens twelve questions about the two men's positions (e.g., "Do you happen to know whether Bush favors or opposes a large cut in personal income taxes?" "Do you happen to know whether Gore favors or opposes expanding Medicare for retirees to cover the costs of prescription drugs?"). Of the twelve questions posed, most respondents could correctly identify candidates' positions on only two issues. Less than half could accurately state the candidates' positions on all of the questions. Studies have documented voters' ignorance of the issues in more recent races as well, and it persists to this day. It's little surprise that the thirty-second commercials produced by candidates and their supporters are failing to educate the electorate given their brevity and, often times, lack of focus on central issues.

What are voters to do, given their spectacular ignorance of basic civics and of the policy differences between candidates? Most do what any good human, voter or nonvoter, does; they use heuristics to help them. Heuristics constitute the mental shortcuts we take when making complex decisions. In the realm of politics, we may rely on shortcuts such as party affiliation to help us decide whom to vote for.

I'll admit that when I went into the voting booth last time, I knew absolutely nothing about candidates running in about half the races. Most of these races were at the local level (e.g., coroner, treasurer). I used the simple mental shortcut of party affiliation to help me decide and chose all of the candidates who shared the party with which I most closely identify. I could have used other shortcuts, such as my newspaper's endorsement or the advice of a friend with similar political opinions.

But what if the electorate is voting based on irrelevant heuristics, like candidates' skin or hair color, attractiveness, or height? Two historical examples provide clues to this question, but modern science has provided some answers to what some voters seem to be zeroing in on to help them decide, at least in part. The answers might surprise you.

*Abraham Lincoln and his
whiskerless face.*

Honest Abe and His Whiskers

Political strategists have long suspected that candidates' appearance might influence how the electorate perceives them. Just a few weeks before the presidential election of 1860, an eleven-year-old girl named Grace Bedell from Westfield, New York, saw a photo of Abraham Lincoln's characteristically gaunt face, which prompted her to write a forthright letter to the future president, as only a child would:

NY
Westfield Chatauque Co
Oct. 15, 1860
Hon A B Lincoln

Dear Sir

My father has just home from the fair and brought home your picture and Mr. Hamlin's. I am a little girl only eleven years old, but want you should be President of the United States very much so I hope you wont think me very bold to write to, such a great man as you are. Have you any little girls about as large as I am if so give them my love and tell her to write to me if you cannot answer this letter. I have got 4 brothers and part of them will vote for you any way, and if you will let your whiskers grow I will try and get the rest of them to vote for you you would look a great deal better for your face is so thin. All the ladies like whiskers and they would tease their husbands to vote for you and then you would be President. My father is a going to vote for you and if I was a man I would vote for you to but I will try and get every one to vote for you that I can I think that rail fence around your picture makes it look very pretty I have got a little baby sister she is nine weeks old and is just as cunning as can be. When you direct your letter direct to Grace Bedell Westfield Chatauque County New York

I must not write any more answer this letter right off Good bye

Grace Bedell

As a young child, Grace intuited that changing his image might improve Lincoln's electoral success. In the midst of his bid for the White House, Lincoln responded to the girl.

Springfield, Ill. Oct. 19, 1860
Miss Grace Bedell

My dear little Miss

Your very agreeable letter of the 15th is received.
I regret the necessity of saying I have no daughters. I have three
sons—one seventeen, one nine, and one seven, years of age. They,
with their mother, constitute my whole family.

As to the whiskers, having never worn any, do you not think people
would call it a piece of silly affection if I were to begin it now?

Your very sincere well wisher

A. Lincoln

Most of us remember Lincoln with a beard (or "whiskers," as Grace Bedell called them).

Lincoln stopped to see Grace in her hometown on his way by train from Springfield, Illinois, to Washington, DC, after winning the presidency. Remembering the event later, the girl said, "He climbed down and sat with me on the edge of the platform. 'Grace,' he said, 'look at my whiskers. I've been growing them for you.' Then he kissed me. I never saw him again." Apparently, the coaxing of an eleven-year-old girl was enough to convince the lawyer from Illinois that one's appearance actually influences others' perceptions.

Kennedy and Nixon face off in 1960 for the presidential nomination.

Kennedy and Nixon Face Off

This lesson would be lost on a Republican running for president one hundred years later. On September 26, 1960, two candidates for president assumed the stage for what would be the first televised debate in US history. A record 60 million viewers sat in front of their black-and-white televisions that night to watch John F. Kennedy, the Democrat, debate Vice President Richard M. Nixon, the Republican. The face-off took place in a Chicago CBS studio, where the candidates stood in front of a moderator and panelists with cameras pointed directly at them. Both Kennedy and Nixon understood the historic nature of the event, as they knew it might make or break their candidacies and set the precedent for future presidential debates (as it did).

The candidates focused on the domestic issues of the day, including education and medical care for the elderly. But rather than their positions on the issues, their contrasting visual appeal defined the debate. Kennedy arrived in Chicago the night before the debate and slept well. That day, he gave a short speech to a group of potential voters, took a nap, rehearsed with his advisors, and ate a relaxed dinner. On the CBS studio stage, Kennedy, clean shaven and tanned from campaigning in California, sported a dark blue suit; he appeared youthful and dynamic. Prior to the event, he had received advice from his advisors on how best to address the camera when he spoke and how best to compose himself when listening to his opponent's responses. Overall, he looked not only in command of the issues but ready to assume the presidency.

Nixon arrived in Chicago late the night before, gave a speech the following morning, and then prepared for the debate alone in his hotel room. Unlike Kennedy's suit, which contrasted well with the studio set on black-and-white television, Nixon's gray suit blended into the background, rendering his image somewhat disembodied. More problematically, he looked fatigued, pale, sweaty, and weary. Though CBS had a cosmetician on hand, both candidates refused her assistance. However, Kennedy's staff applied some makeup to his freshly shaven face; Nixon applied over-the-counter makeup himself, which seemed to accentuate his stubble and pallor. On top of all this, Nixon was also underweight due to his rigorous campaign schedule and a recent stay in the hospital following a serious knee injury. The debate was a debacle for Nixon.

"Kennedy was bronzed beautifully," CBS president Frank Stanton would later recall. "Nixon looked like death because he had been in the hospital. And you could run your hand inside his collar without touching anything—it was that loose. His color was terrible; his beard was not good and he didn't want any makeup. I felt sorry for him." Nixon received immediate feedback, as he would later recall: "After the program, callers, including my own mother, wanted to know if anything was wrong, because I did not look well."

With the help of professionally applied makeup, a clean-shaven face, and numerous milkshakes, Nixon did not suffer the same fate in subsequent debates. Nonetheless, his destiny was sealed, as most people who watched the televised debate thought Kennedy had won. Interestingly, however, people who listened to the debate on the radio were actually more inclined to believe Nixon had won, or at least that his performance had been competitive. Naive undergraduate viewers and listeners with no prior knowledge of the debate have supported this sentiment experimentally. Kennedy's appearance and nonverbal cues seem to influence viewers' perceptions of the candidates.

Did the debate actually influence the votes that citizens would cast about six weeks later? We'll never know for sure, but it's widely thought that Nixon's haggard appearance in that first debate influenced the election significantly. Before the first debate, Nixon had been ahead by one point in polls, but immediately following the debate, Kennedy took the lead by three points. According to a historian of debates at Northeastern University, the subsequent debates did not matter: "Kennedy left such a positive impression in the first debate, it was quite difficult for Nixon to overcome it." Kennedy would go on to win the presidency, of course, but only by a razor-thin margin of victory in the popular vote: 34,220,984 votes versus Nixon's 34,108,157—this is one-sixth of 1 percent difference.

Just How (Ir)rational Are We?

Although the Kennedy-Nixon debate holds an important lesson regarding electoral politics, it only reveals one—perhaps misleading—part of the picture. The debate result suggests that youthfulness and attractiveness influence our perceptions of candidates. Not until relatively recently, however, have researchers investigated the degree to which superficial factors actually do drive voting decisions. As we'll see, the weight of these tells on the outcome of elections is deeper, more complex, and more troubling than most of us would have presumed. We may not be nearly as rational as many political scientists contend. If so, the very electoral process on which our democracy rests could be on shaky ground.

If I had to choose one paper that has rocked the political psychology world most in the last decade, it would be a series of studies published in *Science* conducted by Alexander Todorov and his colleagues at Princeton University. Imagine participating in one of these studies, in which you would sit in front of a computer monitor as pairs of head shots like the

Which person is the more competent?

pair above flashed on the screen. For each of the pairs, you would answer a simple question: "Which person is the more competent?"

Unbeknownst to subjects, all of the pictures showed competing Democrat and Republican congressional candidates. Some elections had not yet taken place before subjects viewed the images. If subjects recognized any of the candidates, their data were not included in the analysis.

If you thought the candidate on the left—the Democrat—was more competent than the candidate on the right—the Republican—you're like most of the Princeton undergrads whom Todorov and his colleagues tested. The Democrat defeated the Republican in the 2004 US Senate race in Wisconsin. In an amazing demonstration of the power of our quick judgments, the Princeton undergraduates' perceptions of competence predicted the congressional elections not only for this race but also for the majority of others; candidates chosen as more competent won 72 percent of the time among US Senate candidates and 67 percent of the time among candidates for the House of Representatives. The researchers were even able to predict the candidates' overall proportion of votes received by examining the competency ratings of subjects. Shockingly, the Princeton undergraduates predicted electoral success even when given just one second to view the photographs.

Although this study demonstrates links between impressions of competency and voting behavior, just as revealing is what qualities are not predictive of electoral success. Todorov and his colleagues also asked subjects to choose which candidates were more honest, trustworthy, charismatic, and likeable. Although the competency ratings (including perceptions of leadership and intelligence) predicted electoral outcomes, none of these other traits did. Appearing competent is much more important than seeming likeable, honest, or charismatic in winning public office.

These findings are especially impressive when you consider that the candidates had been campaigning for months, even years. Without any knowledge of their policy positions, leadership track record, or party affiliation, we can make accurate predictions of their electoral success based on a one-second viewing of a photograph. We like to think that we vote our democratically elected officials into office because they best represent the people's hopes for the future. Yet, Todorov and his colleagues' findings suggest we rely on a heuristic, and a poor one at that.

Who Says Five-Year-Olds Don't Know Anything About Voting?

An equally fascinating, albeit disconcerting, study comes from studying Swiss children. Researchers asked kids between the ages of five and thirteen to play a computer game simulating a ship voyage from Troy to Ithaca. At the end of the game, they showed the children a pair of photographs of the faces of candidates running in French parliamentary elections and asked the following question: "Imagine that you will now sail from Troy to Ithaca. Who would you choose as the captain of your boat?"

If you told your friends that kids as young as five years old could accurately predict who would win the political elections in a different country, they might gaze at you incredulously. But this is exactly what the Swiss team found and reported in *Science*: the children's preferred choice of captain happened to be the winning parliamentary candidate 71 percent of the time. These results are virtually identical to those for adults assessing the same candidates.

As I wrote this chapter, my six-year-old son looked over my shoulder and saw the pictures on the previous page of the candidates for US Senate from the study by Todorov and his colleagues. "Imagine that you were on a large ship and wanted to sail across an ocean," I said to him. "Who would you choose to be your captain?" Isaac immediately replied, "The man on the left, dad. He just looks like a better captain. The other guy looks okay, but he doesn't look like a captain."

In an offshoot of the original study focusing on Swiss youth, the researchers also presented some of the children with pairs of faces that included Barack Obama and John McCain, as well as Barack Obama and

Hillary Clinton. You probably guessed it: children chose Obama 77 percent of the time over McCain and 90 percent of the time over Clinton. The Swiss study suggests that kids may rely on the same perceptual cues that adults do, implying that these perceptual inferences develop relatively early in life.

Judging from these studies and others, "Facial competence is a highly robust and specific predictor of political preferences." Why some faces look competent and others do not is still an open question. People seem to associate competency with candidates whose faces show leadership and intelligence, as well as dependability, attractiveness, and emotional stability. At present, we have little idea how people develop these perceptions.

We do know that we can make such assessments of candidates' faces lightning fast. In one study, subjects' assessments of the competency level of gubernatorial candidates accurately predicted electoral success in one-tenth of one second. And their accuracy was barely less than that of subjects who had as much time as they wanted. Only one instruction led to a detriment in subjects' performance: telling them to think carefully about their competency judgment. When researchers directed subjects to deliberate on their decision, rather than rely on a gut feeling, their overall performance degraded significantly.

Perhaps there's an alternative explanation for the findings that link candidates' appearance to their electoral success. Perhaps more competent-looking candidates supply better pictures of themselves. Perhaps race, gender, or party affiliation drives impressions of competence. Perhaps people see incumbents as more competent, and that's why they win more frequently. Perhaps impressions of competency only matter when conservatives and liberals run against each other. Perhaps subjects rate familiar candidates as more competent, and familiarity leads to greater electoral success. All of these seem like viable alternative explanations, but in general the data do not support them.

It's difficult to tell if impressions of candidates' competence correspond to actual candidate quality, but the available evidence suggests no link. We do know that it's important to "look the part" if one wants to succeed in politics.

Obviously, perceived competence isn't the beginning and end of the story when it comes to predicting electoral success. Some incompetent-looking candidates certainly won, and some competent-looking candidates lost. A number of other appearance-related factors play a role, though none as reliably as competence.

Weird Science: Perfect Candidate Appeal

All of us have movies from our childhoods that are forever seared into our memories. One such movie for me is *Weird Science,* in which two high school teenagers named Wyatt and Gary dream of winning popularity and developing the social prowess to woo girls, though they realize it's probably not going to happen. Out of boredom and curiosity, the boys decide to use their home computer to design a virtual woman who is physically perfect (in their eyes). In order to create this ideal female, they download a plethora of data and pictures, then connect a Barbie doll to the computer to upload her dimensions. Suddenly, a bolt of lightning strikes, and when the smoke clears, a beautiful woman, played by Kelly LeBrock, appears in front of the astonished teenagers. She then proceeds to help them gain the popularity for which they've always longed.

Much like Wyatt and Gary, political strategists, campaign managers, and party leaders hope to mold, develop, and nurture a stable of politically appealing candidates for upcoming elections. Political strategists have always considered candidates' images important, but scientists have identified numerous other tells that both positively and negatively relate to electoral appeal. Let's examine the face, voice, and height, in turn.

THE FACE: The "ideal" candidate's face signals leadership ability in the form of competency, dependability, emotional stability, and intelligence. The older and more familiar a candidate appears, the more votes he or she receives. A host of perceived traits in candidates' faces have no relation to the outcome of elections, including impressions of honesty, anxiety, enthusiasm, warmth, trustworthiness, and likeability.

The perfect candidate should certainly not have a threatening-looking face. When one study asked subjects to choose which appeared the most physically intimidating among two smiling candidates for Congress, the one chosen more frequently was more likely to lose the election.

One might think the ideal candidate would be attractive, but the evidence is mixed, with some studies showing a positive association between this quality and voting behavior and others showing no relationship. One carefully conducted study even showed that candidates with physically attractive faces were more likely to lose elections, but it based this finding primarily on candidates who looked attractive but incompetent. Thus, "attempting to make a candidate look more attractive," said the researchers, "may well backfire if the candidate looks otherwise incompetent."

Finally, the context in which an election takes place may influence the way voters respond to faces. Some evidence suggests that during wartime voters prefer dominant- and masculine-appearing leaders, whereas in peacetime they prefer leaders who appear intelligent and less masculine.

THE VOICE: If male, the ideal presidential candidate's voice sounds deeper than his opponent's. Researchers measured the vocal quality of candidates in nineteen US presidential debates from 1960 until 2000. Of the presidential elections in this period featuring televised debates, candidates with lower-pitched voices (marked by an asterisk in the list below) won the popular vote 100 percent of the time:

2000	Bush II versus Gore*
1996	Clinton* versus Dole
1992	Clinton* versus Bush I
1988	Bush I* versus Dukakis
1984	Reagan* versus Mondale
1980	Reagan* versus Carter
1976	Carter* versus Ford
1960	Kennedy* versus Nixon

Researchers surmised that a low-pitched voice in men is a clue to dominance and high levels of testosterone. Such signals may be preferred because dominance may have been adaptive in our evolutionary history.

HEIGHT: The probability of electoral success for a presidential candidate is also greater if he is tall. Abraham Lincoln, the tallest president ever elected, stood six feet, four inches, while our shortest president, James Madison, stood five feet, four inches. In the forty-six presidential elections between 1796 and 2012, the taller candidate won twenty six times, and the shorter candidate won twenty times. Looking at the popular vote rather than the electoral college, the taller candidate won twenty-nine times and the shorter candidate only seventeen times. Though the vast majority of shorter candidates exceeded the average American height for the time in which they lived, the statistics reveal that taller candidates enjoy a height advantage over their opponents.

Taller Candidates	Shorter Candidates
Barack Obama (2008)	Barack Obama (2012)
William J. Clinton (1996)	George W. Bush (2004)
George H. W. Bush (1988)	George W. Bush (2000)*
Ronald Reagan (1980)	Jimmy Carter (1976)
Ronald Reagan (1984)	Richard Nixon (1972)
Richard Nixon (1968)	Calvin Coolidge (1924)
Lyndon B. Johnson (1964)	Woodrow Wilson (1912)
John F. Kennedy (1960)	William McKinley (1900)
Dwight D. Eisenhower (1956)	
Dwight D. Eisenhower (1952)	
Harry S. Truman (1948)	
Franklin D. Roosevelt (1940)	
Franklin D. Roosevelt (1936)	
Franklin D. Roosevelt (1932)	
Herbert Hoover (1928)	
Warren G. Harding (1920)	
Woodrow Wilson (1916)	
William Howard Taft (1908)	
Theodore Roosevelt (1904)	

This lists the presidential winners when they were the taller candidate (left column) and the shorter candidate (right column).

*Al Gore won the popular vote in 2000 but lost the election due to a Supreme Court decision that decided the winner of Florida's electoral college votes.

Height becomes more strongly associated with electoral success if one examines presidential races in the twentieth and twenty-first centuries, when the impact of political image and media became increasingly important. In the table on page 168, I've listed all the presidents that we know of whose heights differed from that of their opponents. On the left, I've listed the winners who were taller than their opponents, and on the right the winners who were comparatively shorter (presidents' names appear as many times as they won an election). From the electoral college perspective, taller candidates won their presidential bids 70 percent of the time. From the perspective of the popular vote, these statistics become even more suggestive since Al Gore, the taller candidate, won the popular vote over George W. Bush, though he lost the presidency in 2000. From either perspective, the shorter candidates are at a disadvantage to their taller counterparts during most elections. Interestingly, we see no relation between height and electoral success in gubernatorial races.

Researchers have uncovered links between the height of a president and his success in office as well. Periodically, scholars and news networks poll citizens and academics, asking them to rate the degree to which presidents have succeeded in the job. There is no doubt that ranking the greatness of presidents is a tricky business; standings ebb and flow, depending on whom you ask and when. Nonetheless, there is some degree of consistency over time and between respondents; Lincoln and Washington are almost always in the top cluster of presidents, and James Buchanan and Warren Harding are almost at the bottom of the list.

With these caveats in mind, I've listed all of the presidents from George Washington through George W. Bush and graphed their presidential greatness scores on the next page as assessed by presidential scholars in 2005. The balance between liberal and conservative scholars who rated the presidents was equal. I computed a relatively simple statistic and found that the degree to which presidents were taller positively and significantly correlated with their average greatness score. That is, respondents tended to rate taller presidents as more successful than their shorter counterparts. The three "great" presidents, according to the scholars, were George Washington, Abraham Lincoln, and Franklin Roosevelt, whose average height was 6 feet, 2 1/2 inches; the three lowest-ranked presidents—James Buchanan, Warren Harding, and Franklin Pierce—had an average height of 5 feet, 11 1/3 inches; this represents a statistically significant height

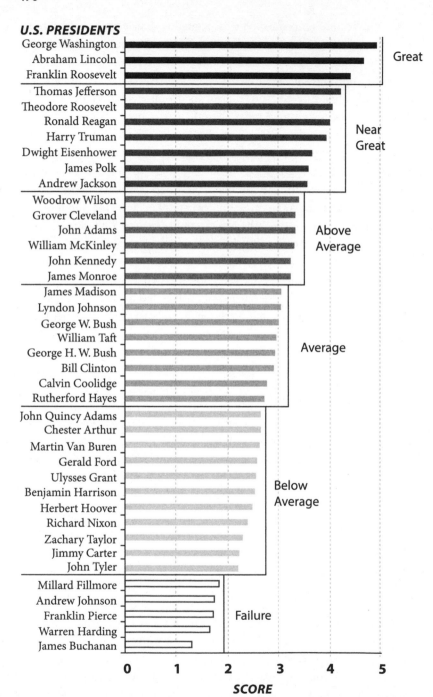

U.S. PRESIDENTS

President		Category
George Washington		Great
Abraham Lincoln		
Franklin Roosevelt		
Thomas Jefferson		Near Great
Theodore Roosevelt		
Ronald Reagan		
Harry Truman		
Dwight Eisenhower		
James Polk		
Andrew Jackson		
Woodrow Wilson		Above Average
Grover Cleveland		
John Adams		
William McKinley		
John Kennedy		
James Monroe		
James Madison		Average
Lyndon Johnson		
George W. Bush		
William Taft		
George H. W. Bush		
Bill Clinton		
Calvin Coolidge		
Rutherford Hayes		
John Quincy Adams		Below Average
Chester Arthur		
Martin Van Buren		
Gerald Ford		
Ulysses Grant		
Benjamin Harrison		
Herbert Hoover		
Richard Nixon		
Zachary Taylor		
Jimmy Carter		
John Tyler		
Millard Fillmore		Failure
Andrew Johnson		
Franklin Pierce		
Warren Harding		
James Buchanan		

0   1   2   3   4   5

SCORE

difference. (Of course, there are exceptions to most statistical trends; Harry Truman and Dwight Eisenhower were both well under six feet tall, but most scholars consider them near-great presidents.)

A number of different evolutionary and environmental explanations might elucidate the relation between height and political success. Because height signals dominance and strength, people may prefer tall leaders over their shorter counterparts. After all, such qualities were important to our ancestors, as having a physically strong leader would improve survival chances in more turbulent environments. It's also possible that tall individuals receive more leadership opportunities and are treated more like leaders throughout childhood, which may lead them to become superior leaders and therefore seek out leadership positions. Whatever the explanation, if I were designing the perfect candidate for president, the person would be at least six feet tall if he were a man. Hopefully in time we'll have enough data to determine the role of height in presidential success for women (and for the other characteristics I've described in this chapter).

The Subtlety of Appearance

The effects of appearance on voting behavior can be subtle and pernicious. Appearance seems to influence our voting behaviors, a tendency often completely lost upon us that yet has lasting impact. When I'm in the voting booth, I feel confident that I'm basing my decisions not on how a candidate looks but on how he or she would govern. By the time we head to the polls we should have replaced our first impressions with something more substantive, like an understanding of candidates' policy positions or past performance. And yet, these first impressions persist in many of our minds and therefore influence our voting behavior. It's the equivalent of having a broken Etch A Sketch; no matter how hard you shake it, the image will not disappear.

Appearance might influence only a small proportion of the votes candidates receive. In the context of policy positions and other candidate variables, it seems unlikely that appearance would matter all that much. Research, however, indicates something different. Subjects in one study watched ten second silent videos of debates between candidates in fifty-eight different gubernatorial elections. Their impressions of the candidates more powerfully predicted the candidates' vote shares than the economic conditions during the campaign, including the unemployment rate, per capita income, and real estate prices. Subjects' impressions were equally as predictive of the popular vote as the incumbency status of the candidates.

Obviously, some voters are buffered from the effects of appearance. My grandfather was a staunch Republican and would have been persuaded to vote for nobody other than Barry Goldwater in the 1964 presidential election. He was a knowledgeable voter who cast votes predominantly along party lines. For voters like him, a candidate's appearance matters little. It's the swing voters and the uninformed voters who are most influenced by a candidate's looks. And in today's political races, it's the undecided voters who can make or break a candidate's chances of victory.

Consider elections in which a few percentage points—or less—can mean the difference between winning and losing. Recall that Kennedy defeated Nixon by a razor-thin margin of one-sixth of 1 percent. More recently, in 2008 Al Franken defeated Norm Coleman for a pivotal Senate seat by a mere 312 votes from the 2,424,946 cast. In the 2000 presidential election, in which the Supreme Court decided that George W. Bush had won Florida's electoral college votes, the popular vote difference between Bush and Gore in Florida was 0.0092 percent, according to the official statistics.

Some Recommendations

The findings I've discussed in this chapter have some significant implications for citizens, political leaders, and society in general. Here I include a few recommendations based on the research linking candidates' appearance to voting behavior.

RECOMMENDATION 1: Turn off the television and read the news. Television exacerbates the influence of candidates' appearances on voting behavior, especially among voters who have the least amount of general political knowledge or understanding of candidates' actual positions on the issues. Becoming more knowledgeable and watching less television will provide you with a greater buffer against the candidates' appearance.

RECOMMENDATION 2: Guard against biased images in the media. One study examined how various Internet news sources depicted George W. Bush and Barack Obama during their presidencies. Some of these sources are preferred by conservatives (FOX.com and *Townhall*) and some by liberals (CNN.com, MSNBC.com, and the *Huffington Post*). Blind coders rated the pictures of Obama as warmer and more competent on the "liberal" media sources compared to the "conservative" media sources. Conversely, the coders rated the pictures of Bush as warmer and more competent on the "conservative" media sources. The bottom line: both the rhetoric and the images on these sources are biased. Be aware of where you're getting your information; the source may be having a greater influence than you realize.

RECOMMENDATION 3: Evaluate the candidates consciously and critically. In the process, actively resist the potential influence of their images. Critically analyze candidates' positions and their potential for leadership to make sound choices, rather than defaulting to heuristics, which likely don't reflect potential future success.

RECOMMENDATION 4: Avoid placement of candidates' photos on ballots. One of the worst things a country can do for its election process is to put photos of candidates on the ballot, and yet numerous countries around the world do. Placing photos of candidates next to their names is an innocent practice to help voters recognize whom they're voting for, but studies show that this may strengthen the impact of candidates' appearance, especially if the voters know little about the candidates.

RECOMMENDATION 5: Hire scientists as political consultants. If I were a political strategist with the power to influence which candidates the party should select to run for office, I'd hire an expert to conduct the type of studies I've discussed in this chapter. With some relatively straightforward study designs and statistics, it's possible to see if a candidate comes off as competent, threatening, and so forth. Strategists could then use this information, along with other more substantive variables, to help decide who might be the best candidate for a particular race. Of course, whether they should do this is another question.

RECOMMENDATION 6: Gamble on your politicians. I offer this last recommendation tongue in cheek. The University of Iowa runs a futures market for elections in which you can win or lose real money depending on the outcome. If you want to win, do not listen to the political pundits' predictions, as studies show they are about as accurate as I am at hitting a golf ball (my success is, regrettably, virtually random). Who needs pundits when we, the people, can accurately predict who will win based on our impressions of candidates? Any one of us may or may not be adept at deciphering which of two candidates is the most competent; thus, it's important to collect a group of friends to help you. Predictive accuracy increases when you average responses across people, as most of the studies I've discussed in this book do. Present candidates faces in pairs and ask your friends who is the more competent. How many people should you ask? Forty, according to the research. Personally, I wouldn't feel comfortable gambling on elections, but if you're going to do so, listening to the collective wisdom of your friends is probably a better bet than listening to pundits.

University committees admit students based largely on their standardized test scores and high school grades, professional sports teams hire athletes based on past performance and physical capacities, and Fortune 500 companies choose CEOs based on leadership potential and vision. But voters' choice for the leader of the free world is based on looks to some degree. Science, it seems, is just now catching up with Plato's contention that in choosing democratically elected leaders, the populace cannot be trusted to make informed, rational decisions. Science, it seems, is just now catching up with Plato's contention that in choosing democratically elected leaders, people cannot be trusted to make rational decisions for the good of the community. In *The Republic*, Plato argued that people in a democratic society would elect leaders not because of their competency, but because they would engender the passions of the voters, in part through their appearance.

Newspaper and magazine opinion pieces lament the role that money plays in who wins political office. Yet, few seem concerned that superficial variables may very well drive the results of many of our elections. In this way, it's not only money that influences elections but candidates' capricious appearances arising from their genetic fortune or misfortune. If you're a candidate running for higher office, you better hope you "look the part."

Party-Worthy Findings

1. **Perceived competence predicts election outcomes:** We can predict electoral winners from perceived competence in as little as one-tenth of a second.

2. **Prediction of election outcomes begins young:** Even kids as young as five years old are capable of predicting who will win elections.

3. **It pays to be tall:** Height predicts not only whether someone will win a presidential election but how "great" a president will be.

THE IMPORTANCE OF PREDICTIVE HUMILITY

I f you've made it this far, I owe you a sincere debt of gratitude for taking the time to read this book. At the outset, I stated that *The Tell* isn't a self-help book that aims to assist you in making accurate predictions in your life. If it helps you in this regard, that's fine, but my main goal is to aid you in becoming a more sophisticated observer of others' nonverbal signals and appearance, as well as to show you the predictive capacities of the mind.

I hope that I've been at least partially successful in meeting these goals. We've learned, for example, what tells in early life predict autism, how photographs betray others' personalities and aggressive inclinations, how smiling predicts marital stability, how microexpressions signal deception, and how facial structure predicts companies' profits and even who wins political elections. I hope you're as impressed as I am by the number of domains in which tells can reveal something about past and future events.

However, I must remind myself—and you—to remain humble. When meeting others we are constantly forming (and updating) impressions of them. Just yesterday, for example, I hung out with one of my son's friends for the first time at our house. On balance, the friend was nice enough, but he seemed excessively aggressive toward my son and on the rowdy side—jumping off our couch, throwing toys, and breaking a knickknack that we have displayed on a shelf. When we have encounters with people, our first impressions have a tendency to stick with us. Why? Because our brains have a propensity to remember evidence that supports our initial impressions and to forget or distort evidence that contradicts them. We need to remember that our impressions and predictions may very well be wrong; we must be constantly on the lookout for information that contradicts rather than merely supports our hunches. The next time my son's friend comes over, I must make a special effort to notice his more civilized behaviors (assuming he demonstrates them) rather than merely attending to rowdy behaviors that confirm my initial impressions.

Another foible of the mind occurs when we think something is much more predictable once it has already happened. Imagine, for example, that you find out that your romantic partner lied to you or a particular candidate won an important election. Both of these events may seem utterly predictable when you look back in time. It's as if you "knew it all along." Unfortunately, our perceived ability to accurately understand and explain the past gives us unwarranted confidence in our capacity to predict future events. We think we're capable of making amazingly accurate predictions, when we're often wrong. And even when we are wrong, we often ignore and distort the evidence.

Numerous studies reliably show that confidence bears virtually no relation to one's predictive accuracy. That is, you might feel confident that you can predict someone's personality, but your confidence level corresponds little, if at all, with how accurate you'll be. You certainly don't want to remain blinded to who people really are merely because your prediction was wrong. Keep reminding yourself—as I try to—that the predictions that science tells us we are capable of making are based on probability and not certainty. My advice is to remember this while being acutely aware of the tells that you witness in those you meet.

What is the future of the science of prediction based on tells? Honestly, it's hard to know for sure, but technology will almost certainly play various roles. We can employ technology more consistently to help detect and interpret the tells I've discussed throughout this book. In essence, it may enhance our ability to use tells to make accurate predictions. We are already beginning to see this in our airports, where authorities are using high-definition cameras and other technology that measures physiology to predict whether someone might be a terrorist.

But just as technology may enhance our abilities, it may also numb our perceptual systems. Social media are playing an increasingly larger role in our lives, whereas face-to-face contact with others is diminishing for many. A friend recently told her daughter to call one of her friends to work out a teenage social squabble. "I'll just text her mom," said the daughter. "I wouldn't even know how to talk to her on the phone. We never talk." With text messaging and other technologies, we no longer have to communicate directly with people to the same degree. It's an open question as to how living with this technology over an entire lifetime will change our perceptive capacities.

Overall, though, I'm optimistic. Yes, technology has the capacity to diminish our capacities, but it can also enhance them. Also, science will continue to identify the tells that truly are predictive versus those we merely think of as such. This should be encouraging news for all of us.

ACKNOWLEDGMENTS

I t's a privilege for book authors to have a built-in mechanism to thank—publicly—the people who have contributed to their work directly and indirectly. It's a rarity to have such an opportunity. Also, if you believe in some form of determinism in life, as I do, rather than free will, you realize that you are not solely responsible for a project. Thus, by logical necessity, it's important to thank those who have influenced who you are and how you think.

First, I thank the institutions I've attended and the people in them who have been influential: the Luther College faculty, especially Simon Hanson and David Bishop, who generously planted intellectual seeds in me, and Dacher Keltner and Joseph Campos at the University of California, Berkeley, who modeled how to ask important questions and conduct rigorous empirical research to answer them.

I also extend gratitude to the faculty and staff of DePauw University. Thanks to my colleagues in the Psychology Department—Susanne Biehle, Ted Bitner, Terri Bonebright, Kevin Moore, Pam Propsom, Michael Roberts, Scott Ross, Sharmin Tunguz, Akshat Vyas, and Christina Wagner—for putting up with me knocking on their doors to run ideas by them and pick their brains. I also thank Amber Taylor and Connie Lambermont for their helpful assistance.

Thanks also to others at DePauw who have been helpful along the way as I wrote this book, including Meryl Altman, Kelly Hall, Jeff Kenney, Manu Raghav, Victor DeCarlo, Ken Owen, Brett O'Bannon, Maryann Gallagher, Harry Brown, Jonathan Nichols-Pethick, Valerie Rudolph, Dana Dudle, Tim Good, Dave Berque, Alexander Komives, Matthew Balensuela, Tom Dickinson, Tiffany Hebb, Matthew Demmings, Dave Bohmer, and Jeanette Johnson-Licon. Thanks, as well, to the students with whom I've worked over the years; my work would not be nearly as meaningful without them. Finally, thanks to Kati Lear, who helped me track down studies, fact-check, and communicate my ideas more clearly and who provided a valuable sounding board throughout the process. I'd also like to acknowledge the support I received from DePauw University via the Fisher Fellowship, the J. William and Katherine C. Asher Endowed Research Fund, and the Mellon Foundation. Of course the views expressed in this book are completely my own.

Second, I thank the many colleagues, friends, and family who read drafts of the chapters in this book. They are so many that it's not feasible to name them all here, but this book has benefited immensely from their input; their feedback saved the reader from numerous errors in thinking and writing. Of course, for any that remain, the fault is entirely my own (I assume you knew a statement like this would be coming at some point as it's virtually ubiquitous in the acknowledgments sections of nonfiction books).

Third, I owe a debt of gratitude to others whom I contacted for this book, including John Antonakis, Eyes for Lies, and several others whom I interviewed but whose names, as well as other inconsequential details, I've changed to maintain confidentiality. Quotes that receive general attribution in the book come from these individuals. Those that do not receive attribution are quotes from my experience and represent my best recollection of what people I've observed actually stated.

Fourth, I'm grateful for the community of researchers whose findings provide the foundation for this book, including, but not limited to, Jerome Kagan, John Gottman, Nicholas Rule, Nalini Ambady, Robert Rosenthal, Mary Main, David Buss, Alexander Todorov, David Kenny, and the late John Bowlby and Mary Ainsworth. This book simply would not have been possible without a cadre of researchers' theoretical, conceptual, and empirical contributions. I have to admit that when I first began this project,

I thought it would be a relatively straightforward task to convey all the nuances of the literature given that a book provides more space than most other venues. I quickly disabused myself of this notion once I began to edit my own prose. I did my best to retain nuance when necessary and possible, but there's no doubt that the details of every study did not make it into the book, given its general intended audience.

Fifth, I am grateful to the team at Basic Books, including Jennifer Kelland, Michele Jacob, and Melissa Veronesi. I'm indebted to my editor, T. J. Kelleher, whose work permeates this book. I'd also like to thank Shannon O'Neill, my literary agent, for her unflagging commitment to this project. She, along with the rest of the team at the Sagalyn Literary Agency, has been instrumental in bringing this book to fruition and helping me navigate the publishing terrain as a neophyte. Her sage advice and ideas regarding content and style have been invaluable.

Finally, I'm grateful to my family: to my grandparents who gave me opportunities I would have never had otherwise, to my parents who taught me the importance of hard work, and especially to my wife and son. Margo is an amazing human being whose creativity, love, and character are a constant inspiration, and Isaac is a steady reminder of what insatiable curiosity and unconditional love look like. I'm thankful that the prediction Margo and I made in the year 2000 is coming to pass.

NOTES

INTRODUCTION

ix   **Unfortunately, we must often answer:** In this book, I use the words "we," "us," and "our" to refer to humans in general, to our species collectively. I realize that human diversity is vast and exceptions will often arise within the human population.

ix   **As a result, we base:** Ambady and Skowronski 2008.

ix   **that occur in a snap of the fingers:** For an edited book that reviews some of the literature in *The Tell*, please see Ambady and Skowronski 2008. For a meta-analysis of some of the work described in this book, see Ambady and Rosenthal 1992.

ix   **about the power of prediction:** I use the word "prediction" in this book to mean linking one event to another event, independent of the timing of those events. In this way, variable x may predict y, with y occurring before or after x. An example may prove helpful. Based on the orbit of the moon (variable x), I could predict a full moon (variable y) at some point in the future, or I could predict a full moon at some point in the past. The latter prediction is sometimes referred to as "postdiction" because of its focus on an event in the past. These are relevant distinctions, but for our purpose here, I'll refer to "prediction" in both the future and past sense. You'll read in the book that some studies predict future events, while others predict past events.

ix   **observations of brief samples:** In the book, I draw on studies in which researchers sample behavior and appearance in as little as a moment (e.g., in a photo) or in as long as about forty-five minutes. Some researchers refer to some of these studies—based on the length and nature of the stimuli—as "thin-slicing" or "zero-acquaintance" studies. For definitions of and distinctions between these types of studies, see Ambady, LaPlante, and Johnson 2001; Kenny and West 2008.

ix   **of others' behavior:** In this book, I use words such as "behavior," "cue," and "signal" in the colloquial sense. Researchers have technical definitions for some of these terms (Shariff and Tracy 2011), but I don't wish to bog the reader down with these.

ix   **Anyone familiar with the game:** Elwood 2012.

x   **You'll form some of these impressions:** For an excellent discussion of rapid versus slow thinking, see Kahneman 2011.

x   *Stumbling on Happiness:* Gilbert 2006.

x   *Predictably Irrational:* Ariely 2008.

x   **we get things wrong:** One person I know quipped that these books represent the "dumb shit we do" genre.

xi   **"I have trained myself":** Doyle 1927, 36.

xii   **according to some, on the fringe:** For a recent debate on this issue in the opinion pages of the *Los Angeles Times*, see Berezow 2012; Wilson 2012.

xii   **Freud might have described as:** Bartlett 2010.

xii   **comprised of 170 billion cells:** Azevedo et al. 2009.

CHAPTER 1: PRIMITIVE PREDICTIONS

3   **"Prediction is very difficult, especially":** Bohr, n.d.

3   **On December 23, 2004, twenty-nine-year-old:** This information came from an interview with the soldier whose name I've changed to protect his confidentiality.

4   **"prediction is indispensable to our lives":** Silver 2012, 14.

4   **The famous physicist Niels Bohr:** Bohr, n.d.

4   **Forecasting future events—whether it's an upcoming:** Halpern 2000.

5   *The Future of Everything:* Orrell 2007.

5   **lists some of these methods:** Adapted from Orrell 2007, 49.

5   **Thanks to the early insights:** Orrell 2007.

5   **Predictions derived from quantum:** Barabasi 2010.

6   **a slew of articles and books:** See, for example, Taleb's *Fooled by Randomness*, Gilbert's *Stumbling on Happiness*, Ariely's *Predictably Irrational*, Chabris and Simons's *The Invisible Gorilla*, Van Hecke's *Blind Spots*, Hallinan's *Why We Make Mistakes*, Brafmans and Brafman's *Sway*, and Shore's *Blunder*.

6   **pick up just about any:** Gray 2011; Myers 2013; Baron, Byrne, and Branscombe 2006; Gazzaniga, Heatherton, and Halpern 2011; Sternberg 2006; Goldstein 2008.

7   **many predict that having children:** Gilbert 2006.

7   **If you ask mothers how:** Kahneman et al. 2004.

7   **The trend continues until:** Gilbert 2006; Walker 1977.

7   **We're having kids for:** Gilbert 2006.

7   **The planning fallacy: We are miserable at:** Kahneman 2011.

7   One study showed that: Holt 2011.
7   researchers asked college students: Buehler, Griffin, and Ross 1994.
8   "if everything went as poorly as it possibly could": Buehler, Griffin, and Ross 1994, 369.
8   the Big Dig in Boston: Amendola 2007.
8   installing a new government in Iraq: Herszenhorn 2008.
8   Cramer's predictive skills are merely: Allpert 2009; CXO Advisory Group 2009; CXO Advisory Group 2013.
8   In fact, one recent study: CXO Advisory Group 2013.
8   "A blindfolded chimpanzee throwing": Malkiel 2003, 17.
9   prognosticators are no better: Tetlock 2005. For an exception, read Nate Silver's New York Times blog "FiveThirtyEight." The mathematical algorithm he uses to predict political outcomes is most often spot on.
9   the mind is largely flawed: Obviously, some authors have given a more even-handed treatment of our predictive capacities. See, for example, Myers's Intuition, Gladwell's Blink, Kahneman's Thinking, Fast and Slow, Pinker's How the Mind Works and Gigerenzer's Gut Feelings.
9   mind is a "prediction machine": Clark, in press; Hawkins and Blakeslee 2004; Bubic, von Cramon, and Schubotz 2010; Friston 2010; Kveraga, Ghuman, and Bar 2007; Kurzweil 2012.
9   "Prediction is not just one": Hawkins and Blakeslee 2004, 89.
9   our brains work to identify: Shermer 2011.
9   The origins of our predictive: Ambady and Hallahan 2002; Schaller 2008.
9   being able to detect swiftly: Schaller 2008.
9   assessing the personalities of those: Haselton and Funder 2006.
9   Operating over multiple generations: Schaller 2008.
9   beginning to understand the neural mechanisms: Clark, in press.
9   we are well underway: Rule and Ambady 2008c.
10   remarkable ability to learn: Gopnik 2009; Gopnik, Meltzoff, and Kuhl 1999.
10   infant brains are approximately: Papalia, Feldman, and Martorell 2012.
10   By maturity, our brains: Azevedo et al. 2009.
10   Developmental psychologists sometimes refer: Gopnik 2009.
10   The job of science: Lillienfeld, 2012.
10   "to within about one part in 10^{10}": Barabasi 2010, 66. The specific property to which I'm referring is the "magnetic dipole moment of an electron" (Barabasi 2010, 66).
10   In the behavioral sciences, virtually all relationships: Lilienfeld 2012; Stanovich 2010.
11   just because you know a person: Stanovich 2010.
11   relation between longevity and conscientiousness: Kern and Friedman 2008; Bogg 2004.
11   who these highly conscientious people: Gosling 2008.
11   These same people would never: Stanovich 2010.
11   conscientious people being likelier: Kern and Friedman 2008; Bogg 2004.
11   other variables—like the fact: Bogg 2004.

12   **"brevity is the soul of wit":** Shakespeare 1992, 46.
12   **In his *Principia Mathematica*:** Newton 1729.
12   **"Hypotheses non fingo":** Leahey 1994, 6.
12   **Newton refused to provide:** Leahey 1994.
12   **Thanks to Albert Einstein:** Einstein 1916.

CHAPTER 2: THE GENES IN ALL OF US

13   **"We can work with our givens":** Pipher 2009, 35.
13   **approximately 108 billion times:** Haub 2011.
14   **a group of neurodevelopmental disorders characterized:** American Psychiatric Association 2000.
14   **1 in every 110 children:** Dawson and Burner 2011.
14   **four times higher in boys:** Ingersoll 2011.
14   **Research has shown ASD:** Happé, Ronald, and Plomin 2006.
14   **If one identical twin has autism:** Bailey et al. 1995.
15   **most children don't ultimately get:** Zwaigenbaum et al. 2009.
15   **building the brain over time from the bottom up:** Papalia, Olds, and Feldman 2007.
15   **we know that brain plasticity:** Papalia, Olds, and Feldman 2007.
15   **A growing body of evidence demonstrates:** Dawson and Burner 2011; Ingersoll 2011; Reichow 2012; LeBlanc and Gillis 2012.
15   **"What you ultimately might be":** Dembosky 2010.
16   **catch the condition in its earliest:** Rose 2011. Preventing the onset of mental disease rather than trying to treat it after it occurs represents a new paradigm shift in many ways. A recent article published in *Science* highlighted efforts to try to prevent Alzheimer's disease before it ever begins (Greg Miller 2012).
16   **researchers have begun to identify:** Ingersoll 2011; Zwaigenbaum et al. 2009; Rogers 2009. I'm indebted to the researchers who conduct these studies.
16   **The bad news is that:** Progress is being made on this front, however. Researchers have found differences in brain connectivity as early as six months between kids who go on to develop autism versus those who do not (Wolff et al. 2012).
16   **At first, they relied on:** Rogers 2009.
16   **Finally, in the early 1990s:** Adrien et al. 1991.
16   **But this method also had:** Ingersoll 2011; Rogers 2009.
16   **only 5 in 10,000 children:** Yirmiya and Ozonoff 2007.
16   **teams in the United States, England, Sweden, and Israel:** Yirmiya and Ozonoff 2007.
16   **They identified children with ASD:** Ingersoll 2011; Rogers 2009.
17   **The table on page 18 includes a list:** This table is adapted from Zwaigenbaum et al. 2009, 1385.
17   **People sometimes consider autism a:** Rogers 2009.

17   **not formally possible until:** Zwaigenbaum et al. 2009.

17   **empirically supported behavioral therapies:** For a review of effective interventions, read LeBlanc and Gillis 2012.

17   **However, when it came to:** Of course, parents of children with autism shouldn't feel guilty if they didn't identify autism early. In reality, the onset of autism is quite variable, and the signs are often subtle. Furthermore, even with early intervention, some children may not show signs of improvement.

19   **a combination of the two?:** If there's one thing we know, it's almost always the case that genes and environments interact dynamically.

19–20 **cry less after the first two:** Field 2007.

20   **During that first year, I:** I'm indebted to J. Kagan and others whose work inspired part of this chapter and many of the ideas it contains.

20   **kids who exhibit vigilance:** Chen et al. 2009.

20   **Researchers attribute this behavioral:** Hirshfeld-Becker et al. 2008; Kagan et al. 2007.

20   **Kagan's pioneering research shows:** Kagan et al. 2007; Kagan 2010; Kagan and Snidman 2004.

20   **His and other research:** For a review of some of this work, see Fox et al. 2005.

20   **One of Kagan's most famous studies:** Kagan et al. 2007; Kagan 2010.

20   **Kagan and his colleagues were interested:** Kagan et al. 2007.

20   **"extend their arms and legs":** Kagan, Snidman, and Arcus 1992, 172.

21   **Two in every five:** Kagan et al. 2007.

21   **Kagan invited many of these:** Kagan et al. 2007; Kagan and Snidman 2004; Schwartz et al. 2010.

21   **Like others who study behavioral:** Hirshfeld-Becker et al. 2008; Kagan et al. 2007.

21   *Galen's Prophecy*: Kagan et al. 1994.

21   **Low-reactive infants were significantly:** Kagan et al. 2007.

21   **Kagan describes a subject:** Kagan et al. 1994.

21   **As a toddler and young child:** Kagan et al. 1994.

22   **When experimenters interviewed the fifteen-year-old:** Kagan et al. 2007.

22   **Kagan describes one fifteen-year-old:** Kagan et al. 2007.

22   **"invites the conclusion that his high-reactive temperament":** Kagan et al. 2007, 52. Although most high-reactives will not be diagnosed with a social anxiety disorder (Kagan et al. 2007), children who show high levels of behavioral inhibition early in life are at heightened risk for developing the disorder (Hirshfeld-Becker et al. 2008). The probability of developing an anxiety disorder is even greater when researchers identify kids high in behavioral inhibition who are born to parents diagnosed with an anxiety disorder (Hirshfeld-Becker et al. 2008). Although the data are not as clear, there is some evidence that behaviorally inhibited kids are more likely to develop depression as well (Hirshfeld-Becker et al. 2008). At Kagan's fifteen-year follow-up of his sample, severe depression

was relatively uncommon, but among the nine cases of clinical depression identified, four subjects were high-reactive babies, whereas only one was a low-reactive infant (the others were neither high- nor low-reactives) (Kagan et al. 2007).

22   **Kagan and others have uncovered:** Kagan et al. 2007; Marshall, Reeb, and Fox 2009.

22   **When the infants in Kagan's studies:** Kagan et al. 2007.

22   **electroencephalogram activation, associated:** Buss et al. 2003; Tops et al. 2005; Wittling and Pflüger 1990; Kagan and Fox 2006.

22   **The cardiovascular systems of high- and low-reactives:** Kagan et al. 2007.

23   **Finally, adults who were high-reactive:** Schwartz et al. 2010.

23   **Located within the base of the temporal lobe:** Johansen et al. 2010.

23   **In a landmark study published:** Schwartz et al. 2003.

23   **Were the amygdalae of the adults who had been inhibited:** Schwartz et al. 2003.

23   **"Our findings," remarked one of Kagan's colleagues:** *Science Daily* 2003. Results held even when data from the two participants who had been diagnosed with generalized social phobia—both of whom were inhibited children—were excluded from the statistical analyses (Schwartz et al. 2003). Of course, one doesn't know if adults' amygdalae in this study are differentially reactive as infants or not, given the study design. However, one study shows that differences in amygdala reactivity between inhibited and uninhibited children appear as early as age thirteen (Pérez-Edgar et al. 2007).

23   **Kagan and his colleagues think:** Kagan et al. 2007.

23   **That high-reactives experience this more strongly:** Even the thought of unfamiliar events, according to Kagan, is believed to trigger this biological response, resulting in heightened anxiety (Kagan et al. 2007).

24   **At present, this is a provisional explanation:** Recent research is implicating brain differences in the striatal circuitry, a part of the reward system of the brain (Helfinstein, Fox, and Pine 2011). Clearly, more than one brain system is likely at work to produce highly inhibited children and adults.

24   **biology is not destiny:** Kagan 2010; Kagan and Snidman 2004.

24   **Not all high-reactives remained shy:** Kagan et al. 2007; Kagan and Snidman 2004.

24   **By these ages, kids can control:** Hirshfeld-Becker et al. 2008; Kagan and Snidman 2004.

24   **By age eleven, according to Kagan:** Kagan and Snidman 2004.

24   **Kagan proposes several possibilities:** Kagan 2010; Kagan and Snidman 2004.

25   **"Heredity deals the cards":** Brewer 1990.

26   **Prediction of autism:** Zwaigenbaum et al. 2009.

26   **Prevention of autism:** Ingersoll 2011.

26   **Stability of temperament:** Kagan 2010; Kagan et al. 1994.

CHAPTER 3: STRANGE SITUATIONS:
GROWING UP IN A THIN-SLICED WORLD

27   "What is learned in the cradle": French proverb, n.d.

28   Questions like these have occupied: I'm indebted to the late J. Bowlby and M. Ainsworth, as well as M. Main, A. Sroufe, and others whose work inspired this chapter and many of the ideas it contains.

28   For much of the twentieth century: Cassidy 2008.

28   Theorists from the psychoanalytic camp: Blount and Hertenstein 2006; Bretherton 1992.

28   Learning theorists, such as B. F. Skinner: Blount and Hertenstein 2006; Bretherton 1992.

28   For both camps, provision of food: Cassidy 2008.

28   Nobel Prize–winning biologist Konrad Lorenz: Lorenz 1957.

28   Another set of ingenious studies conducted by Harry Harlow: Harlow 1958; Harlow and Harlow 1966; Harlow and Suomi 1970; Harlow and Zimmermann 1959.

28   Pulling from Lorenz, Harlow, and others: Bowlby 1958, 1969, 1973, 1980.

29   By genetically prewiring into our brains: Cassidy 2008; Blount and Hertenstein 2006.

29   Unlike many other animals that flee: Bowlby 1969. For critiques of attachment theory, as well as how it's indexed, read Lewis 1997; Kagan 1998; Lamb 2005; Lewis 2005.

29   While formulating his theory, Bowlby: Ainsworth and Marvin 1995.

29   In her most well-known: Ainsworth et al. 1978.

29   She noted how infants emitted: Ainsworth et al. 1978; Ainsworth and Bowlby 1991.

29   At the end of the year: Ainsworth et al. 1978; Ainsworth and Bowlby 1991.

29   The procedure was meant: Blount and Hertenstein 2006.

29   akin to going to the doctor's: Weinfield et al. 2008.

30   Ainsworth identified three primary: Ainsworth et al. 1978.

30   Mary Main and her colleagues: Main and Morgan 1996; Main and Solomon 1986; Main and Solomon 1990. Although there is some controversy in the field, researchers have observed all the categories of attachment in all cultures studied. Culture does, however, influence the specific proportion of children in each, as one might expect (van IJzendoorn and Sagi-Schwartz 2008).

30   The first category I describe: Most research on attachment has studied infants and mothers for many reasons. Nonetheless, studies that do examine fathers draw similar conclusions (Haidt 2006).

30   I remember one child: The examples I describe in this section come from strange situation films I've seen in various classes I've taken, at research conferences, and in pedagogical media. I mention no identifying characteristics to maintain confidentiality.

30   **Touch is the ultimate:** Hertenstein 2002; Main 1990.

30   **Harlow taught us with his monkeys:** Harlow 1958; Harlow and Harlow 1966; Harlow and Suomi 1970; Harlow and Zimmermann 1959.

30   **After his mother had soothed him:** Ainsworth and Bowlby 1991; Weinfield et al. 2008.

31   **The majority of US children:** When we classify a child using the strange situation, we don't know if he truly belongs in the designated category. We only know that he behaved in a way consistent with that category. Thus, when I indicate in this chapter that researchers have "deemed" a child to have a given attachment status, I'm referring only to his behavior in the strange situation; I'm not making a definitive statement about the true attachment style of the child.

31   **he showed signs of missing:** van IJzendoorn and Sagi-Schwartz 2008.

31   **These parents respond promptly:** Ainsworth et al. 1978; Belsky and Fearon 2008; Simpson and Belsky 2008.

31   **generally available and warm:** Although most of the studies conducted linking maternal behavior to attachment security are correlational, some experimental studies show that the caregiver's behavior actually causes differences in attachment (Bakermans-Kranenburg, van IJzendoorn, and Juffer 2005; van den Boom 1990).

31   **These children often have attachment figures:** Ainsworth et al. 1978; Hertenstein 2002; Belsky and Fearon 2008; Simpson and Belsky 2008.

31   **They show distress both:** Ainsworth et al. 1978; Simpson and Belsky 2008.

32   **Strikingly bizarre behaviors like these:** van IJzendoorn, Schuengel, and Bakermans-Kranenburg 1999.

32   **Researchers deem these children "disorganized-disoriented":** Infants in this category are also given a secondary classification consisting of one of the three others (Main and Solomon 1990).

32   **Infants who behave oddly:** Belsky and Fearon 2008; Lyons-Ruth and Jacobvitz 2008; Main and Hesse 1990.

32   **On identifying their attachment status:** van IJzendoorn, Schuengel, and Bakermans-Kranenburg 1999.

32   **In one study, for example:** Carlson et al. 1989.

32   **investigators categorized 82 percent of maltreated infants:** It should also be noted that other risk factors—low income, single motherhood, low education, and substance abuse—also increase the risk of classification as disorganized-disoriented (Cyr et al. 2010).

32   **about three of every four:** Dobrova-Krol et al. 2010; St. Petersburg—USA Orphanage Research Team 2008; Zeanah et al. 2005.

32   **The figure above illustrates:** Adapted from van IJzendoorn and Bakermans-Kranenburg 2009, 3.

33   **Several studies suggest the outcome:** Lyons-Ruth and Jacobvitz 2008; Lyons-Ruth, Bronfman, and Parsons 1999.

33   **Researchers theorize that unlike infants:** Lyons-Ruth and Jacobvitz 2008; Main and Hesse 1990; Hesse and Main 2006.

33   **In contrast, theorists think there is a breakdown:** Main and Hesse 1990; Hesse and Main 2006.

33   **For these kids, their caregivers:** Main and Hesse 1990.

33   **The paradox causes them:** Main, Hesse, and Kaplan 2005.

33   **the strange situation represents:** Of course, a myriad of other factors beyond one's attachment status influence who one becomes.

34   **secure attachment signifies a host:** Thompson 2008.

34   **Children deemed secure are significantly:** Weinfield et al. 2008; Sroufe 2005; Sroufe et al. 2005.

34   **Children deemed insecure have a history:** Weinfield et al. 2008.

34   **The emotional lives of children:** Weinfield et al. 2008.

34   **Kids who behave angrily:** Weinfield et al. 2008.

34   **more likely to be securely attached:** Weinfield et al. 2008.

34   **studies examining emotions and peer interaction:** Troy and Sroufe 1987.

35   **"bugger nose," "bugger face," and "hey poop":** Troy and Sroufe 1987, 168.

35   **Children deemed secure are:** Weinfield et al. 2008.

35   **Throughout childhood and into adulthood:** Weinfield et al. 2008; Sroufe 2005; Englund et al. 2000.

35   **A team led by Jay Belsky:** Belsky, Houts, and Fearon 2010.

35   **"An evolutionary biology perspective says":** Rochman 2010.

36   **Girls who go through puberty:** Copeland et al. 2010; Negriff, Susman, and Trickett 2011.

36   **Early-maturing girls are also at risk:** Copeland et al. 2010.

36   **"predicts and perhaps programs the timing":** Belsky, Houts, and Fearon 2010, 1198. I appreciate this quote because it emphasizes that while attachment history predicts the outcome, it doesn't necessarily cause it. These studies, like most of the others I've discussed, are correlational, so one must be very careful not to assume that attachment causes these outcomes.

36   **There are a number of potential pathways:** Cicchetti and Rogosch 1996.

36   **Moreover, few, if any, psychiatric disorders:** Greenberg, Speltz, and DeKlyen 1993.

36   **Studies show that having a secure:** Weinfield et al. 2008; Sroufe 2005.

37   **Individuals classified as avoidant or ambivalent-resistant:** Sroufe 2005; DeKlyen and Greenberg 2008.

37   **Infants deemed ambivalent-resistant:** Sroufe 2005; Warren et al. 1997.

37   **infants classified as avoidant are:** Pasco Fearon and Belsky 2011; Renken et al. 1989.

37   **The majority of these individuals don't:** Weinfield et al. 2008; Sroufe 2005.

37   **"strong predictor of later disturbance":** Sroufe 2005, 360.

37   **"is far stronger than for":** Sroufe 2005, 360.

37   **Infants deemed disorganized-disoriented:** Weinfield et al. 2008.

37   **link is between the disorganized-disoriented:** Harari, Bakermans-Kranenburg, and van IJzendoorn 2007.

37   **Dissociation, which falls into three:** Ogawa et al. 1997.

37   **Dissociative symptoms run the continuum:** Ray 2000.

37   **a history of infant disorganized:** Ogawa et al. 1997; Lyons-Ruth et al. 2006; Carlson 1998.

38   **Importantly, one's infant attachment status:** Weinfield et al. 2008; Ogawa et al. 1997.

38   **the best early predictor we have:** Carlson 1998; Hesse 2008.

38   **"may be artificial, but so is":** Talbot 1998, 46.

38   **Thankfully, researchers have developed:** Berlin, Zeanah, and Lieberman 2008.

38   **In one study, the researcher:** van den Boom 1994.

39   **Imagine that a researcher has:** The description of the Adult Attachment Interview (AAI) and its questions are abbreviated from Hesse 2008. The direct quotes and the interpretation of those quotes come from this source as well. Hesse wrote the quotes to be typical of subjects' responses; they are not direct quotes.

39   **In the mid-1980s, Mary Main and her colleagues:** Main, Kaplan, and Cassidy 1985.

39   **Researchers worldwide have given:** Bakermans-Kranenburg and van IJzendoorn 2009.

39   **If someone administered the AAI:** Hesse 2008; van IJzendoorn 1995.

39   **Based on how people describe:** Hesse 2008.

39   **four primary adult attachment classifications:** A "cannot classify" category is also available to researchers who have difficulty placing a particular interview into one of the four primary classifications (Hesse 2008).

40   **These adults are able to reflect:** Hesse 2008.

40   **Troublesome. Well, she was troublesome:** Hesse 2008, 560.

40   **This interviewee provided a well-reasoned:** Hesse 2008.

40   **These adults tend to describe:** Hesse 2008.

41   **Sobbed through her aunt's funeral:** Hesse 2008, 560.

41   **This person's response brusquely dismissed:** Hesse 2008.

41   **These adults focus intensely:** Hesse 2008.

41   **"Great mother. Well, not really":** Hesse 2008, 568.

41   **"That was an understatement":** Hesse 2008, 560.

41   **Here, the interviewer requested:** Hesse 2008.

42   **Adults classified as "unresolved/disorganized":** Hesse 2008.

42   **"It was almost better":** Hesse 2008, 570.

42   **"She died because I forgot":** Hesse 2009.

42   **"She was young, she was":** Hesse and Main 2000, 1113.

42   **Overall, people who are unable:** AAI transcripts categorized as unresolved/disorganized also receive a secondary classification of one of the other three categories (Hesse 2008).

42   **Main and her colleagues interviewed men:** Main, Kaplan, and Cassidy 1985.

42   **In contrast, adults not deemed:** Main, Hesse, and Kaplan 2005; Main, Kaplan, and Cassidy 1985.

42   Others drawing upon samples in other cultures: Hesse 2008. As one leading researcher put it, the "predictive validity of the AAI is a replicated fact" (van IJzendoorn 1995, 387).

43   Researchers have also given the AAI: Benoit and Parker 1994; Fonagy, Steele, and Steele 1991; Steele, Steele, and Fonagy 1996.

43   Among pregnant mothers deemed secure-autonomous: Benoit and Parker 1994.

43   The explanation largely resides: Hesse 2008.

43   Adults judged secure-autonomous: Hesse 2008; van IJzendoorn 1995.

43   Parents deemed unresolved/disorganized: Hesse 2008; Abrams, Rifkin, and Hesse 2006; Ballen et al. 2010.

44   At least four studies show: Hesse 2008.

44   Main and her colleagues reported: Main, Hesse, and Kaplan 2005.

44   Of course circumstances derail some: Main, Hesse, and Kaplan 2005.

44   However, barring major life trauma: Main, Hesse, and Kaplan 2005; Hesse 2008; Fraley 2002; Van Ryzin, Carlson, and Sroufe 2011.

44   Instead, it's *how* you mentally understand: Main, Hesse, and Kaplan 2005.

44   "In theory, then," writes Mary Main: Main, Hesse, and Kaplan 2005, 268.

45   Early puberty: Belsky, Houts, and Fearon 2010.

45   Prediction of psychopathology: Ogawa et al. 1997; Lyons-Ruth et al. 2006; Carlson 1998.

45   Prediction of attachment: Benoit and Parker 1994; Fonagy, Steele, and Steele 1991; Steele, Steele, and Fonagy 1996.

CHAPTER 4: WHO ARE YOU ANYWAY?

49   "It is only shallow people": Wilde 1988.

50   we size people up based: Ambady and Skowronski 2008; Todorov, Said, and Verosky 2011.

50   Virtually all of us feel: I'm indebted to a number of researchers for inspiring this chapter and the ideas it contains, including, but not limited to, L. Zebrowitz, A. Todorov, P. Borkenau, D. Kenny, A. Little, D. Perrett, J. Carré, M. Stirrat, and N. Ambady.

50   The study of how physical: Valla, Ceci, and Williams 2011; Zebrowitz 1997.

50   The scientific investigation of physiognomy: Valla, Ceci, and Williams 2011.

50   "we shall then be able to": Aristotle, n.d.

50   Since then, physiognomy has waxed: Zebrowitz 1997; Highfield 2009; Penton-Voak et al. 2006.

50   We make snap judgments: Gladwell 2005; Todorov, Pakrashi, and Oosterhof 2009.

50   showing remarkable consensus in: Todorov, Said, and Verosky 2011; Penton-Voak et al. 2006; Hollingworth 1922; Zebrowitz and Montepare 2008.

50   **baby-faced people than mature-looking individuals:** Zebrowitz and McDonald 1991.

51   **juries are more likely to impose the death penalty:** Eberhardt et al. 2006.

51   **most famous visitor, Charles Darwin:** Darwin 1958; Darwin 1950.

51   **The English naturalist was there:** Darwin 1958, 76.

51   **But history very nearly took:** For those who know the history of the events surrounding Darwin's announcement of evolution via natural selection, I could have very easily been following in the footsteps of one of Darwin's contemporaries, Alfred Wallace, who devised his own theory of natural selection on the Maluku islands off the coast of Indonesia (Slotten 2004).

51   **The captain of the HMS Beagle:** Zebrowitz 1997.

51   **"an exact relationship exists between":** Zebrowitz 1997, 41.

51   **The captain of the Beagle:** Zebrowitz 1997; Highfield 2009; Todorov et al. 2005.

51   **"He was an ardent disciple":** Darwin 1958, 72.

51   **We have come a long:** Albright, Kenny, and Malloy 1988; Borkenau and Liebler 1992; Borkenau and Liebler 1993; Kenny et al. 1992; Levesque and Kenny 1993; Norman and Goldberg 1966.

51   **Whether we're observing someone:** Piff et al. 2012.

51   **A seminal study done:** Norman and Goldberg 1966.

52   **Investigators in Germany videotaped subjects:** Borkenau and Liebler 1992.

52   **Subjects generally identify the latter:** Kenny and West 2008; Albright, Kenny, and Malloy 1988; Borkenau and Liebler 1992; Borkenau and Liebler 1993; Levesque and Kenny 1993; Beer and Watson 2008; Gray 2008.

52   **In the work sphere:** Hill 2012.

52   **In one study at the University of Texas:** Naumann et al. 2009.

53   **The "+" signs indicate:** Based on data from Naumann et al. 2009, Table 1. To derive this table, I rounded the correlation coefficients to the nearest tenth's place. A correlation of 0.2 received "++," a correlation of 0.3 received "+++," and a correlation of 0.4 received "++++." All correlation coefficients were positive and statistically significant.

53   **So, what cues did people:** Gosling 2008.

53   **On page 54, I've indicated the cues:** The researchers, who knew nothing about the subjects' personalities, recorded these cues. I've included only some of the personality traits studied.

54   **Bold italicized cues were both valid:** Data are from Naumann et al. 2009, Tables 3 and 4. I'm indebted to Sam Gosling for giving me the idea to present data in this format as he did in his book, *Snoop*.

55   **Though there is nothing wrong:** Naumann et al. 2009.

55   **people whose appearances vary more:** Naumann et al. 2009.

55   **This study has another implication:** Naumann et al. 2009.

55   **If you wish to come across:** Naumann et al. 2009.

55   **Even when we examine only:** Penton-Voak et al. 2006; Borkenau et al. 2009; Little and Perrett 2007.

55   **We need view a photograph for only:** Borkenau et al. 2009.

55 Curiously, we're also adept: Kramer, King, and Ward 2011.

55 we should never "judge a": Zebrowitz and Montepare 2008; Verplaetse, Vanneste, and Braeckman 2007.

55 a kernel of truth: Penton-Voak et al. 2006; Naumann et al. 2009; Naylor 2007.

55 We sometimes assess people's: Murphy, Hall, and Colvin 2003.

56 One team videotaped people: Borkenau et al. 2004.

56 From just three minutes: Two validated tests measured targets' intelligence.

56 Researchers at Northeastern University videotaped: Murphy, Hall, and Colvin 2003.

56 The researchers then obtained: The researchers employed one validated measure of IQ. I'm well aware that some do not believe these indices are indicative of intellectual ability per se. In the field of psychology, there is heated debate about what is meant, exactly, by the word "intelligence." Here, I use the term like the authors did in the study.

57 eye gaze: Murphy, Hall, and Colvin 2003.

57 vocal qualities: Borkenau and Liebler 1995.

57 level of attractiveness: Zebrowitz and Montepare 2008; Zebrowitz et al. 2002; Zebrowitz and Rhodes 2004.

57 People who look others: Murphy, Hall, and Colvin 2003.

57 Some evidence indicates that those: Borkenau and Liebler 1995.

57 Finally, the perceived attractiveness of individuals: Zebrowitz and Montepare 2008; Zebrowitz et al. 2002; Zebrowitz and Rhodes 2004.

57 "faces in the lower half": Zebrowitz and Montepare 2008, 179.

57 simply by "appearing smart": Murphy 2007, 325.

57 For about one hundred days: Banks 2006.

58 "the Oskar Schindler of Africa": Banks 2006.

58 "There was no other solution": Owen 2005.

59 The question is whether we: Fetchenhauer, Groothuis, and Pradel 2010.

59 Although the data are still: Verplaetse, Vanneste, and Braeckman 2007; Brosig 2002; Frank, Gilovich, and Regan 1993; Pradel, Euler, and Fetchenhauer 2009.

59 One group of researchers in Germany: Fetchenhauer, Groothuis, and Pradel 2010.

59 A remarkable study took these: Kogan et al. 2011.

59 This neuropeptide, as well as: Kosfeld et al. 2005; Barraza et al. 2011; Rodrigues et al. 2009; Tost et al. 2010.

60 "people can't see genes," said Kogan: Science Daily 2011.

60 As the study authors acknowledge: Kogan et al. 2011.

60 "I had to listen to my": Owen 2005.

60 The next time you have: The ability to identify the prosocial among us has benefits from an evolutionary perspective (Fetchenhauer, Groothuis, and Pradel 2010). The capacity to recognize prosocial individuals, for example, helps us choose mates (Miller 2000), as it may signal how good a parent or relationship partner another might be (Fetchenhauer, Groothuis, and

Pradel 2010). Furthermore, it can also help us choose whom to work with on projects and obstacles that we encounter (Fetchenhauer, Groothuis, and Pradel 2010; Frank 1988, 2008). It seems evolution has shaped our ability to perceive who is dedicated to him- or herself versus others.

60   **"Get the fuck out of here":** This quote comes from my friend's recollection of the event.

61   **These faces differ in their:** These illustrative faces come from Carré, McCormick, and Mondloch 2009, 1195.

61   **Justin Carré and his colleagues:** Carré, McCormick, and Mondloch 2009, 1195.

61   **Prior to asking this question:** Carré and McCormick 2008.

61   **Moreover, the judges could accurately:** Carré, McCormick, and Mondloch 2009. Although, see Özener 2012.

61   **Interestingly, these facial ratios have:** Carré and McCormick 2008.

61   **Specifically, the judges' assessments:** Carré, McCormick, and Mondloch 2009; Carré et al. 2010.

61   **ratio between the men's:** The width of the face is measured from the right and left zygion, and the height is measured from the lip to the brow (Carré and McCormick 2008).

61   **a measure independent of body size:** Weston, Friday, and Liò 2007; Haselhuhn and Wong 2011; Verdonck et al. 1999; Stirrat, Stulp, and Pollet 2012.

62   **Carré and his team manipulated:** Carré et al. 2010.

62   **Lying and cheating:** Haselhuhn and Wong 2011.

62   **"Our findings suggest that some":** Connor 2011.

62   **Exploitation of others:** Stirrat and Perrett 2010.

63   **Death of slim-faced males:** Stirrat, Stulp, and Pollet 2012.

63   **A slew of other variables:** Todorov et al. 2008.

63   **Nonetheless, these studies demonstrate:** Carré, McCormick, and Mondloch 2009.

63   **It's unclear if our evolutionary:** Short et al. 2012.

64   **Research shows that this:** Zebrowitz and Montepare 2008.

64   **According to Leslie Zebrowitz:** Zebrowitz and Montepare 2008.

64   **"more naive, submissive, physically":** Zebrowitz and Montepare 2008, 181.

64   **Some studies confirm these stereotypes:** Berry 1991; Berry and Brownlow 1989; Berry and Landry 1997.

64   **others do not:** Zebrowitz et al. 1998.

64   **According to the study on which:** Zebrowitz, Tenenbaum, and Goldstein 1991.

65   **Also in this study, men were preferred over:** Zebrowitz 1997.

65   **Other work shows that women:** Zebrowitz 1997; Collins and Zebrowitz 1995.

65   **There's even evidence that baby-faced:** Mueller and Mazur 1996.

65   **according to one study:** Zebrowitz, Tenenbaum, and Goldstein 1991.

65   **"The effect of the defendants'":** Zebrowitz 1997, 113.

66   **Predicting who is going:** Americans are very good at putting people in prison; in fact, we're the best at it in the world (I hope you sense my sarcasm). Over 2.2 million people reside in US prisons, which represents about 25 percent of the entire world's prison population and amounts to about one in every one hundred US adults (PEW 2012). This is a staggeringly high rate compared to all other countries in the world (Liptak 2008).

66   **Researchers at the University of Colorado:** Blair, Judd, and Chapleau 2004.

66   **Florida has taken explicit:** Blair, Judd, and Chapleau 2004.

66   **"the degree to which each":** Blair, Judd, and Chapleau 2004, 676.

66   **these features as "Afrocentric features":** According to the authors, "Afrocentric features are those physical features that are perceived as typical of African Americans (e.g., dark skin, wide nose, full lips)" (Blair, Judd, and Chapleau 2004, 674).

66   **regardless of race, the perceived:** It's important to note that in this and the subsequent study I discuss, researchers measured only the perceptions of Afrocentric facial features, not actual differences in facial structure.

66   **Despite the fact that the judges:** Blair, Judd, and Chapleau 2004.

66   **Other researchers examined perceived Afrocentric:** Eberhardt et al. 2006.

66   **Some think that when:** Blair, Judd, and Chapleau 2004.

67   **This faulty linkage of traits to facial:** The origins of this linkage are unclear given the empirical evidence.

67   **The problem is that people:** Blair, Judd, and Chapleau 2004.

67   **Prediction of intelligence:** Murphy, Hall, and Colvin 2003.

67   **Prediction of genes:** Kogan et al. 2011.

67   **Linkage of severity of prison sentences:** Blair, Judd, and Chapleau 2004.

CHAPTER 5: THE TARGETS OF OUR ATTRACTION

69   **"I must be giving off":** *Ellen* 1998.

69   **I learned later from someone:** Frankly, whether he was gay or not made no difference to me then; nor does it make any difference to me now.

70   **Although one's age, gender:** Rule et al. 2008. Obviously, we do not always infer everyone's age, gender, and ethnicity accurately.

70   **"invisible in plain sight":** This quote comes from a person I interviewed.

70   **People sometimes refer to the ability to infer if a person is gay:** LeVay 2011; Rieger et al. 2010. In this chapter, I refer to as "gay" (in the case of men and women), "lesbian" (in the case of women), and "same-sex preference" those who are exclusively or nearly exclusively attracted to their own sex. I refer to as "straight" those who are exclusively or nearly exclusively attracted to the opposite sex. I refer as "bisexual" those who are exclusively or nearly exclusively attracted to both sexes. These definitions map roughly onto some others in the field (e.g., LeVay 2011).

70   **If there is, in fact:** LeVay 2011. For that matter, we could refer to virtually any accurate perception of a trait as *xdar* (e.g., relationshipdar, personalitydar, agedar, ethnicdar, brunettedar, blondar—you get my point).

70   **We must acknowledge that:** I realize that the very topic of this chapter—perceiving sexual orientation—rubs some peoples' sensibilities the wrong way; in many ways, it challenges my sensibilities as well. Nonetheless, I think that the topic is a legitimate one to consider, and it represents a lively field of inquiry in my discipline. I have made a concerted effort to try to make this chapter as inclusive and respectful as I know how. I'll leave it up to the reader as to whether he or she buys the science on which this chapter rests.

70   **Some think gaydar is an:** Woolery 2007.

70   **People who think they:** Reuter 2002.

70   **As you'll see, however:** I'm indebted to N. Rule and N. Ambady and others whose work inspired this chapter and many of the ideas it contains.

70   **science has largely demystified gaydar:** Tabak and Zayas 2012b.

71   **Noticing potential mates for potential:** Miller 2000.

71   **"Adults with normal perceptual abilities":** Tabak and Zayas 2012b.

71   **In the McCarthy era:** Freeman et al. 2010; Loughery 1998.

71   **"With the Soviets on the":** Loughery 1998, 204.

71   **"purge of the perverts":** Loughery 1998, 208.

71   **Whereas US policy during McCarthyism:** Ambady, Hallahan, and Conner 1999.

72   **One of the most infamous:** Bumiller 2011.

72   **"that sexual orientation is evident":** Ambady, Hallahan, and Conner 1999, 538.

72   **"in the armed forces would":** United States Government, 10 U. S. C. § 654.

72   **And a recent study actually:** Palm Center 2012.

72   **And that fear was legitimate:** Bender 2009.

72   **"I constantly was always thinking":** Considine 2011.

72   **The repeal of Don't Ask, Don't Tell:** Considine 2011.

72   **To my knowledge no professional:** Jason Collins, a professional basketball player, recently came out as gay publicly. He was the first to do so in his sport. See Medina 2013.

73   **These initial perceptions frame:** Ambady, Bernieri, and Richeson 2000; Greenwald and Banaji 1995.

73   **humans do not perceive and:** Ambady, Bernieri, and Richeson 2000; Greenwald and Banaji 1995.

73   **Gay people are the US minority:** Potok 2010.

73   **And the trend is growing:** Romney 2011.

73   **Researchers at the University of Toronto:** Remedios et al. 2011.

73   **"To the average Canadian":** Remedios et al. 2011, 1313.

73   **Straight white men were significantly:** Remedios et al. 2011. Here, I'm adopting the terms "black" and "white" as the researchers of the study used them.

73   **Remember that the researchers did:** Remedios et al. 2011.

74   **unconscious perceptions of sexual orientation:** Remedios et al. 2011.

74   **Although the University of Toronto:** Remedios et al. 2011.

74   **Estimates vary, but about 3 percent:** Chandra, Mosher, and Copen 2011; Herbenick et al. 2010.

74   **Approximately 85 to 90 percent of:** LeVay and Baldwin 2012.

74   **"an essential survival strategy":** This quote comes from a person I interviewed.

74   **"Women *had* to develop gaydar":** Carroll 2009, e10.

74   **Can we accurately infer sexual:** By "accurate" I mean significantly above chance.

74   **And what tells lead to:** These are fundamental questions relating to how members of our species perceive each other; in my humble opinion they are also tractable questions worth pursuing using the scientific method. As mentioned, I fully acknowledge that no one study is perfect, but taken as a whole, they have taught us a lot about how the mind distinguishes the sexual orientation of others.

74   **Several researchers have examined:** LeVay 2011; Rieger et al. 2010; Ambady, Hallahan, and Conner 1999.

74   **In one study, they separately:** Rieger et al. 2010.

74   **interviews with each subject :** The authors wrote, "We videotaped targets for 20 min during a casual interview about their lifestyle" (Rieger et al. 2010, 129). They did not mention the nature of the questions asked in this study to my knowledge.

75   **Subjects accurately perceived the:** Rieger et al. 2010.

75   **This study, among others:** Ambady, Hallahan, and Conner 1999.

75   **"Raters tended to be very":** Rieger et al. 2010, 129.

75   **"I've never been wrong!":** This quote comes from a person I interviewed.

75   **After all, they may be:** LeVay 2011; Rieger et al. 2010.

75   **"We have learned antennae":** These quotes come from a person I interviewed.

75   **It turns out that the data:** LeVay 2011; Rieger et al. 2010.

75   **some studies find that:** Rule et al. 2007.

75   **others find no difference:** Smyth, Jacobs, and Rogers 2003.

75   **If gay people can detect:** Rieger et al. 2010.

76   **Is it possible to do so successfully?:** Johnson et al. 2007.

76   **Since the face often reveals:** Rule et al. 2008; Freeman et al. 2010; Rule and Ambady 2008a; Rule, Ambady, and Hallett 2009.

76   **To find out, male and:** Rule et al. 2008.

76   **First, subjects accurately identified the:** Subsequent research has shown that we can even infer sexual orientation accurately when faces are shown to us upside down (Tabak and Zayas 2012a).

76   **Finally, multiple features of the face:** Rule et al. 2008.

76   **Interestingly, judgments based on hairstyle:** Rule et al. 2008.

77   **Such studies suggest that at least:** Rule et al. 2008; Rule, Ambady, and Hallett 2009.

77   **Other work indicates that body:** Johnson et al. 2007.

77   **Policies like Don't Ask, Don't Tell:** Tabak and Zayas 2012a.

77   **people identified as gay, both:** LeVay 2011; Rieger et al. 2010; Freeman et al. 2010; Johnson et al. 2007.

77   **others sometimes judge as gay:** LeVay 2011.

77   **On average—and "average" is:** Although there are differences between men and women, especially physical differences, most studies show that psychologically and behaviorally, men and women show much more overlap than difference (Hyde 2005).

77   **women's bodies are shaped differently:** Johnson and Tassinary 2005.

77   **women's voices and vocal patterns:** Smyth, Jacobs, and Rogers 2003; Pierrehumbert et al. 2004.

77   **In relation to men's faces:** Freeman et al. 2010; LeVay and Baldwin 2012.

77   **I'll call these empirical generalizations:** I reject the notion that pointing out average differences between men and women implies that one sex or gender is superior to the other. These differences can be observed in the population of humans and, if anything, should be valued and appreciated. Nonetheless, from a statistical perspective, the average values for some physical traits differ between men and women. Moreover, I fully acknowledge that sex and gender are not always dichotomously arranged. There are clearly spectrums when it comes to sex, gender, and sexuality.

77   **Researchers think the degree to which:** Rieger et al. 2010.

78   **The term "sex atypical":** In keeping with much of the literature, I've opted to use the term "sex atypical" (e.g., Rieger et al. 2010).

78   **Men on average do not:** Researchers sometimes refer to this as "gender-inversion" (Freeman et al. 2010), "sex atypical" (Rieger et al. 2010), or "gender atypical" (Johnson and Ghavami 2011).

78   **Gay men have faces that:** Freeman et al. 2010.

78   **The more sex atypical someone's:** Freeman et al. 2010. Recent evidence shows that when evaluating sexual orientation people who are politically liberal are less likely to rely on features that are gender atypical in certain contexts compared to individuals who are politically conservative (Stern et al. 2012).

78   **Sex-atypical body shape:** LeVay 2011; Rieger et al. 2010; Johnson et al. 2007; Smyth, Jacobs, and Rogers 2003.

78   **Body type is diagnostic:** Johnson et al. 2007.

78   **Self-identified "butch" women:** Singh et al. 1999.

78   **Research has also linked walking:** Johnson et al. 2007.

78   **This effect is most powerfully:** Johnson et al. 2007.

78   **Of course, not all people:** LeVay 2011.

78   **Although the voice is diagnostic:** LeVay 2011; Rieger et al. 2010; Smyth, Jacobs, and Rogers 2003; Pierrehumbert et al. 2004.

78   **"mostly in the direction of":** LeVay 2011, 240–241.

78   **"Many gay men have 'straight-sounding'":** LeVay 2011, 241.

79   **Hudson, it was later discovered:** *New York Times* 1989; Langley 2001.

79   **Therefore, even though having sex-atypical:** Freeman et al. 2010.

79   This teaches us that while: Rule et al. 2008; Rieger et al. 2010; Ambady, Hallahan, and Conner 1999; Johnson et al. 2007; Rule and Ambady 2008a; Rule, Ambady, and Hallett 2009; Rule, Ishii, et al. 2011.

79   *we are undoubtedly wrong sometimes*: Freeman et al. 2010.

79   One involves examining the origins: LeVay 2011.

79   Some researchers hold that the: Johnson et al. 2007.

79   The fact that a man swings: LeVay 2011.

79   From this perspective, the findings: LeVay 2011; Johnson et al. 2007.

79   Others, however, think such cues: Rieger et al. 2010.

79   I refer the reader to a provocative book: LeVay 2011.

79   studies conducted at the University of Toronto: Rule, Rosen, et al. 2011.

80   The figure below depicts the general pattern: Adapted from Rule, Rosen, et al. 2011, 3.

80   Astonishingly, the closer women were: Rule, Rosen, et al. 2011

80   The subjects could accurately distinguish: Rule, Rosen, et al. 2011.

81   This hypothesis gained further: Rule, Rosen, et al. 2011.

81   After seeing men's and women's faces: Rule and Ambady 2008a; Rule, Ambady, and Hallett 2009.

81   our perceptual systems are finely: Rule and Ambady 2008a; Rule, Ambady, and Hallett 2009.

81   The ability to detect sexual: Rule, Ishii, et al. 2011; Valentova et al. 2011.

81   In one study, men and women: Rule, Ishii, et al. 2011.

81   People from Japan—where homosexuality: Rule, Ishii, et al. 2011.

81   along with other data: Valentova et al. 2011.

81   It is important to note: Rieger et al. 2010; Ambady, Hallahan, and Conner 1999; Rule, Ambady, and Hallett 2009; Rule, Ishii, et al. 2011; Valentova et al. 2011; Jordan-Young 2010.

82   Few examine people who are bisexual: For an exception, see Ding and Rule 2012.

82   "I must be giving off one": *Ellen* 1998.

82   Facial structure: Rule et al. 2008.

82   Ovulation and detection of sexual orientation: Rule, Rosen, et al. 2011.

82   Blink-of-the-eye prediction of sexual orientation: Rule and Ambady, 2008a; Rule, Ambady, and Hallett, 2009.

CHAPTER 6: FROM DATING TO MATING

85   "Who ever loved that loved": Shakespeare 1922.

85   The answers to these questions: I'm indebted to several researchers who inspired this chapter and the ideas it contains, including, but not limited to, D. Kenrick, D. Keltner, M. Kraus, R. Thornhill, J. Gottman, and K. Grammer. I'm particularly indebted to Buss (2011) and Cartwright (2008), who have reviewed much of this literature. Some of what follows comes from these reviews.

85   **our brains come preprogrammed:** Buss 2011; Cartwright 2008. This chapter focuses on heterosexual preferences, but this emphasis is not intended to discount the importance, reality, and validity of other types relationships. For a review of the literature pertaining to gay men's and women's preferences, see Kenrick 2011.

85   **evolutionary theory suggests that:** Dawkins 1976.

85   **we are dating in a:** Davis 2009.

85   **with Stone Age minds:** I don't want to overstate the case that evolution in any way determines who we are. One need only look at individuals who choose to remain celibate to see that evolution is in no way deterministic; natural individual differences, choices, and cultures all shape our preferences and goals as well.

86   **According to evolutionary theory:** Cartwright 2008; Buss 2003.

86   **costly to women in terms:** In this book, I use the words "men" and "women" colloquially to refer to the genders/sexes. Moreover, I realize that there will always be diversity and exceptions within each gender/sex, but when I use these words, I'm referring to generalizations and averages.

86   **These selection pressures:** Buss 2011; Cartwright 2008; Buss 2003.

86   **In a now famous study:** Buss 1994, 2011.

86   **In a different study, researchers:** Pawlowski and Koziel 2002.

86   **One study indicates that:** Judge 2004.

86   **In short, women carry the:** Buss 2003, 2011.

86   **Women prefer men who:** Buss 2011.

87   **As *New York Times* columnist:** Brooks 2011.

87   **Women desire stick-around dads:** Myers 2013.

87   **Just because we have:** Buss 2003.

87   **does not mean they are "good":** It's important to steer clear of the naturalistic fallacy, which holds as good or right that which occurs in nature (Kanazawa 2012). Scientists and consumers of science alike must take care not to think that we should necessarily design policies or construct our values based on what we find in nature. Likewise, it's important that we avoid the moralistic fallacy, which holds that the world actually is as we think it should be (Kanazawa 2012). That is, we shouldn't disbelieve scientific claims based solely on the fact that the findings do not necessarily accord with how we wish reality to be. Some of the findings in this book and others in science run against my personal beliefs, but to the best of my ability, I try to separate personal values from scientific observations. Of course, 100 percent objectivity is virtually impossible to attain, but science is at its best when personal beliefs do not enter into the equation.

87   **Are women able to predict:** Of course, men may also be interested in examining other men for these qualities.

87   **first impressions count:** Ambady and Skowronski 2008.

87   **If you're like most people:** Grammer and Thornhill 1994.

87   **This tendency holds true across races:** Some factors influence preference for symmetry. For example, research has shown the menstrual cycle

to influence the degree of preference for men's faces (Little, Jones, et al. 2007).

88 **most faces contain such misalignments:** Gallup and Frederick 2010.
88 **Both men and women prefer:** Cartwright 2008.
88 **Any number of factors:** Buss 2011; Cartwright 2008.
88 **According to evolutionary psychology, we should prefer:** Buss 2003, 2011; Cartwright 2008.
89 **Men with symmetrical faces:** Shackelford and Larsen 1997.
89 **These men also have sex:** Buss 2011.
89 **And physically attractive men are stronger:** Gangestad and Thornhill 1997; Henderson and Anglin 2003.
89 **A group of researchers photographed:** Soler et al. 2003.
89 **Among the most fascinating:** Thornhill et al. 2003.
89 **they have fewer respiratory illnesses:** Thornhill and Gangestad 2006.
89 **people in New York and Los Angeles:** Terrill 2012.
90 **It turns out that heterosexual women:** Rhodes 2006.
90 **Researchers are still investigating why:** Buss 2011.
90 **masculine faces signal greater health:** Johnston et al. 2001.
90 **greater dominance, another quality:** Boothroyd et al. 2007.
90 **David Buss, an "enormous":** Buss 2011, 114.
90 **In fact, according to one study, women:** Buss 2011; Kenrick et al. 1990.
90 **Women also prefer men who:** Buss 2011.
91 **Sociologists and psychologists define social class:** Kraus, Piff, and Keltner 2011.
91 **Further, social class actually affects:** Kraus, Piff, and Keltner 2011.
91 **Those from lower-class backgrounds:** Kraus, Piff, and Keltner 2011.
91 **Michael Kraus and Dacher Keltner:** Kraus and Keltner 2009.
91 **First, subjects from high-class backgrounds:** Kraus, Piff, and Keltner 2011.
92 **"Nonverbal displays of the capacity":** Kraus and Keltner 2009, 99.
92 **On the evolutionary savannah:** Buss 2001; Cartwright 2008.
92 **women paired wisely, whereas men:** Myers 2000.
93 **It turns out, males commit:** Buss 2011.
93 **men around the world prefer women:** Buss 2003.
93 **One of the most salient cues:** Buss 2011.
94 **From an evolutionary view, a man:** Buss 2011.
94 **according to the data, he almost:** Kenrick et al. 1996.
94 **the more symmetrical her face:** Buss 2011.
94 **this is thought to be:** Perrett, May, and Yoshikawa 1994.
94 **we don't know the degree:** Of course, it's Jolie's and anyone else's prerogative to have plastic surgery as he or she sees fit.
94 **These women also have significantly:** Smith et al. 2006.
94 **Interestingly though, men's preferences:** Sugiyama 2005.
94 **But there is scant evidence:** Jasieńska et al. 2004.
95 **Two different waist-to-hip ratios:** Figure from Kościński 2012.

95   **to women's ability to breast-feed:** Cartwright 2008.
95   **that the ratio of the woman's:** Kościński 2012.
95   **Men worldwide prefer women:** Singh et al. 2010.
95   **the more a woman's WHR:** Singh 1993.
95   **I've computed the WHRs:** Ratios were computed based on values available at http://www.famemeasurements.com. Of course, the list I provide is not representative, but for illustration only.
96   **In one seminal study, a researcher:** Singh 1993.
96   **This procedure presented a unique opportunity:** Platek and Singh 2010.
97   **Before puberty, men and women:** Cartwright 2008.
97   **The WHR really measures:** Cartwright 2008.
97   **Women with elevated WHR are:** Cartwright 2008; Nelson et al. 1999.
97   **These findings explain why the World Health Organization:** World Health Organization 2008.
97   **A low WHR signals that:** Gallace and Spence 2010.
97   **As a woman goes through menopause:** Aréchiga et al. 2001.
97   **women with lower WHRs menstruate:** van Hooff et al. 2000.
97   **ovulate more frequently:** Jasieńska et al. 2004.
97   **apt to conceive via artificial:** Zaadstra et al. 1993.
97   **and in vitro fertilization:** Wass et al. 1997.
97   **One study showed that women:** Wass et al. 1997.
97   **Perhaps one of the most novel:** Lassek and Gaulin 2008.
98   **Consider what some women do:** Culture, no doubt, influences some women to take such actions as well.
98   **One of the first cosmetic surgeries:** Morris 1967.
98   **For hundreds of years, women:** Steele 2001.
98   **The *New York Times* recently featured:** Nir 2012.
98   **Despite the fact that ideals:** Buss 2011.
98   **Take the iconic Barbie:** Maine 2000.
98   **In 2011, Galia Slayen wrote:** See Slayen 2011.
98   **If one were to extrapolate Barbie's:** Slayen 2011.
99   **Convincing experimental evidence shows that:** Dittmar, Halliwell, and Ive 2006.
99   **Evolutionary theory and everyday experience:** Miller 2009.
99   **After the mid-twenties, their eyes:** Miller 2009.
99   **Many women overcome these physical:** Miller 2009.
100   **Americans spend an astounding $10.1 billion:** American Society of Plastic Surgeons 2010a.
100   **Breast augmentation, nose reshaping, liposuction:** American Society of Plastic Surgeons 2010b.
100   **While they account for only 9 percent:** American Society of Plastic Surgeons 2010a.
101   **And, as in women, injection:** American Society of Plastic Surgeons 2010a.
101   **In his fascinating book *The Mating Mind*:** Miller 2000.

101   **One study showed that men:** Kruger 2008.
101   **differentiate between honest and dishonest signals:** Miller 2000; Gallace and Spence 2010.
101   **Like the NutraSweet I consume:** Gallace and Spence 2010.
102   **Over the years I've surreptitiously:** Most of the time these conversations are forced upon us whether we want them to be or not.
103   **John Gottman knows the answers:** Gottman 1994; Gottman et al. 2002.
103   **"Von Frisch discovered the language":** Brockman 2004.
103   **In a typical lab study, Gottman:** Gottman et al. 1998; Gottman and Krokoff 1989; Gottman and Levenson 2000.
103   **Based on the interactions of these:** Gottman et al. 1998; Gottman and Levenson 2000; Buehlman, Gottman, and Katz 1992.
103   **Gottman can make these predictions:** Carrère and Gottman 1999.
104   **For the vast majority of couples:** Gottman 1994.
104   **When a person singles out:** Gottman 1994.
104   **Emotional and verbal expressions of contempt:** Gottman 1994; Gottman and Levenson 1999.
105   **lifting on only one side:** Matsumoto 2005.
105   **Defensiveness is another key:** Gottman and Levenson 1992.
105   **Stonewalling constitutes another revealing tell:** Gottman 1994.
105   **When a person's heart rate exceeds:** Gottman and Levenson 1992.
105   **amount of positive and negative emotionality:** Carrère and Gottman 1999; Gottman and Levenson 1992.
105   **So the golden ratio for marital bliss:** Gottman and Levenson 1992.
105   **One of my intellectual heroes:** Galton 1869. My field owes a great debt to Galton; directly or indirectly, he pioneered work in facial morphing, statistical techniques, cognitive tests, and quantitative genetics, to name only a few (Miller 2012). Regrettably, he also pioneered the intellectually bankrupt idea of eugenics (Medin 2012; Galton 1904).
105   **from intelligence to an audience's boredom:** Silverman 2013.
106   **His program teaches couples healthy:** For information regarding Gottman's marital therapy program, see http://www.gottman.com.
106   **Research links divorce to a host:** Hughes and Waite 2009.
107   **One study indicated that adults:** Friedman and Martin 2011.
107   **but they predicted divorce:** Hertenstein et al. 2009.
107   **evidence of a so-called Duchenne smile:** Ekman 2007.
107   **More recently, researchers examined photos:** Abel and Kruger 2010.
108   **Eddie Mathews—the great baseball Hall of Famer:** These players did not necessarily participate in the described study. I mention them here only for illustration.
109   **The explanation with the most support:** Harker and Keltner 2001; Seder and Oishi 2012.
109   **LeeAnne Harker and Dacher Keltner:** Harker and Keltner 2001.
109   **Another study showed that people:** Seder and Oishi 2012.

109   **Smelly T-shirts and sperm:** Soler et al. 2003; Thornhill et al. 2003.
109   **Prediction of divorce:** Gottman 1994; Hertenstein et al. 2009.
109   **Prediction of longevity from smiles:** Abel and Kruger 2010.

CHAPTER 7: DETECTING DECEPTION

111   **"Actions lie louder than words":** Wells, n.d.
112   **despite encountering so many lies:** I'm indebted to P. Ekman, M. Frank, C. Bond, B. DePaulo, A. Vrij, the late M. O'Sullivan, and others whose work inspired this chapter and many of the ideas it contains.
112   **Natural-Born Lie Detectors We Are Not:** Smith 2005.
112   **It stands to reason that:** Ekman 2009.
112   **others barrage us constantly with lies:** For this chapter, I've adopted Paul Ekman's definition of a lie: "one person intends to mislead another, doing so deliberately, without prior notification of this purpose, and without having been explicitly asked to do so by the target" (Ekman 2009, 28). I use related words such as "deception" to mean the same thing, but researchers sometimes distinguish between the terms in the literature (Frank and Svetieva 2013).
112   **In one study, researchers individually:** Lewis 1993; Lewis, Stanger, and Sullivan 1989.
112   **"Did you peek?":** Lewis, Stanger, and Sullivan 1989, 440.
112   **"Everybody lies—every day":** Twain 1885.
112   **On average, people lie:** DePaulo et al. 1996.
112   **showers we take in a lifetime:** We can compute this using the equation (1)(365)[(78.5)–(3)]: 1 is the number of lies told per day (a conservative estimate); 365 is the number of days per year; 78.5 is the average life expectancy of a person in the United States (National Center for Health Statistics 2012); 3 is the first three years of life in which children, arguably, do not deliberately deceive.
112   **"And the Lord said unto":** Genesis 4:9, King James Bible.
113   **Although scientists currently employ functional:** Miller 2010; Vrij, Granhag, and Porter 2010.
113   **the vast majority of us:** Bond and DePaulo 2006.
113   **explanations for our meager abilities:** O'Sullivan 2003.
113   **but most boil down to:** See O'Sullivan 2003 and Vrij 2008 for a more complete list of reasons.
113   **It's so much easier going:** Ekman 2009.
113   **Making false accusations and doubting:** Ekman 2009.
113   **The behavioral and verbal cues:** Vrij, Granhag, and Porter 2010; DePaulo et al. 2003.
113   **When emitted in the complex:** Ekman 2009.
113   **the clues we do pick up:** Ekman 2009; Vrij, Granhag, and Porter 2010.

113   **Finally, there is no telltale:** Ekman 2009; Vrij, Granhag, and Porter 2010; DePaulo et al. 2003; Leach 2012.
114   **We may be poor at detecting:** Ekman 2009.
114   **rather than teaching their children:** Ekman 2009; O'Sullivan 2003.
114   **We're rarely given any feedback:** O'Sullivan 2003.
115   **Fidgeting with the pencil:** DePaulo et al. 2003.
115   **Biting her lip:** Ekman 2009.
115   **Presenting a friendly demeanor:** DePaulo et al. 2003.
115   **Touching her nose:** DePaulo et al. 2003.
115   **Touching her ears:** Ekman 2009.
115   **Tapping her foot rapidly:** Ekman 2009.
115   **Averting her gaze:** O'Sullivan 2003; Vrij 2008; Temple-Raston 2007.
115   **Looking to the left:** Gladstone 2009.
115   **Shifting her posture:** Ekman 2009; Vrij 2008; DePaulo et al. 2003.
116   **we think we know what:** Vrij, Granhag, and Porter 2010; Frank 2009; Santarcangelo 2008. Hartwig and Bond (2011) believe that it's not that we don't know what the cues are but that the cues to deceit are too subtle for people to perceive.
116   **Researchers asked people in fifty-eight:** Global Deception Team 2006.
116   **no reliable link exists between:** DePaulo et al. 2003.
116   **Researchers showed a number of subjects:** Ekman and O'Sullivan 1991.
117   **other groups guessed at about chance levels:** Subsequent research has identified a relatively small subset of individuals in other law-related occupations who are also adept at detecting deception (Ekman 2009; Ekman, O'Sullivan, and Frank 1999; O'Sullivan and Ekman 2004; O'Sullivan 2009b), especially high-stakes lies (O'Sullivan et al. 2009).
117   **most police officers, including those:** O'Sullivan 2009b.
117   **Consider the fate of Jerry Watkins:** Innocence Project, n.d.
117   **most people in law enforcement:** Ekman 2007; Leach 2012; Frank and Feeley 2003.
117   **or are flat-out wrong:** Ekman 2007; Leach 2012.
117   **First, all of the tells:** Ekman 2009; Frank 2009; Vrij 2004.
117   **despite much consensus among researchers:** Ekman 2009; Vrij, Granhag, and Porter 2010; Bond and DePaulo 2006; Vrij 2008; DePaulo et al. 2003; Frank and Feeley 2003.
118   **People telling high-stakes lies:** Ekman 2009.
118   **The first, "thinking clues," result:** Vrij 2008; DePaulo et al. 2003; Frank 2009; Trivers 2011; Frank and Ekman 2004; Frank, Menasco, and O'Sullivan 2010.
118   **This additional mental work:** Vrij 2008.
118   **reflecting the cognitive load she's experiencing:** Ekman 2009; Vrij 2008; DePaulo et al. 2003; Frank, Menasco, and O'Sullivan 2010.
118   **As a result, they provide "emotional:** Frank 2009; Frank and Ekman 2004; Frank, Menasco, and O'Sullivan 2010.

119   **No one has studied the "emotional:** Krelster 2004.

119   **"teaching us how to recognize":** Taylor 2009.

119   **The serendipitous origins of Ekman's:** The two colleagues with whom he has published most frequently on the topic of deceit are Mark Frank (University of Buffalo) and the late Maureen O'Sullivan (University of San Francisco).

119   **Early in his career he:** Ekman 2007.

119   **"When a patient who had":** Ekman 2007, 213.

119   **Mary had a history of trying:** Ekman tells the story of Mary in Ekman 2007, 2009.

119   **Ekman and one of his colleagues went on:** Ekman 2007, 2009.

120   **In some of his latest work:** Ekman 2009.

120   **When analyzing videotape that includes:** Ekman 2009; Frank, Yarbrough, and Ekman 2006.

120   **So here's what the data tell us:** Ekman 2007, 2009; Frank 2009. If you're interested in delving deeper into the study of emotion and deceit, check out two of Ekman's books: *Emotions Revealed* (2007) and *Telling Lies* (2009). The presentation of the signals here was inspired in some measure by Meyer (2010), although she parses the work differently than me.

120   **Microexpressions: When people lie:** Ekman 2007, 2009; Porter and ten Brinke 2008.

120   **One of Ekman's colleagues analyzed:** See David Matsumoto (San Francisco State University) analyze the video clip at Humintell 2009. He also analyzes other clues of deceit at Humintell 2010.

120   **Ekman has developed a short program:** Ekman 2009; Hurley 2012. If you're interested in learning more about his training program, visit www .paulekman.com. And, no, I have no financial stake in Ekman's products.

120   **"Reliable" muscles: Some muscles of:** Ekman 2007, 2009.

121   **Silver medalists' smiles:** Why don't silver medalists contract the muscle around their eyes when bronze medal winners do? Researchers think that bronze medalists are actually happier than silver medalists because of counterfactual thinking (Medvec, Madey, and Gilovich 1995). In essence, bronze medalists are simply happy to have medaled at the Olympic games; after all, they were only one place away from not receiving a medal whatsoever. In contrast, silver medalists are likely comparing the other way and thinking that they barely missed the gold medal. Such thinking engenders less satisfaction among silver medalists compared to those winning the bronze.

121   **Systematic studies in which:** Matsumoto and Willingham 2006. This study focused on Olympic Judo athletes, specifically.

121   **Squelched expressions: One elderly woman:** Ekman 2007, 2009.

121   **Lopsided facial displays: If a person:** Ekman 2007, 2009.

121   **look to see if her smile is:** Ekman, Hager, and Friesen 1981.

121   **Timing of the emotional display: If you've:** Ekman 2009.

122   **several people in the blogosphere:** Hamptonroads.com 2008; Schlesinger 2008.

122   **Observations like these led *The Onion*:** Onion 2008.

122   **"Unless someone is having a peak":** Ekman 2009, 148.
122   **The relationship between facial displays:** Ekman 2009.
122   **The eyes: Although there is some disagreement:** See Vrij 2008; DePaulo et al. 2003.
122   **evidence indicates that when we prevaricate:** Ekman 2009; DePaulo et al. 2003.
122   **because our nervous system is aroused:** DePaulo et al. 2003.
123   **The voice: People who lie:** Ekman 2009; DePaulo et al. 2003; Frank 2009; Streeter et al. 1977.
123   **One group of people walking:** O'Sullivan and Ekman 2004; O'Sullivan 2009b.
123   **truth wizards:** O'Sullivan 2009b. These wizards of deception detection are not deemed wizards because they have magical abilities but rather because of their unique capacities to tell if someone is lying (Frank, Menasco, and O'Sullivan 2010; O'Sullivan 2007a).
123   **Whereas most people correctly identify:** There is some debate about whether truth wizards actually exist or are merely statistical anomalies. My take on the data is that they are real, but to learn more about the debate, see the following: Bond and DePaulo 2008a, 2008b; Bond and Uysal 2007; Bond 2008; O'Sullivan 2007b, 2008.
123   **To date, researchers have identified:** O'Sullivan 2009b.
123   **One such truth wizard is:** Most of the material in this chapter about EFL comes from an e-mail interview I conducted with her, though some comes from her website at www.eyesforlies.com.
124   **As I write:** August 8, 2012.
124   **Truth wizards share one common:** O'Sullivan and Ekman 2004; O'Sullivan 2007b, 2009b.
124   **They analyze the subtleties of:** O'Sullivan and Ekman 2004; O'Sullivan 2007b, 2009b.
125   **"Our wizards are extraordinarily attuned":** McDonald 2004.
125   **Are truth wizards innately gifted:** O'Sullivan 2009a.
125   **The answer is probably a combination:** O'Sullivan and Ekman 2004; O'Sullivan 2009a, 2009b.
125   **Truth wizards are likely the same:** O'Sullivan 2007b.
125   **It's important to look for a cluster:** Ekman 2009; Vrij 2004.
125   **We are always revising probabilities:** Silver 2012.
125   **Instead, such a pattern should:** Frank 2009.
126   **Not much better than chance:** Bond and DePaulo 2006.
126   **Accurate analysis of tells:** Ekman 2009; Frank, Yarbrough, and Ekman 2006.
126   **Truth Wizards among us:** O'Sullivan 2009b.

CHAPTER 8: THE POWER OF ENTHUSIASM

129   **"Good teaching is one-fourth preparation":** Godwin, n.d.
130   **Consider one study in which students:** Laws et al. 2010.

131   **In other words, students form:** Laws et al. 2010.
131   **But what if students' impressions:** I'm indebted to N. Ambady, R. Rosenthal, S. Ceci, and others whose work inspired this chapter and many of the ideas it contains.
132   **In a seminal study, Nalini Ambady:** Ambady and Rosenthal 1993.
132   **"Rate the quality of the section":** Ambady and Rosenthal 1993, 433).
132   **"Rate section leader's performance overall":** Ambady and Rosenthal 1993, 433.
132   **In a study they dubbed:** Ambady and Rosenthal 1993.
133   **And, if you're wondering:** Researchers conducted a follow-up study to expand on Ambady and Rosenthal's original study but examined a relatively large sample of seasoned professors who taught in Israel (Babad, Avni-Babad, and Rosenthal 2004). The researchers allowed judges to hear the instructor's voice intonation while observing the clips, allowing non-Hebrew-speaking judges to assess the vocal qualities of the faculty without comprehending the content of their speech. Finally, the researchers coded more specific nonverbal behaviors exhibited by the faculty while teaching than that of the original study. Overall, the results replicated the general findings of Ambady and Rosenthal (Babad, Avni-Babad, and Rosenthal 2004): strangers' evaluations of brief clips of lectures predicted students' ratings of the instructors, including for humor, enthusiasm, clarity, and overall evaluation at the end of the semester.
133   **"What exactly happens in those":** Babad, Avni-Babad, and Rosenthal 2004.
133   **"are very expressive in their faces":** Babad, Avni-Babad, and Rosenthal 2004, 27.
133   **Fortunately, a team at Cornell University:** Williams and Ceci 1997.
134   **As you can see in the following:** Graphs adapted from Williams and Ceci, 1997, table 1.
135   **In terms of the course itself:** Williams and Ceci 1997.
136   **"Among courses that you have":** Williams and Ceci 1997, 21.
136   **Although not a perfect:** Given that the design of this study is a pre- versus post-test comparison, it's always possible that other factors might play a role in explaining the difference between the fall and spring terms.
137   **Nothing could be further:** Of course, institutions vary to some degree in terms of the amount of weight they give to evaluations. My institution, for example, does not rely solely on evaluations to assess teaching quality, but some likely do. Others pay little attention to evaluations.
137   **These evaluations often have:** Weinberg, Hashimoto, and Fleisher 2009. My goal is not to definitively weigh the evidence regarding the use and appropriateness of evaluations, as there are sound arguments on both sides of the issue. Nonetheless, I do think these studies illustrate that evaluations measure not only student learning but other extraneous variables as well.
137   **tenure, promotion, and salary decisions:** Clayson 2009; Wilson 1998.
137   **"If I trust one source of data":** Seldin 1999, 15.
137   **Should some institutions reconsider the weight:** Babad, Avni-Babad, and Rosenthal 2004.

137   **The gravity placed on evaluations:** Love and Kotchen 2010.
137   **in 2008, 43 percent of grades:** Rojstaczer and Healy 2012.
138   **evaluations play such an important role:** Love and Kotchen 2010.
138   **"the research almost universally finds":** Clayson 2009, 26.
138   **"If you make people think":** Clayson 2009, 27.
138   **something called the "expressivity halo":** Bernieri et al. 1996.
138   **people who are expressive and animated:** Bernieri et al. 1996.
138   **"I think I figured out how":** For the record, this faculty member recognized the ethical quandaries surrounding this issue.
139   **"what is expressive is good":** Bernieri et al. 1996, 124.
139   **goes beyond education:** Bernieri et al. 1996.
139   **at least one set of studies:** Ambady et al. 2002.
139   **which patients would improve most:** Of course, the correlational nature of this study doesn't allow us to infer that expressivity caused these patients' improvements.
139   **most people do not recognize:** Bernieri et al. 1996.
140   **The problem is that the effects:** Bernieri et al. 1996.
140   **Parallels between first- and:** Laws et al. 2010.
140   **Six seconds to a quality professor:** Ambady and Rosenthal 1993.
140   **The power of enthusiasm:** Williams and Ceci 1997.

CHAPTER 9: CATCHING THE CUES OF THE CASH COW

141   **"One of the hardest tasks of leadership":** Flom, n.d.
142   **"While the law of competition":** Carnegie, n.d.
142   **According to Carnegie and:** I thank my colleague Manu Raghav for our discussion about these economists.
142   **Herbert Spencer, a nineteenth-century:** Schultz and Schultz 2004.
142   **A well-known scholar of his day:** Regrettably, Spencer adapted the concept of natural selection too far, formulating what is known as social Darwinism.
142   **what he termed "survival of the fittest":** Schultz and Schultz 2004.
142   **Though companies such as Betamax:** Business Pundit 2009.
142   **Walt Disney's family-oriented emphasis:** Ranft et al. 2006.
142   **In 1980, CEOs made about:** Rasmus 2004.
142   **by 2010 they earned a whopping:** Lazonick 2011.
143   **Even the academic studies:** For example, some studies find that charisma, an extremely ephemeral quality, is important, whereas others do not (Agle et al. 2006).
143   **Neither the popular nor the academic:** Agle et al. 2006; Tosi et al. 2004.
143   **accomplishments of CEOs—at least as:** I'm indebted to N. Rule and N. Ambady and others whose work inspired this chapter and many of the ideas it contains.
143   **In a landmark study, Nicholas Rule:** Rule and Ambady 2008b.
143   **The researchers asked subjects:** Researchers cropped pictures tightly around the head so as not to reveal clothing and other adornments.

Although the authors do not reveal the ethnicity of the CEOs to my knowledge, virtually all of them were likely Caucasian.

143   **"How good would this person":** Rule and Ambady 2008b, 109.

143   **CEOs with faces perceived as powerful:** This finding held true even when researchers controlled for ratings of leadership.

144   **CEOs whom subjects thought:** This finding held true even when researchers controlled for ratings of power.

144   **A follow-up study showed:** Rule and Ambady 2009.

144   **"The ability to infer success":** Rule and Ambady 2009, 651.

144   **"These findings," wrote the authors:** Rule and Ambady 2008b, 110.

144   **In fact, most previous studies:** Agle et al. 2006.

144   **In contrast, Rule and Ambady's study:** Rule and Ambady 2008b; Rule and Ambady 2009.

145   **To answer the first question:** Rule, Moran, et al. 2011.

145   **The researchers propose that these CEOs' faces:** Rule, Moran, et al. 2011.

145   **Response of the left amygdala:** The figure is from Rule, Moran, et al. 2011, 736.

145   **One team at the University of Wisconsin:** Wong, Ormiston, and Haselhuhn 2011.

145   **the photos of fifty-five male CEOs:** Ninety-eight percent of the CEOs were Caucasian.

145   **a trait linked to aggression:** Carré, McCormick, and Mondloch 2009.

145   **psychological perception of power:** Haselhuhn and Wong 2011.

146   **The authors reported that although:** Wong, Ormiston, and Haselhuhn 2011.

146   **Are the differences in facial appearance:** Rule, Moran, et al. 2011; Rule and Ambady 2011b.

146   **One hypothesis—let's call it:** Collins and Zebrowitz 1995; Rule, Moran, et al. 2011.

146   **From this perspective, looking successful:** Rule, Moran, et al. 2011.

146   **This effect can occur in any:** Rule and Ambady 2011b.

146   **People may treat powerful-looking people:** Langlois et al. 1995.

146   **A second hypothesis—let's call it:** Rule, Moran, et al. 2011; Rule and Ambady 2011a.

146   **"success begets a face" hypothesis:** This is sometimes called the "Dorian Gray effect" in the literature (Zebrowitz, Collins, and Dutta 1998).

146   **Some evidence suggests that repeated:** Zebrowitz, Collins, and Dutta 1998; Malatesta, Fiore, and Messina 1987.

147   **Data also suggest that the facial structures:** Zajonc et al. 1987.

147   **Although no definitive evidence exists:** Rule, Moran, et al. 2011.

147   **First, consider the above study:** Wong, Ormiston, and Haselhuhn 2011.

147   **Researchers asked subjects to assess:** Rule and Ambady 2011b.

147   **Just as in their studies of CEOs:** Rule and Ambady 2008b.

147   **In contrast, no such possibility exists:** Rule and Ambady 2011b.

147   **not true for companies in Japan:** Rule, Ishii, and Ambady 2011.

147   **For instance, Japanese:** Rule and Ambady 2008b; Rule et al. 2010.

148   **Black CEOs who display a warmer:** Livingston and Pearce 2009. The researchers did not examine whether facial characteristics correlated to company profitability to my knowledge.

149   **Individuals who make their living:** Ambady, Krabbenhoft, and Hogan 2006.

149   **Researchers asked upper management:** Ambady, Krabbenhoft, and Hogan 2006.

150   **The eight judges readily differentiated:** Ambady, Krabbenhoft, and Hogan 2006.

150   **"No computer network with pretty":** Stoll 1995, 21.

150   **According to one estimate, businesses spent:** Kantar Media 2013.

150   **As they have only a thin:** Ambady, Krabbenhoft, and Hogan 2006.

150   **considering the implications of these studies:** Ambady, Krabbenhoft, and Hogan 2006.

151   **CEO power predicts company profitability:** Rule and Ambady 2008b.

151   **Brain activity predicts company profitability:** Rule, Moran, et al. 2011.

151   **We can predict success in sales:** Ambady, Krabbenhoft, and Hogan 2006.

CHAPTER 10: POLITICAL PUNDITRY: ANY KID CAN DO IT

153   **"Democracy is the theory that":** Mencken, n.d.

153   **preference in candidates solely the result:** Todorov et al. 2005; Rule et al. 2010; Little, Burriss, et al. 2007; Riggio and Riggio 2010.

154   **But, as you'll see, superficial variables:** I'm indebted to a number of researchers, including A. Todorov and J. Antonakis, whose work inspired this chapter and many of the ideas it contains.

154   **Humans are unique within:** Little, Burriss, et al. 2007.

154   **Moreover, elections are a relatively:** Shively 2012.

154   **Elections are the linchpin between:** Shea, Connor Green, and Smith 2011; Wayne 2011.

154   **They give elected officials:** Wayne 2011.

154   **Political scientists suggest that:** Shively 2012.

154   **In a presidential election year:** Bipartisan Policy Center 2012.

154   **during a nonpresidential year:** Roskin et al. 2012; Wasserman 2011.

155   **And, of course, none of:** Smith et al. 2010.

155   **"There are two things that":** Shields 2010.

155   **The amount of money spent:** Center for Responsive Politics 2011.

155   **They spend millions of dollars:** Todorov et al. 2005.

155   **place their lives on hold:** Brooks 2012.

155   **For decades, political science and economics:** Downs 1957; Olivola and Todorov 2010; Shenkman 2008b; Quattrone and Tversky 1988.

155   **that they base their decisions:** Wasserman 2011; Zaino 2012.

155   **But could some people vote:** Kelley and Mirer 1974.

155   **More than at any other:** Olivola and Todorov 2010.

155   **people are working longer hours:** Bureau of Labor Statistics 2011.

155   **for less pay:** Chandra and Matthews 2010; Pear 2011.
155   **and getting less sleep:** Bureau of Labor Statistics 2011.
156   **So even though we have:** Shenkman 2008b.
156   **An astounding 60 percent of Americans:** Shenkman 2008a.
156   **Less than a third of Americans:** Craig and Martinez 2010.
156   **Only 25 percent of Americans can name:** Craig and Martinez 2010.
156   **Curiously, one in five people think:** Associated Press 2006.
156   **If deciding whom to vote:** Craig and Martinez 2010. Obviously, I'm not arguing that governments should require citizens to take a test of their civic knowledge.
156   **When it comes to awareness:** Shenkman 2008b; Craig and Martinez 2010.
156   **"Do you happen to know":** Shenkman 2008b, 31.
156   **voters' ignorance of the issues:** Craig and Martinez 2010.
156   **It's little surprise that:** Shenkman 2008a.
157   **they use heuristics to help them:** Todorov et al. 2005; Olivola and Todorov 2010; Shenkman 2008b; Craig and Martinez 2010; Hayes 2010; Olivola and Todorov 2009.
157   **such as my newspaper's endorsement:** Shenkman 2008b.
158   **Just a few weeks before:** *New York Times* 1966.
158   **"My father has just home":** Trump 1977.
159   **"My dear little Miss":** Trump 1977.
160   **"He climbed down and sat with me":** Bedell 1860.
160   **On September 26, 1960, two candidates:** Plissner 1999; Maynard 2010.
160   **A record 60 million viewers:** Plissner 1999.
160   **The face-off took place in:** Germond and Witocover 1979.
160   **Both Kennedy and Nixon understood:** Plissner 1999.
161   **including education and medical care:** Plissner 1999.
161   **But rather than their positions on the issues:** Plissner 1999; Maynard 2010; Germond and Witocover 1979; Kirkpatrick 1979.
161   **Kennedy arrived in Chicago the:** Germond and Witocover 1979.
161   **On the CBS studio stage, Kennedy:** Maynard 2010.
161   **Prior to the event, he:** Plissner 1999.
161   **Overall, he looked not only in:** Ironically, Kennedy was actually in much worse health than Nixon. According to Robert Dallek (2002), Kennedy suffered from several serious medical issues, including Addison's disease.
161   **Nixon arrived in Chicago late:** Germond and Witocover 1979.
161   **Unlike Kennedy's suit, which contrasted:** Plissner 1999; Maynard 2010; Germond and Witocover 1979.
161   **However, Kennedy's staff applied some:** Plissner 1999; Maynard 2010; Germond and Witocover 1979.
161   **On top of all this, Nixon was:** Plissner 1999.
161   **and a recent stay in the hospital:** Maynard 2010.
161   **"Kennedy was bronzed beautifully":** Stanton 2000.
161   **"After the program, callers, including":** Plissner 1999, 132.
161   **With the help of professionally:** Plissner 1999.

161   **Nonetheless, his destiny was sealed:** Germond and Witocover 1979.
162   **people who listened to the debate on the radio:** Plissner 1999; Maynard 2010; Germond and Witocover 1979; Hellweg, Pfau, and Brydon 1992. There has been some disagreement on this point, however (Vancil and Pendell 1987).
162   **Naive undergraduate viewers and listeners:** Druckman 2003.
162   **it's widely thought that Nixon's:** Maynard 2010; Kirkpatrick 1979.
162   **Before the first debate, Nixon:** Germond and Witocover 1979.
162   **Kennedy left such a positive impression:** Maynard 2010.
162   **Kennedy would go on to win:** Leip 2012.
162   **is one-sixth of 1 percent:** Plissner 1999.
162   **the weight of these tells on the outcome:** Rosenberg, Kahn, and Tran 1991.
162   **We may not be nearly as rational:** Olivola and Todorov 2010; Shenkman 2008b.
162   **studies published in** *Science* **conducted by Alexander Todorov:** Todorov et al. 2005.
162   **pairs of head shots like the pair:** The image is from Todorov et al. 2005.
163   **Todorov and his colleagues also asked:** Todorov et al. 2005.
164   **Without any knowledge of their:** Researchers have replicated Todorov's general findings in other countries and also at various levels of electoral politics, such as gubernatorial elections (Rule et al. 2010; Olivola and Todorov 2010; Atkinson 2009; Ballew and Todorov 2007).
164   **Researchers asked kids between:** Antonakis and Dalgas 2009.
164   **"Imagine that you will now":** Antonakis and Dalgas 2009.
164   **pictures of the candidates for US Senate:** Todorov et al. 2005.
165   **children chose Obama 77 percent:** Antonakis, personal communication. The children may have been familiar with the candidates in this study, which may have influenced the results. Also, gender and age may obviously be confounding factors in the children's decisions.
165   **The Swiss study suggests that:** Antonakis and Dalgas 2009.
165   **"Facial competence is a highly":** Olivola and Todorov 2010, 83.
165   **People seem to associate competency:** Todorov et al. 2005.
165   **dependability, attractiveness, and emotional stability:** Olivola and Todorov 2010.
165   **In one study, subjects' assessments:** Ballew and Todorov 2007.
165   **When researchers directed subjects to deliberate on:** Ballew and Todorov 2007.
165   **All of these seem like viable:** Lenz and Lawson 2011. There is some evidence, albeit limited in my opinion, that competent-looking candidates may run in less competitive races (Atkinson 2009).
165   **It's difficult to tell if impressions:** Olivola and Todorov 2010; Lenz and Lawson 2011. Although, see Atkinson 2009, which suggests that candidates with competent faces may possess more wealth and human capital.
165   **We do know that it's:** Lenz and Lawson 2011; Lawson et al. 2010.

166   **A number of other appearance-related:** Olivola and Todorov 2010.
166   **One such movie for me:** IMDB, n.d.
166   **The ideal candidate's face signals:** Todorov et al. 2005; Olivola and Todorov 2010.
166   **The older and more familiar:** Olivola and Todorov 2010.
166   **A host of perceived traits in:** Olivola and Todorov 2010.
166   **When one study asked subjects:** Mattes et al. 2010.
166   **One might think the ideal:** Armstrong et al. 2010; Miller and Lundgren 2010.
166   **some studies showing a positive association:** Olivola and Todorov 2010; King and Leigh 2009; Poutvaara, Jordahl, and Berggren 2009.
166   **others showing no relationship:** Rule et al. 2010; Riggle et al. 1992.
166   **One carefully conducted study:** Mattes et al. 2010. Most of the candidates in this study were male.
167   **"attempting to make a candidate":** Mattes et al. 2010, 55.
167   **Some evidence suggests that during:** Little, Burriss, et al. 2007.
167   **If male, the ideal presidential candidate's:** Gregory and Gallagher 2002; Tigue et al. 2012.
167   **Researchers measured the vocal quality:** Gregory and Gallagher 2002.
167   **Of the presidential elections in:** Lyndon Johnson and Barry Goldwater did not debate each other in 1964. Richard Nixon declined to debate his opponents in 1968 and 1972.
167   **Researchers surmised that a low-pitched:** Tigue et al. 2012.
167   **The probability of electoral success:** Gillis 1982.
167   **In the forty-six presidential elections:** All heights for this chapter are from Wikipedia, n.d.
168   **taller candidate won twenty-nine times:** There have been times in history when the taller candidate won the popular vote but lost the election (e.g., 2000: George W. Bush versus Al Gore; 1888: Benjamin Harrison versus Grover Cleveland; 1876: Rutherford Hayes versus Samuel Tilden).
168   **Though the vast majority of shorter:** Gillis 1982.
168   **Al Gore won the popular vote:** Supreme Court of the United States 2009.
169   **we see no relation between height:** Benjamin 2009.
169   **Researchers have uncovered links between:** Sommers 2002.
169   **presidential greatness scores:** Graph based on data reported by Taranto 2005. According to Taranto, James Lindgren of Northwestern University Law School collected the data.
169   **I computed a relatively simple:** $p < .05$.
169   **this represents a statistically significant height difference:** $p < .05$.
171   **A number of different evolutionary:** Murray and Schmitz 2011.
171   **Appearance seems to influence our voting:** Todorov et al. 2005; Olivola and Todorov 2010; Ballew and Todorov 2007.
171   **we should have replaced our first impressions:** Todorov et al. 2005; Antonakis and Dalgas 2009.

171   It's the equivalent of having: Thanks are in order to one of Mitt Romney's advisors for inspiring this analogy. See Shear 2012.

171   Subjects in one study watched ten-second: Benjamin 2009.

172   It's the swing voters and the uninformed: Olivola and Todorov 2010; Ballew and Todorov 2007; Lenz and Lawson 2011.

172   Recall that Kennedy defeated Nixon: Plissner 1999.

172   Al Franken defeated Norm Coleman: Minnesota Secretary of State 2008.

172   In the 2000 presidential election: Federal Election Comission 2008.

172   Here I include a few recommendations: Olivola and Todorov 2010; Lenz and Lawson 2011; Armstrong et al. 2010.

172   Recommendation 1: Olivola and Todorov 2010; Lenz and Lawson 2011.

172   Television exacerbates the influence: Lenz and Lawson 2011.

173   One study examined how various Internet: Hehman et al. 2012.

173   Recommendation 3: Riggio and Riggio 2010.

173   Recommendation 4: Olivola and Todorov 2010.

173   studies show that this may strengthen: Olivola and Todorov 2010; Banducci et al. 2008; Buckley, Collins, and Reidy 2007.

173   Strategists could then use this information: Armstrong et al. 2010.

174   Recommendation 6: Armstrong et al. 2010.

174   The University of Iowa runs: University of Iowa Tippie College of Business 2012.

174   as studies show they are: Tetlock 2005; Barrie 2011; Begley 2009.

174   Predictive accuracy increases when you: Olivola and Todorov 2010; Surowiecki 2004.

174   Present candidates faces in pairs: Todorov et al. 2005.

174   Forty, according to the research: Olivola and Todorov 2010.

174   listening to the collective wisdom: Surowiecki 2004.

174   better bet than listening to pundits: Taylor 2011.

174   In *The Republic*: Bloom 1991.

174   Plato argued that people: Antonakis and Dalgas 2009.

175   Perceived competence predicts election: Ballew and Todorov 2007.

175   Prediction of election outcomes begins: Antonakis and Dalgas 2009.

175   It pays to be tall: Gillis 1982.

CONCLUSION: THE IMPORTANCE OF PREDICTIVE HUMILITY

177   When meeting others we are: Ambady and Skowronski 2008; Ambady, Bernieri, and Richeson 2000.

178   Because our brains have: Ifould 2009. Psychologists refer to this as confirmation bias because we are biased to confirm our preconceived views (Mendel et al. 2011).

178   Another foible of the mind: Psychologists refer to this as hindsight bias because we are biased to believe we knew something the whole time when we really didn't (Myers 2013; Kahneman 2011; Roese and Vohs 2012).

178   you "knew it all along": Roese and Vohs 2012, 411.
178   unwarranted confidence in our capacity: Kahneman 2011; Taleb 2010.
178   Numerous studies reliably show that: Kahneman 2011.
179   "I'll just text her mom": These quotes come from a conversation I had
       with a friend.

REFERENCES

Abel, E. L., & Kruger, M. L. (2010). Smile intensity in photographs predicts longevity. *Psychological Science, 21,* 542–544.

Abrams, K. Y., Rifkin, A., & Hesse, E. (2006). Examining the role of parental frightened/frightening subtypes in predicting disorganized attachment within a brief observational procedure. *Development and Psychopathology, 18,* 345–361.

Adrien, J. L., Perrot, A., Hameury, L., & Martineau, J. (1991). Family home movies: Identification of early autistic signs in infants later diagnosed as autistics. *Brain Dysfunction, 4,* 355–362.

Agle, B. R., Nagarajan, N. J., Sonnenfeld, J. A., & Srinivasan, D. (2006). Does CEO charisma matter? An empirical analysis of the relationships among organizational performance, environmental uncertainty, and top management team perceptions of CEO charisma. *Academy of Management Journal, 49,* 161–174.

Ainsworth, M. D. S., Blehar, M. C., Waters, E., & Wall, S. (1978). *Patterns of attachment: A psychological study of the strange situation.* Hillsdale, NJ: Erlbaum.

Ainsworth, M. D. S., & Bowlby, J. (1991). An ethological approach to personality development. *American Psychologist, 46,* 333–341.

Ainsworth, M. D. S., & Marvin, R. S. (1995). On the shaping of attachment theory and research: An interview with Mary D. S. Ainsworth (Fall 1994). *Monographs of the Society for Research in Child Development, 60,* 3–21.

Albright, L., Kenny, D. A., & Malloy, T. E. (1988). Consensus in personality judgments at zero acquaintance. *Journal of Personality and Social Psychology, 55,* 387–395.

Allpert, B. (2009, February 9). Cramer's star outshines his stock picks. *Barron's.* Retrieved from http://online.barrons.com/article/SB123397107399659271 .html#articleTabs_article%3D1.

Ambady, N., Bernieri, F. J., & Richeson, J. A. (2000). Toward a histology of social behavior: Judgmental accuracy from thin slices of the behavioral stream. In M. P. Zanna (Ed.), *Advances in experimental social psychology* (Vol. 32, pp. 201–271). San Diego, CA: Academic Press.

Ambady, N., & Hallahan, M. (2002). Using nonverbal representations of behavior: Perceiving sexual orientation. In A. M. Galaburda, S. M. Kosslyn & C. Yves (Eds.), *The languages of the brain* (pp. 320–332). Cambridge, MA: Harvard University Press.

Ambady, N., Hallahan, M., & Conner, B. (1999). Accuracy of judgments of sexual orientation from thin slices of behavior. *Journal of Personality and Social Psychology, 77,* 538–547.

Ambady, N., Koo, J., Rosenthal, R., & Winograd, C. H. (2002). Physical therapists' nonverbal communication predicts geriatric patients' health outcomes. *Psychology and Aging, 17,* 443–452.

Ambady, N., Krabbenhoft, M. A., & Hogan, D. (2006). The 30-sec sale: Using thin-slice judgments to evaluate sales effectiveness. *Journal of Consumer Psychology, 16,* 4–13.

Ambady, N., LaPlante, D., & Johnson, E. (2001). Thin-slice judgments as a measure of interpersonal sensitivity. In J. A. Hall & F. J. Bernieri (Eds.), *Interpersonal sensitivity: Theory and measurement* (pp. 89–101). Mahwah, NJ: Erlbaum.

Ambady, N., & Rosenthal, R. (1992). Thin slices of expressive behavior as predictors of interpersonal consequences: A meta-analysis. *Psychological Bulletin, 111,* 256–274.

Ambady, N., & Rosenthal, R. (1993). Half a minute: Predicting teacher evaluations from thin slices of nonverbal behavior and physical attractiveness. *Journal of Personality and Social Psychology, 64,* 431–441.

Ambady, N., & Skowronski, J. J. (Eds.). (2008). *First impressions.* New York: Guilford Press.

Amendola, E. (2007, December 25). Boston's $14.8 big dig finally complete. *USA Today.* Retrieved from http://usatoday30.usatoday.com/news/nation/2007-12-25-big-dig_N.htm.

American Psychiatric Association. (2000). *Diagnostic and statistical manual of mental disorders* (4th ed., text rev.). Washington, DC: Author.

American Society of Plastic Surgeons. (2010a). 2010 cosmetic surgery gender distribution. *Report of the 2010 plastic surgery statistics.* Retrieved from http://www.plasticsurgery.org/Documents/news-resources/statistics/2010-statisticss/Male-vs-Female/2010-men-cosmetic-surgery-minimally-invasive-statistics.pdf.

American Society of Plastic Surgeons. (2010b). 2010 quick facts: Cosmetic and reconstructive plastic surgery trends. *Report of the 2010 plastic surgery statistics.* Retrieved from http://www.plasticsurgery.org/Documents/news-resources/statistics/2010-statisticss/Male-vs-Female/2010-women-cosmetic-surgery-minally-invasive-statistics.pdf.

Antonakis, J., & Dalgas, O. (2009). Predicting elections: Child's play! *Science, 323,* 1183.

Aréchiga, J., Prado, C., Cantó, M., & Carmenate, M. (2001). Women in transition—menopause and body composition in different populations. *Collective Anthropology, 25,* 443–448.

Ariely, D. (2008). *Predictably irrational: The hidden forces that shape our decisions.* New York: HarperCollins.

Aristotle. (n.d.). Prior analytics. Logos Virtual Library. Retrieved from http://www.logoslibrary.org/aristotle/prior/227.html.

Armstrong, J. S., Green, K. C., Jones, R. J., & Wright, M. J. (2010). Predicting elections from politicians' faces. *International Journal of Public Opinion Research, 22,* 1–12.

Associated Press. (2006, March 1). D'oh! More know Simpsons than constitution. Retrieved from http://www.msnbc.msn.com/id/11611015/ns/us_news-life/t/doh-more-know-simpsons-constitution/#.T9ot15jSl8E.

Atkinson, M. D. (2009). Candidate faces and election outcomes: Is the face-vote correlation caused by candidate selection? *Quarterly Journal of Political Science, 4,* 229–249.

Azevedo, F. A. C., Carvalho, L. R. B., Grinberg, L. T., Farfel, J. M., Ferretti, R. E. L., Leite, R. E. P., . . . Herculano-Houzel, S. (2009). Equal numbers of neuronal and nonneuronal cells make the human brain an isometrically scaled-up primate brain. *Journal of Comparative Neurology, 513,* 532–541.

Babad, E., Avni-Babad, D., & Rosenthal, R. (2004). Prediction of students' evaluations from brief instances of professors' nonverbal behavior in defined instructional situations. *Social Psychology of Education, 7,* 3–33.

Bailey, A., Le Couteur, A., Gottesman, I., & Bolton, P. (1995). Autism as a strongly genetic disorder: Evidence from a British twin study. *Psychological Medicine, 25,* 63–77.

Bakermans-Kranenburg, M. J., & van IJzendoorn, M. H. (2009). The first 10,000 adult attachment interviews: Distributions of adult attachment representations in clinical and non-clinical groups. *Attachment and Human Development, 11,* 223–263.

Bakermans-Kranenburg, M. J., van IJzendoorn, M. H., & Juffer, F. (2005). Disorganized infant attachment and preventive interventions: A review and meta-analysis. *Infant Mental Health Journal, 26,* 191–216.

Ballen, N., Bernier, A., Moss, E., Tarabulsy, G. M., & St-Laurent, D. (2010). Insecure attachment states of mind and atypical caregiving behavior among foster mothers. *Journal of Applied Developmental Psychology, 31,* 118–125.

Ballew, C. C., & Todorov, A. (2007). Predicting political elections from rapid and unreflective face judgments. *Proceedings of the National Academy of Sciences of the United States of America, 104,* 17948–17953.

Banducci, S. A., Karp, J. A., Thrasher, M., & Rallings, C. (2008). Ballot photographs as cues in low-information elections. *Political Psychology, 29,* 903–917.

Banks, D. (2006, April 6). Paul Rusesabagina, no "ordinary man." National Public Radio. Retrieved from http://www.npr.org/templates/story/story.php?storyId=5324187.

Barabasi, A.-L. (2010). *Bursts: The hidden pattern behind everything we do.* New York: Dutton.

Baron, R. A., Byrne, D., & Branscombe, N. R. (2006). *Social psychology* (11th ed.). Boston, MA: Pearson Education, Inc.

Barraza, J. A., McCullough, M. E., Ahmadi, S., & Zak, P. J. (2011). Oxytocin infusion increases charitable donations regardless of monetary resources. *Hormones and Behavior, 60,* 148–151.

Barrie, V. (2011, May 2). Pundits predict no more accurately than a coin toss. Hamilton. Retrieved from http://www.hamilton.edu/news/story/pundits-as-accurate-as-coin-toss-according-to-study.

Bartlett, T. (2010, February 8). Physics envy: Or why no one respects psychologists. *Chronicle of Higher Education.* Retrieved from http://chronicle.com/blogs/percolator/physics-envy-or-why-no-one-respects-psychologists/21108.

Bedell, G. (1860, October 18). [Letter to Abraham Lincoln]. Biggest Apple. Retrieved from http://www.biggestapple.net/images/uploads/bedell.jpg.

Beer, A., & Watson, D. (2008). Personality judgment at zero acquaintance: Agreement, assumed similarity, and implicit simplicity. *Journal of Personality Assessment, 90,* 250–260.

Begley, S. (2009, February). Why pundits get things wrong. *Newsweek.* Retrieved from http://www.thedailybeast.com/newsweek/2009/02/13/why-pundits-get-things-wrong.html.

Belkin, A., Ender, M., Frank, N., Furia, S., Lucas, G. R., Packard, . . . Segal, D. R. (2012). One year out: An assessment of DADT repeal's impact on military readiness. Palm Center. Retrieved from http://www.palmcenter.org/files/One%20Year%20Out_0.pdf.

Belsky, J., & Fearon, R. M. P. (2008). Precursors of attachment security. In J. Cassidy & P. R. Shaver (Eds.), *Handbook of attachment: Theory, research, and clinical applications* (2nd ed., pp. 295–316). New York: Guilford Press.

Belsky, J., Houts, R. M., & Fearon, R. M. P. (2010). Infant attachment security and the timing of puberty: Testing an evolutionary hypothesis. *Psychological Science, 21,* 1195–1201.

Bender, B. (2009, May 20). Continued discharges anger "Don't Ask, Don't Tell" critics: Gay-rights groups urge reversal now. *Boston Globe.* Retrieved from http://www.boston.com/news/nation/washington/articles/2009/05/20/continued_discharges_anger_dont_ask_dont_tell_critics.

Benjamin, D., & Shapiro, J. M. (2009). Thin-slice forecasts of gubernatorial elections. *Review of Economics and Statistics, 91,* 523–536.

Benoit, D., & Parker, K. C. H. (1994). Stability and transmission of attachment across three generations. *Child Development, 65,* 1444–1456.

Berezow, A. B. (2012, July 13). Why psychology isn't science. *Los Angeles Times.* Retrieved from http://www.latimes.com/news/opinion/opinion-la/la-ol-blow back-pscyhology-science-20120713,0,1641705.story.

Berlin, L. J., Zeanah, C. H., & Lieberman, A. F. (2008). Prevention and intervention programs for supporting early attachment security. In J. Cassidy & P. R. Shaver (Eds.), *Handbook of attachment: Theory, research, and clinical applications* (2nd ed., pp. 745–761). New York: Guilford Press.

Bernieri, F. J., Gillis, J. S., Davis, J. M., & Grahe, J. E. (1996). Dyad rapport and the accuracy of its judgment across situations: A lens model analysis. *Journal of Personality and Social Psychology, 71,* 110–129.

Berry, D. S. (1991). Accuracy in social perception: Contributions of facial and vocal information. *Journal of Personality and Social Psychology, 61,* 298–307.

Berry, D. S., & Brownlow, S. (1989). Were the physiognomists right? Personality correlates of facial babyishness. *Personality and Social Psychology Bulletin, 15,* 266–279.

Berry, D. S., & Landry, J. C. (1997). Facial maturity and daily social interaction. *Journal of Personality and Social Psychology, 72,* 570–580.

Bipartisan Policy Center. (2012, November 8). 2012 Voter turnout. Retrieved from http://bipartisanpolicy.org/library/report/2012-voter-turnout.

Blair, I. V., Judd, C. M., & Chapleau, K. M. (2004). The influence of Afrocentric facial features in criminal sentencing. *Psychological Science, 15,* 674–679.

Bloom, A. (1991). *The Republic of Plato: Translated, with notes and an interpretive essay.* New York: Basic Books.

Blount, K., & Hertenstein, M. J. (2006). Attachment. In N. Salkind (Ed.), *Encyclopedia of human development* (Vol. 1, pp. 126–133). Thousand Oaks, CA: Sage.

Bogg, T., & Roberts, B. W. (2004). Conscientiousness and health-related behaviors: A meta-analysis of the leading behavioral contributors to morality. *Psychological Bulletin, 130,* 887–919.

Bohr, N. (n.d.). Niels Bohr quotes. Goodreads. Retrieved from http://www.good reads.com/author/quotes/821936.Niels_Bohr.

Bond, C. F., Jr., & DePaulo, B. M. (2006). Accuracy of deception judgments. *Personality and Social Psychology Review, 10,* 214–234.

Bond, C. F., Jr., & DePaulo, B. M. (2008a). Individual differences in judging deception: Accuracy and bias. *Psychological Bulletin, 134,* 477–492.

Bond, C. F., Jr., & DePaulo, B. M. (2008b). Individual differences in judging deception: Reply to O'Sullivan (2008) and Pigott and Wu (2008). *Psychological Bulletin, 134,* 501–503.

Bond, C. F., Jr., & Uysal, A. (2007). On lie detection "wizards." *Law and Human Behavior, 31,* 109–115.

Bond, G. D. (2008). Deception detection expertise. *Law and Human Behavior, 32,* 339–351.

Boothroyd, L. G., Jones, B. C., Burt, D. M., & Perrett, D. I. (2007). Partner characteristics associated with masculinity, health, and maturity in male faces. *Personality and Individual Differences, 43,* 1161–1173.

Borkenau, P., Brecke, S., Möttig, C., & Paelecke, M. (2009). Extraversion is accurately perceived after a 50-ms exposure to a face. *Journal of Research in Personality, 43,* 703–706.

Borkenau, P., & Liebler, A. (1992). Trait inferences: Sources of validity at zero acquaintance. *Journal of Personality and Social Psychology, 62,* 645–657.

Borkenau, P., & Liebler, A. (1993). Convergence of stranger ratings of personality and intelligence with self-ratings, partner ratings, and measured intelligence. *Journal of Personality and Social Psychology, 65,* 546–553.

Borkenau, P., & Liebler, A. (1995). Observable attributes as manifestations and cues of personality and intelligence. *Journal of Personality, 63,* 1–25.

Borkenau, P., Mauer, N., Riemann, R., Spinath, F. M., & Angleitner, A. (2004). Thin slices of behavior as cues of personality and intelligence. *Journal of Personality and Social Psychology, 86,* 599–614.

Bowlby, J. (1958). The nature of a child's tie to his mother. *International Journal of Psychoanalysis, 39,* 350–373.

Bowlby, J. (1969). *Attachment and loss, vol. 1, Attachment.* New York: Basic Books.

Bowlby, J. (1973). *Attachment and loss, vol. 2, Separation: Anxiety and anger.* New York: Basic Books.

Bowlby, J. (1980). *Attachment and loss, vol. 3, Loss, sadness, and depression.* New York: Basic Books.

Brafman, O., & Brafman, R. (2008). *Sway: The irresistible pull of irrational behavior.* New York: Doubleday.

Bretherton, I. (1992). The origins of attachment theory: John Bowlby and Mary Ainsworth. *Developmental Psychology, 28,* 759–775.

Brewer, C. L. (1990). Heredity quotes, quotations, and sayings. World of Quotes. Retrieved from http://www.worldofquotes.com/topic/heredity/index.html.

Brockman, J. (2004, April 14). The mathematics of love: A talk with John Gottman. *Edge.* Retrieved from http://edge.org/3rd_culture/gottman05/gottman05 _index.html.

Brooks, D. (2011, January 17). Social animal: How the new sciences of human nature can help make sense of a life. *New Yorker.* Retrieved from http://www .newyorker.com/reporting/2011/01/17/110117fa_fact_brooks.

Brooks, D. (2012, April 30). Warfare or courtship in 2012? *New York Times.* Retrieved from http://www.nytimes.com/2012/05/01/opinion/brooks-warfare -or-courtship-in-2012.html.

Brosig, J. (2002). Identifying cooperative behavior: Some experimental results in a prisoner's dilemma game. *Journal of Economic Behavior and Organization, 47,* 275–290.

Bubic, A., Yves von Cramon, D., & Schubotz, R. I. (2010). Prediction, cognition and the brain. *Frontiers in Human Neuroscience, 4,* 1–15.

Buckley, F., Collins, N., & Reidy, T. (2007). Ballot paper photographs and low-information elections in Ireland. *Politics, 27,* 174–181.

Buehler, R., Griffin, D., & Ross, M. (1994). Exploring the "planning fallacy": Why people underestimate their task completion times. *Journal of Personality and Social Psychology, 67,* 366–381.

Buehlman, K. T., Gottman, J. M., & Katz, L. F. (1992). How a couple views their past predicts their future: Predicting divorce from an oral history interview. *Journal of Family Psychology, 5,* 295–318.

Bumiller, E. (2011, July 22). Obama ends "Don't Ask, Don't Tell" policy. *New York Times.* Retrieved from http://www.nytimes.com/2011/07/23/us/23military .html?_r=1.

Bureau of Labor Statistics. (2011, December 2). Charts from the American time use survey. Retrieved from http://www.bls.gov/tus/charts.

Business Pundit. (2009). The 25 worst business failures in history. Retrieved from http://www.businesspundit.com/the-25-worst-business-failures-in-history.

Buss, D. M. (1994). The strategies of human mating. *American Scientist, 82,* 238–249.

Buss, D. M. (2003). *The evolution of desire: Strategies of human mating* (4th ed.). New York: Basic Books.

Buss, D. M. (2011). *Evolutionary psychology: The new science of the mind* (4th ed.). Boston, MA: Allyn & Bacon.

Buss, K. A., Schumacher, J. R. M., Dolski, I., Kalin, N. H., Goldsmith, H. H., & Davidson, R. J. (2003). Right frontal brain activity, cortisol, and withdrawal behavior in 6-month-old infants. *Behavioral Neuroscience, 117,* 11–20.

Carlson, E. A. (1998). A prospective longitudinal study of attachment disorganization/disorientation. *Child Development, 69,* 1107–1128.

Carlson, V., Cicchetti, D., Barnett, D., & Braunwald, K. (1989). Disorganized/disoriented attachment relationships in maltreated infants. *Developmental Psychology, 25,* 525–531.

Carnegie, A. (n.d.). Andrew Carnegie quotes. Brainy Quote. Retrieved from http://www.brainyquote.com/quotes/authors/a/andrew_carnegie.html.

Carré, J. M., & McCormick, C. M. (2008). In your face: Facial metrics predict aggressive behaviour in the laboratory and in varsity and professional hockey players. *Proceedings of the Royal Society B, 275,* 2651–2656.

Carré, J. M., McCormick, C. M., & Mondloch, C. J. (2009). Facial structure is a reliable cue of aggressive behavior. *Psychological Science, 20,* 1194–1198.

Carré, J. M., Morrissey, M. D., Mondloch, C. J., & McCormick, C. M. (2010). Estimating aggression from emotionally neutral faces: Which facial cues are diagnostic? *Perception, 39,* 356–377.

Carrère, S., & Gottman, J. M. (1999). Predicting divorce among newlyweds from the first three minutes of a marital conflict discussion. *Family Process, 38,* 293–301.

Carroll, J. (2009, March 17). Gaydar revisited. *San Francisco Chronicle.* Retrieved from http://www.sfgate.com/entertainment/article/Gaydar-revisited-3168302.php.

Cartwright, J. (2008). *Evolution and human behavior: Darwinian perspectives on human nature* (2nd ed.). Cambridge, MA: MIT Press.

Cassidy, J. (2008). The nature of the child's ties. In J. Cassidy & P. R. Shaver (Eds.), *Handbook of attachment: Theory, research, and clinical applications* (2nd ed., pp. 3–22). New York: Guilford Press.

Center for Responsive Politics. (2011, May 20). Price of admission. Retrieved from http://www.opensecrets.org/bigpicture/stats.php?cycle=2010.

Chabris, C., & Simons, D. (2009). *The invisible gorilla: How our intuitions deceive us.* New York: Broadway Paperbacks.

Chandra, A., Mosher, W. D., & Copen, C. (2011, March 3). Sexual behavior, sexual attraction, and sexual identity in the United States: Data from the 2006–2008 National Survey of Family Growth. *National Health Statistics Reports 36.* Centers for Disease Control and Prevention. Retrieved from http://www.cdc.gov/nchs/data/nhsr/nhsr036.pdf.

Chandra, S., & Matthews, S. (2010, October 3). Falling wages threatening US as consumers may cut spending. *Businessweek*. Retrieved from http://www .businessweek.com/news/2011-10-03/falling-wages-threatening-u-s-as-consumers-may-cut-spending.html.

Chen, X., Chen, H., Li, D., & Wang, L. (2009). Early childhood behavioral inhibition and social and school adjustment in Chinese children: A 5-year longitudinal study. *Child Development, 80*, 1692–1704.

Cicchetti, D., & Rogosch, F. A. (1996). Equifinality and multifinality in developmental psychopathology. *Development and Psychopathology, 8*, 597–600.

Clark, A. (in press). Whatever next? Predictive brains, situated agents, and the future of cognitive science. *Behavioral and Brain Sciences*.

Clayson, D. E. (2009). Student evaluations of teaching: Are they related to what students learn? A meta-analysis and review of the literature. *Journal of Marketing Education, 31*, 16–30.

Collins, M. A., & Zebrowitz, L. A. (1995). The contributions of appearance to occupational outcomes in civilian and military settings. *Journal of Applied Social Psychology, 25*, 129–163.

Connor, S. (2011, July 6). The bare-faced truth about big fat liars. *Independent*. Retrieved from http://www.independent.co.uk/news/science/the-barefaced -truth-about-big-fat-liars-2307552.html.

Considine, A. (2011, October 14). Coming out to the world on the web. *New York Times*. Retrieved from http://www.nytimes.com/2011/10/16/fashion /after-dont-ask-dont-tell-coming-out-on-the-web.html?ref=dontaskdonttell.

Copeland, W., Shanahan, L., Miller, S., Costello, E. J., Angold, A., & Maughan, B. (2010). Outcomes of early pubertal timing in young women: A prospective population-based study. *American Journal of Psychiatry, 167*, 1218–1225.

Craig, S. C., & Martinez, M. D. (2010). Voter competence. In S. C. Craig & D. B. Hill (Eds.), *The electoral challenge: Theory meets practice* (2nd ed., pp. 62–90). Washington, DC: CQ Press.

CXO Advisory Group. (2009, June 15). Jim Cramer deconstructed. Retrieved from http://www.cxoadvisory.com/2809/individual-gurus/jim-cramer.

CXO Advisory Group. (2013, March 5). Guru grades. Retrieved from http://www .cxoadvisory.com/gurus.

Cyr, C., Euser, E. M., Bakermans-Kranenburg, M. J., & van IJzendoorn, M. H. (2010). Attachment security and disorganization in maltreating and high-risk families: A series of meta-analyses. *Development and Psychopathology, 22*, 87–108.

Dallek, R. (2002). The medical ordeals of JFK. *Atlantic Monthly*. Retrieved from http://www.theatlantic.com/past/docs/issues/2002/12/dallek.htm.

Darwin, C. R. (1950). *The voyage of the Beagle*. London: J. M. Dent and Sons, Ltd. (Original work published in 1906).

Darwin, C. R. (1958). The autobiography. In N. Barlow (Ed.), *The autobiography of Charles Darwin*. London: Collins Clear-Type Press.

Davis, H. (2009). *Caveman logic: The persistence of primitive thinking in a modern world*. Amherst, NY: Prometheus Books.

Dawkins, R. (1976). *The selfish gene*. Oxford: Oxford University Press.

Dawson, G., & Burner, K. (2011). Behavioral interventions in children and adolescents with autism spectrum disorder: A review of recent findings. *Current Opinion in Pediatrics, 23,* 616–620.

DeKlyen, M., & Greenberg, M. T. (2008). Attachment and psychopathology in childhood. In J. Cassidy & P. R. Shaver (Eds.), *Handbook of attachment: Theory, research, and clinical applications* (2nd ed., pp. 637–665). New York: Guilford Press.

Dembosky, A. (2010, November 1). At the age of peekaboo, in therapy to fight autism. *New York Times.* Retrieved from http://www.nytimes.com/2010/11/02/health/02autism.html.

DePaulo, B. M., Kashy, D. A., Kirkendol, S. E., Wyer, M. M., & Epstein, J. A. (1996). Lying in everyday life. *Journal of Personality and Social Psychology, 70,* 979–995.

DePaulo, B. M., Lindsay, J. J., Malone, B. E., Muhlenbruck, L., Charlton, K., & Cooper, H. (2003). Cues to deception. *Psychological Bulletin, 129,* 74–118.

Ding, J. Y. C., & Rule, N. O. (2012). Gay, straight, or somewhere in between: Accuracy and bias in the perception of bisexual faces. *Journal of Nonverbal Behavior, 36,* 165–176.

Dittmar, H., Halliwell, E., & Ive, S. (2006). Does Barbie make girls want to be thin? The effect of experimental exposure to images of dolls on the body image of 5- to 8-year-old girls. *Developmental Psychology, 42,* 283–292.

Dobrova-Krol, N. A., Bakermans-Kranenburg, M. J., van IJzendoorn, M. H., & Juffer, F. (2010). The importance of quality of care: Effects of perinatal HIV infection and early institutional rearing on preschoolers attachment and indiscriminate friendliness. *Journal of Child Psychology and Psychiatry, 51,* 1368–1376.

Downs, A. (1957). *An economic theory of democracy.* New York: Harper & Row.

Doyle, A. C. (1927). The adventure of the blanched soldier. *The case-book of Sherlock Holmes.* London: Stratus Books.

Druckman, J. N. (2003). The power of television images: The first Kennedy-Nixon debate revisited. *Journal of Politics, 65,* 559–571.

Eberhardt, J. L., Davies, P. G., Purdie-Vaughns, V. J., & Johnson, S. L. (2006). Looking deathworthy: Perceived stereotypicality of black defendants predicts capital-sentencing outcomes. *Psychological Science, 17,* 383–386.

Einstein, A. (1916). Die grundlage der allgemeinen relativitätstheorie [The foundation of the general theory of relativity]. *Annalen der Physik, 49,* 769–822.

Ekman, P. (2007). *Emotions revealed: Recognizing faces and feelings to improve communication and emotional life.* New York: St. Martin's Press.

Ekman, P. (2009). *Telling lies: Clues to deceit in the marketplace, politics, and marriage.* New York: W. W. Norton (Original work published in 1985).

Ekman, P., Hager, J. C., & Friesen, W. V. (1981). The symmetry of emotional and deliberate facial actions. *Psychophysiology, 18,* 101–106.

Ekman, P., & O'Sullivan, M. (1991). Who can catch a liar? *American Psychologist, 46,* 913–920.

Ekman, P., O'Sullivan, M., & Frank, M. G. (1999). A few can catch a liar. *Psychological Science, 10,* 263–266.

Ellen. (1998, January 17). The puppy episode. TVshows.de. Retrieved from http://www.tvshows.de/ellen/deutsch/puppyepisode.html.

Elwood, Z. (2012). *Reading poker tells*. Portland, OR: Via Regia.

Englund, M. M., Levy, A. K., Hyson, D. M., & Sroufe, L. A. (2000). Adolescent social competence: Effectiveness in a group setting. *Child Development, 71,* 1049–1060.

Federal Election Commission. (2008). 2000 official presidential general election results. Retrieved from http://www.fec.gov/pubrec/2000presgeresults.htm.

Fetchenhauer, D., Groothuis, T., & Pradel, J. (2010). Not only states but traits—humans can identify permanent altruistic dispositions in 20 seconds. *Evolution and Human Behavior, 31,* 80–86.

Field, T. (2007). *The amazing infant*. Malden: Blackwell Publishing.

Flom, E. L. (n.d.). Edward L. Flom quotation details. Quotations Page. Retrieved from http://www.quotationspage.com/quote/40118.html.

Fonagy, P., Steele, H., & Steele, M. (1991). Maternal representations of attachment during pregnancy predict the organization of infant-mother attachment at one year of age. *Child Development, 62,* 891–905.

Fox, N. A., Henderson, H. A., Marshall, P. J., Nichols, K. E., & Ghera, M. M. (2005). Behavioral inhibition: Linking biology and behavior within a developmental framework. *Annual Review of Psychology, 56,* 235–262.

Fraley, R. C. (2002). Attachment stability from infancy to adulthood: Meta-analysis and dynamic modeling of developmental mechanisms. *Personality and Social Psychology Review, 6,* 123–151.

Frank, M. G. (2009). Thoughts, feelings, and deception. In B. Harrington (Ed.), *Deception: From ancient empires to Internet dating* (pp. 55–73). Stanford, CA: Stanford University Press.

Frank, M. G., & Ekman, P. (2004). Nonverbal detection of deception in forensic contexts. In W. T. O'Donohue & E. R. Levensky (Eds.), *Handbook of forensic psychology: Resource for mental health and legal professionals* (pp. 635–653). New York: Elsevier Science.

Frank, M. G., & Feeley, T. H. (2003). To catch a liar: Challenges for research in lie detection training. *Journal of Applied Communication Research, 31,* 58–75.

Frank, M. G., Menasco, M. A., & O'Sullivan, M. (2010). Human behavior and deception detection. In J. C. Voeller (Ed.), *Wiley Handbook of science and technology for homeland security* (Vol. 3, pp. 1455–1465). New York: John Wiley.

Frank, M. G., & Svetieva, E. (2013). Deception. In D. Matsumoto, M. G. Frank & H. S. Hwang (Eds.), *Nonverbal communication: Science and applications* (pp. 121–143). Thousand Oaks, CA: Sage.

Frank, M. G., Yarbrough, J. D., & Ekman, P. (2006). Investigative interviewing and the detection of deception. In T. Williamson (Ed.), *Investigative interviewing: Rights, research, regulation* (pp. 229–255). Devon, UK: Willan Publishing.

Frank, R. H. (1988). *Passions within reason: The strategic role of the emotions*. New York: W. W. Norton.

Frank, R. H. (2008). On the evolution of moral sentiments. In C. Crawford & D. Krebs (Eds.), *Foundations of evolutionary psychology* (pp. 371–379). New York: Taylor & Francis Group/Lawrence Erlbaum Associates.

Frank, R. H., Gilovich, T., & Regan, D. T. (1993). The evolution of one-shot cooperation: An experiment. *Ethology and Sociobiology, 14,* 247–256.

Freeman, J. B., Johnson, K. L., Ambady, N., & Rule, N. O. (2010). Sexual orientation perception involves gendered facial cues. *Personality and Social Psychology Bulletin, 36,* 1318–1331.

French proverb. (n.d.). Wise Old Sayings. Retrieved from http://www.wiseold sayings.com/wosdirectoryw.htm.

Friedman, H. S., & Martin, L. R. (2011). *The longevity project: Surprising discoveries for health and long life from the landmark eight-decade study.* New York: Hudson Street Press.

Friston, K. (2010). The free-energy principle: A unified brain theory? *Nature Reviews: Neuroscience, 11,* 127–138.

Gallace, A., & Spence, C. (2010). The science of interpersonal touch: An overview. *Neuroscience and Biobehavioral Reviews, 34,* 246–259.

Gallup, G. G., & Frederick, D. A. (2010). The science of sex appeal: An evolutionary perspective. *Review of General Psychology, 14,* 240–250.

Galton, F. (1869). *Hereditary genius: An inquiry into its laws and consequences.* London: Macmillan.

Galton, F. (1904). Eugenics: Its definition, scope, and aims. *American Journal of Sociology, 10,* 1–6.

Gangestad, S. W., & Thornhill, R. (1997). Human sexual selection and developmental stability. In J. A. Simpson & D. T. Kenrick (Eds.), *Evolutionary social psychology* (pp. 169–196). Hillsdale, NJ: Lawrence Erlbaum Associates, Inc.

Gazzaniga, M., Heatherton, T., & Halpern, D. (2011). *Psychological science* (4th ed.). New York: W. W. Norton.

Germond, J. W., & Witocover, J. (1979). Presidential debates: An overview. In A. Ranney (Ed.), *The past and future of presidential debates* (pp. 191–201). Washington, DC: American Enterprise Institute for Public Policy and Research.

Gigerenzer, G. (2007). *Gut feelings: The intelligence of the unconscious.* London: Penguin Books.

Gilbert, D. (2006). *Stumbling on happiness.* New York: Knopf.

Gillis, J. S. (1982). *Too tall, too small.* Champaign, IL: Institute for Personality and Ability Testing.

Gladstone, B. (2009, January 23). The face never lies: Transcript. On the Media. Retrieved from http://www.onthemedia.org/2009/jan/23/the-face-never-lies /transcript.

Gladwell, M. (2005). *Blink: The power of thinking without thinking.* New York: Little, Brown and Company.

Global Deception Team. (2006). A world of lies. *Journal of Cross-Cultural Psychology, 37,* 60–74.

Godwin, G. (n.d.). Quotations about teachers. Quote Garden. Retrieved from http://www.quotegarden.com/teachers.html.

Goldstein, B. E. (2008). *Cognitive psychology: Connecting mind, research, and everyday experience* (2nd ed.). Belmont, CA: Wadsworth.

Gopnik, A. (2009). *The philosophical baby: What children's minds tell us about truth, love, and the meaning of life.* New York: Farrar, Straus, and Giroux.

Gopnik, A., Meltzoff, A. N., & Kuhl, P. K (1999). *The scientist in the crib: What early learning tells us about the mind.* New York: HarperCollins.

Gosling, S. (2008). *Snoop: What your stuff says about you.* New York: Basic Books.

Gottman, J. M. (1994). *What predicts divorce? The relationship between marital processes and marital outcomes.* Hillsdale, NJ: Lawrence Erlbaum Associates.

Gottman, J. M., Coan, J., Carrere, S., & Swanson, C. (1998). Predicting marital happiness and stability from newlywed interactions. *Journal of Marriage and the Family, 60,* 5–22.

Gottman, J. M., & Krokoff, L. J. (1989). Marital interaction and satisfaction: A longitudinal view. *Journal of Consulting and Clinical Psychology, 57,* 47–52.

Gottman, J. M., & Levenson, R. W. (1992). Marital processes predictive of later dissolution: Behavior, physiology, and health. *Journal of Personality and Social Psychology, 63,* 221–233.

Gottman, J. M., & Levenson, R. W. (1999). What predicts change in marital interaction over time? A study of alternative medicine. *Family Process, 38,* 143–158.

Gottman, J. M., & Levenson, R. W. (2000). The timing of divorce: Predicting when a couple will divorce over a 14-year period. *Journal of Marriage and the Family, 62,* 737–745.

Gottman, J. M., Murray, J. D., Swanson, C. C., Tyson, R., & Swanson, K. R. (2002). *The mathematics of marriage: Dynamic nonlinear models.* Cambridge, MA: MIT Press.

Grammer, K., & Thornhill, R. (1994). Human (Homo sapiens) facial attractiveness and sexual selection: The role of symmetry and averageness. *Journal of Comparative Psychology, 108,* 233–242.

Gray, H. M. (2008). To what extent, and under what conditions, are first impressions valid? In N. Ambady & J. J. Skowronski (Eds.), *First impressions* (pp. 106–128). New York: Guilford Press.

Gray, P. (2011). *Psychology* (6th ed.). New York: Worth.

Greenberg, M. T., Speltz, M. L., & DeKlyen, M. (1993). The role of attachment in the early development of disruptive behavior problems. *Development and Psychopathology, 5,* 191–213.

Greenwald, A. G., & Banaji, M. R. (1995). Implicit social cognition: Attitudes, self-esteem, and stereotypes. *Psychological Review, 102,* 4–27.

Gregory, S. W., Jr., & Gallagher, T. J. (2002). Spectral analysis of candidates' nonverbal vocal communication: Predicting US presidential election outcomes. *Social Psychology Quarterly, 65,* 298–308.

Haidt, J. (2006). *The happiness hypothesis: Finding modern truth in ancient wisdom.* New York: Basic Books.

Hallinan, J. T. (2009). *Why we make mistakes: How we look without seeing, forget things in seconds, and are all pretty sure we are way above average.* New York: Broadway Books.

Halpern, P. (2000). *The pursuit of destiny: A history of prediction.* New York: Perseus Publishers.

Happé, F., Ronald, A., & Plomin, R. (2006). Time to give up on a single explanation for autism. *Nature Neuroscience, 9,* 1218–1220.

Harari, D., Bakermans-Kranenburg, M. J., & van IJzendoorn, M. J. (2007). Attachment, disorganization, and dissociation. In E. Vermetten, M. Dorahy &

D. Spiegel (Eds.), *Traumatic dissociation: Neurobiology and treatment* (pp. 31–54). Arlington, VA: American Psychiatric Publishing, Inc.

Harker, L., & Keltner, D. (2001). Expressions of positive emotion in women's college yearbook pictures and their relationship to personality and life outcomes across adulthood. *Journal of Personality and Social Psychology, 80,* 112–124.

Harlow, H. F. (1958). The nature of love. *American Psychologist, 13,* 673–685.

Harlow, H. F., & Harlow, M. K. (1966). Learning to love. *American Scientist, 54,* 244–272.

Harlow, H. F., & Suomi, S. J. (1970). Nature of love: Simplified. *American Psychologist, 25,* 161–168.

Harlow, H. F., & Zimmermann, R. R. (1959). Affectional responses in the infant monkey. *Science, 130,* 421–432.

Hartwig, M., & Bond, C. F., Jr. (2011). Why do lie-catchers fail? A lens model meta-analysis of human lie judgments. *Psychological Bulletin, 137,* 643–659.

Haselhuhn, M. P., & Wong, E. M. (2011). Bad to the bone: Facial structure predicts unethical behavior. *Proceedings of the Royal Society B, 279,* 571–576.

Haselton, M. G., & Funder, D. C. (2006). The evolution of accuracy and bias in social judgment. In M. Schaller, J. A. Simpson & D. T. Kenrick (Eds.), *Evolution and social psychology* (pp. 15–37). New York: Psychology Press.

Haub, C. (2011, October). How many people have ever lived on earth? Population Reference Bureau. Retrieved from http://www.prb.org/Articles/2002/HowManyPeopleHaveEverLivedonEarth.aspx.

Hawkins, J., & Blakeslee, S. (2004). *On intelligence.* New York: Holt.

Hayes, D. (2010). Trait voting in US senate elections. *American Politics Research, 38,* 1102–1129.

Hehman, E., Graber, E. C., Hoffman, L. H., & Gaertner, S. L. (2012). Warmth and competence: A content analysis of photographs depicting American presidents. *Psychology of Popular Media Culture, 1,* 46–52.

Helfinstein, S. M., Fox, N. A., & Pine, D. S. (2011). Approach-withdrawal and the role of the striatum in the temperament of behavioral inhibition. *Developmental Psychology, 48,* 815–826.

Hellweg, S. A., Pfau, M., & Brydon, S. R. (1992). *Televised presidential debates: Advocacy in contemporary America.* New York: Praeger.

Henderson, J. J. A., & Anglin, J. M. (2003). Facial attractiveness predicts longevity. *Evolution and Human Behavior, 24,* 351–356.

Herbenick, D., Reece, M., Schick, V., Sanders, S. A., Dodge, B., & Fortenberry, J. D. (2010). Sexual behaviors, relationships, and perceived health status among adult women in the United States: Results from a national probability sample. *Journal of Sexual Medicine, 7,* 277–290.

Herszenhorn, D. M. (2008, March 19). Estimates of the Iraq War cost were not so close to ballpark. *New York Times.* Retrieved from http://www.nytimes.com/2008/03/19/washington/19cost.html?_r=0.

Hertenstein, M. J. (2002). Touch: Its communicative functions in infancy. *Human Development, 45,* 70–94.

Hertenstein, M. J., Hansel, C. A., Butts, A. M., & Hile, S. N. (2009). Smile intensity in photographs predicts divorce later in life. *Motivation and Emotion, 33,* 99–105.

Hesse, E. (2008). The Adult Attachment Interview: Protocol, method of analysis, and empirical studies. In J. Cassidy & P. R. Shaver (Eds.), *Handbook of attachment: Theory, research, and clinical applications* (2nd ed., pp. 552–598). New York: Guilford Press.

Hesse, E. (2009). The unresolved/disorganized category of the AAI: Related to frightening parental behavior, and to offspring disorganized attachment status. Paper presented at the Adult Attachment and the Adult Attachment Interview Conference, Beverly Hills Country Club, Los Angeles, CA.

Hesse, E., & Main, M. (2000). Disorganized infant, child, and adult attachment: Collapse in behavioral and attentional strategies. *Journal of the American Psychoanalytic Association, 48,* 1097–1127.

Hesse, E., & Main, M. (2006). Frightened, threatening, and dissociative parental behavior in low-risk samples: Description, discussion, and interpretations. *Development and Psychopathology, 18,* 309–343.

Highfield, R. (2009, February). How your looks betray your personality. *New Scientist,* 2695. Retrieved from http://www.newscientist.com/article/mg20126957.300 -how-your-looks-betray-your-personality.html.

Hill, K. (2012, March). Facebook can tell you if a person in worth hiring. *Forbes.* Retrieved from http://www.forbes.com/sites/kashmirhill/2012/03/05/facebook -can-tell-you-if-a-person-is-worth-hiring.

Hirshfeld-Becker, D. R., Micco, J., Henin, A., Bloomfield, A., Biederman, J., & Rosenbaum, J. (2008). Behavioral inhibition. *Depression and Anxiety, 25,* 357–367.

Hollingworth, H. L. (1922). *Judging human character.* New York: D. Appleton and Company.

Holt, J. (2011, November 25). Two brains running. *New York Times.* Retrieved from http://www.nytimes.com/2011/11/27/books/review/thinking-fast-and-slow -by-daniel-kahneman-book-review.html?pagewanted=all.

Hughes, M. E., & Waite, L. J. (2009). Marital biography and health at mid-life. *Journal of Health and Social Behavior 50,* 344–358.

Humintell. (2009). Dr. David Matsumoto explains microexpressions. YouTube. Retrieved from http://www.youtube.com/watch?v=bu3ayOWHX0w.

Humintell. (2010). How to tell a lie with the naked eye. YouTube. Retrieved from http://www.youtube.com/watch?v=zagJayUYqqY.

Hurley, C. M. (2012). Do you see what I see? Learning to detect micro expressions of emotion. *Motivation and Emotion, 36,* 371–381.

Hyde, J. S. (2005). The gender similarities hypothesis. *American Psychologist, 60,* 581–592.

Ifould, R. (2009, March 6). Acting on impulse. *Guardian.* Retrieved from http://www .guardian.co.uk/lifeandstyle/2009/mar/07/first-impressions-snap-decisions -impulse.

IMDB. (n.d.). Weird science (1985). Retrieved from http://www.imdb.com/title/tt 0090305.

Ingersoll, B. (2011). Recent advances in early identification and treatment of autism. *Current Directions in Psychological Science, 20,* 335–339.

Innocence Project. (n.d.). Jerry Watkins. Retrieved from http://www.innocence project.org/Content/Jerry_Watkins.php.

Jasieńska, G., Ziomkiewicz, A., Ellison, P. T., Lipson, S. F., & Thune, I. (2004). Large breasts and narrow waists indicate high reproductive potential in women. *Proceedings: Biological Sciences, 271*, 1213–1217.

Johansen, J. P., Tarpley, J. W., LeDoux, J. E., & Blair, H. T. (2010). Neural substrates for expectation-modulated fear learning in the amygdala and periaqueductal gray. *Nature Neuroscience, 13*, 979–986.

Johnson, K. L., & Ghavami, N. (2011). At the crossroads of conspicuous and concealable: What race categories communicate about sexual orientation. *PLoS ONE, 6*, e18025.

Johnson, K. L., Gill, S., Reichman, V., & Tassinary, L. G. (2007). Swagger, sway, and sexuality: Judging sexual orientation from body motion and morphology. *Journal of Personality and Social Psychology, 93*, 321–334.

Johnson, K. L., & Tassinary, L. G. (2005). Perceiving sex directly and indirectly: Meaning in motion and morphology. *Psychological Science, 16*, 890–897.

Johnston, V. S., Hagel, R., Franklin, M., Fink, B., & Grammer, K. (2001). Male facial attractiveness: Evidence for hormone-mediated adaptive design. *Evolution and Human Behavior, 22*, 251–267.

Jordan-Young, R. M. (2010). *Brainstorm: The flaws in the science of sex differences*. Cambridge, MA: Harvard University Press.

Judge, T. A., & Cable, D. M. (2004). The effect of physical height on workplace success and income: Preliminary test of a theoretical model. *Journal of Applied Psychology, 89*, 428–441.

Kagan, J. (1998). *Three seductive ideas*. Cambridge, MA: Harvard University Press.

Kagan, J. (2010). *The temperamental thread: How genes, culture, time, and luck make us who we are*. Washington, DC: Dana Press.

Kagan, J., & Fox, N. A. (2006). Biology, culture, and temperamental biases. In N. Eisenberg, W. Damon & R. M. Lerner (Eds.), *Handbook of child psychology, vol. 3, Social, emotional, and personality development* (6th ed., pp.167–225). Hoboken, NJ: John Wiley.

Kagan, J., & Snidman, N. (2004). *The long shadow of temperament*. Cambridge, MA: Belknap Press.

Kagan, J., Snidman, N., & Arcus, D. M. (1992). Initial reactions to unfamiliarity. *Current Directions in Psychological Science, 1*, 171–174.

Kagan, J., Snidman, N., Arcus, D., & Reznick, J. S. (1994). *Galen's prophecy: Temperament in human nature*. New York: Basic Books.

Kagan, J., Snidman, N., Kahn, V., & Towsley, S. (2007). The preservation of two infant temperaments into adolescence. *Monographs of the Society for Research in Child Development, 72*, 1–75.

Kahneman, D. (2011). *Thinking, fast and slow*. New York: Farrar, Straus and Giroux.

Kahneman, D., Krueger, A. B., Schkade, D. A., Schwarz, N., & Stone, A. A. (2004). A survey method for characterizing daily life experience: The day reconstruction method. *Science, 306*, 1776–1780.

Kanazawa, S. (2012). *The intelligence paradox: Why the intelligent choice isn't always the smart one*. Hoboken, NJ: John Wiley.

Kantar Media. (2013). Kantar Media reports US advertising expenditures increased 3 percent in 2012. Retrieved from http://kantarmediana.com/intelligence /press/us-advertising-expenditures-increased-3-percent-2012.

Kelley, S., Jr., & Mirer, T. W. (1974). The simple act of voting. *American Political Science Review, 68,* 572–591.

Kenny, D. A., Horner, C., Kashy, D. A., & Chu, L.-C. (1992). Consensus at zero acquaintance: Replication, behavioral cues, and stability. *Journal of Personality and Social Psychology, 62,* 88–97.

Kenny, D. A., & West, T. V. (2008). Zero acquaintance: Definitions, statistical model, findings, and process. In N. Ambady & J. J. Skowronski (Eds.), *First impressions* (pp. 129–146). New York: Guilford Press.

Kenrick, D. T. (2011). *Sex, murder, and the meaning of life: A psychologist investigates how evolution, cognition, and complexity are revolutionizing our view of human nature.* New York: Basic Books.

Kenrick, D. T., Gabrielidis, C., Keefe, R. C., & Cornelius, J. S. (1996). Adolescents' age preferences for dating partners: Support for an evolutionary model of life-history strategies. *Child Development, 67,* 1499–1511.

Kenrick, D. T., Sadalla, E. K., Groth, G., & Trost, M. R. (1990). Evolution, traits, and the stages of human courtship: Qualifying the parental investment model. *Journal of Personality, 58,* 97–116.

Kern, M. L., & Friedman, H. S. (2008). Do conscientious individuals live longer? A quantitative review. *Health Psychology, 27,* 505–512.

King, A., & Leigh, A. (2009). Beautiful politicians. *KYKLOS, 62,* 579–593.

Kirkpatrick, E. M. (1979). Presidential candidate "debates": What can we learn from 1960? In A. Ranney (Ed.), *The past and future of presidential debates* (pp. 1–50). Washington, DC: American Enterprise Institute for Public Policy Research.

Kogan, A., Saslow, L. R., Impett, E. A., Oveis, C., Keltner, D., & Saturn, S. R. (2011). Thin-slicing study of the oxytocin receptor (OXTR) gene and the evaluation and expression of the prosocial disposition. *PNAS Proceedings of the National Academy of Sciences of the United States of America, 108,* 19189–19192.

Kościński, K. (2012). Mere visual experience impacts preference for body shape: Evidence from male competitive swimmers. *Evolution and Human Behavior, 33,* 137–146.

Kosfeld, M., Heinrichs, M., Zak, P. J., Fischbacher, U., & Fehr, E. (2005). Oxytocin increases trust in humans. *Nature, 435,* 673–676.

Kramer, R. S. S., King, J. E., & Ward, R. (2011). Identifying personality from the static, nonexpressive face in humans and chimpanzees: Evidence of a shared system for signaling personality. *Evolution and Human Behavior, 32,* 179–185.

Kraus, M. W., & Keltner, D. (2009). Signs of socioeconomic status: A thin-slicing approach. *Psychological Science, 20,* 99–106.

Kraus, M. W., Piff, P. K., & Keltner, D. (2011). Social class as culture: The convergence of resources and rank in the social realm. *Current Directions in Psychological Science, 20,* 246–250.

Krelster, H. (2004). Face to face: The science of reading faces. Institute of International Studies, University of California, Berkeley. Retrieved from http://globetrotter.berkeley.edu/people4/Ekman/ekman-con1.html.

Kruger, D. J. (2008). Male financial consumption is associated with higher mating intentions and mating success. *Evolutionary Psychology, 6,* 603–612.

Kurzweil, R. (2012). *How to create a mind: The secret of human thought revealed.* New York: Viking.

Kveraga, K., Ghuman, A. S., & Bar, M. (2007). Top-down predictions in the cognitive brain. *Brain and Cognition, 65,* 145–168.

Lamb, M. E. (2005). Attachments, social networks, and developmental contexts. *Human Development, 48,* 108–112.

Langley, W. (2001, January 9). Ladies who lie together . . . *Telegraph.* Retrieved from http://www.telegraph.co.uk/culture/4720951/Ladies-who-lie-together.html.

Langlois, J. H., Ritter, J. M., Casey, R. J., & Sawin, D. B. (1995). Infant attractiveness predicts maternal behaviors and attitudes. *Developmental Psychology, 31,* 464–472.

Lassek, W. D., & Gaulin, S. J. C. (2008). Waist-hip ratio and cognitive ability: Is gluteofemoral fat a privileged store of neurodevelopmental resources? *Evolution and Human Behavior, 29,* 26–34.

Laws, E. L., Apperson, J. M., Buchert, S., & Bregman, N. J. (2010). Student evaluations of instruction: When are enduring first impressions formed? *North American Journal of Psychology, 12,* 81–92.

Lawson, C., Lenz, G. S., Baker, A., & Myers, M. (2010). Looking like a winner: Candidate appearance and electoral success in new democracies. *World Politics, 62,* 561–593.

Lazonick, W. (2011, July 25). The reason CEOs make 350 times more money than their workers—and why that's terrible for the economy. AlterNet. Retrieved from http://www.alternet.org/economy/151767/the_reason_ceos_make_350_times_more_money_than_their_workers_—_and_why_that%27s_terrible_for_the_economy.

Leach, A.-M. (2012). Detecting deception. In B. L. Cutler (Ed.), *Conviction of the innocent: Lessons from psychological research* (pp. 35–52). Washington, DC: American Psychological Association.

Leahey, T. H. (1994). *A history of modern psychology* (2nd ed.). Englewood Cliffs, NJ: Prentice Hall.

LeBlanc, L. A., & Gillis, J. M. (2012). Behavioral interventions for children with autism spectrum disorders. *Pediatric Clinics of North America, 59,* 147–164.

Leip, D. (2012). 1960 presidential general election results. Dave Leip's Atlas of US Presidential Elections. Retrieved from http://uselectionatlas.org/RESULTS/national.php?year=1960.

Lenz, G. S., & Lawson, C. (2011). Looking the part: Television leads less informed citizens to vote based on candidates' appearance. *American Journal of Political Science, 55,* 574–589.

LeVay, S. (2011). *Gay, straight, and the reason why: The science of sexual orientation.* New York: Oxford University Press.

LeVay, S., & Baldwin, J. (2012). *Human sexuality* (4th ed.). Sunderland, MA: Sinauer Associates.

Levesque, M. J., & Kenny, D. A. (1993). Accuracy of behavioral predictions at zero acquaintance: A social relations analysis. *Journal of Personality and Social Psychology, 65,* 1178–1187.

Lewis, M. (1993). The development of deception. In M. Lewis & C. Saarni (Eds.), *Lying and deception in everyday life* (pp. 90–105). New York: Guilford Press.

Lewis, M. (1997). *Altering fate: Why the past does not predict the future.* New York: Guilford Press.

Lewis, M. (2005). The child and its family: The social network model. *Human Development, 48,* 8–27.

Lewis, M., Stanger, C., & Sullivan, M. W. (1989). Deception in 3-year-olds. *Developmental Psychology, 25,* 439–443.

Lilienfeld, S. O. (2012). Public skepticism of psychology: Why many people perceive the study of human behavior as unscientific. *American Psychologist, 67,* 111–129.

Liptak, A. (2008, April 23). Inmate count in US dwarfs other nations'. *New York Times.* Retrieved from http://www.nytimes.com/2008/04/23/us/23prison .html?pagewanted=all.

Little, A. C., Burriss, R. P., Jones, B. C., & Roberts, S. C. (2007). Facial appearance affects voting decisions. *Evolution and Human Behavior, 28,* 18–27.

Little, A. C., Jones, B. C., Burt, D. M., & Perrett, D. I. (2007). Preferences for symmetry in faces change across the menstrual cycle. *Biological Psychology, 76,* 209–216.

Little, A. C., & Perrett, D. I. (2007). Using composite images to assess accuracy in personality attribution to faces. *British Journal of Psychology, 98,* 111–126.

Livingston, R. W., & Pearce, N. A. (2009). The teddy-bear effect: Does having a baby face benefit black chief executive officers? *Psychological Science, 20,* 1229–1236.

Lorenz, K. (1957). The nature of instinct. In C. H. Schiller (Ed.), *Instinctive behavior: The development of a modern concept* (pp. 129–175). New York: International Universities Press.

Loughery, J. (1998). *The other side of silence: Men's lives and gay identities—a twentieth-century history.* New York: Holt.

Love, D. A., & Kotchen, M. J. (2010). Grades, course evaluations, and academic incentives. *Eastern Economic Journal, 36,* 151–163.

Lyons-Ruth, K., Bronfman, E., & Parsons, E. (1999). Maternal frightened, frightening, or atypical behavior and disorganized infant attachment patterns. *Monographs of the Society for Research in Child Development, 64,* 67–96.

Lyons-Ruth, K., Dutra, L., Schuder, M. R., & Bianchi, I. (2006). From infant attachment disorganization to adult dissociation: Relational adaptations or traumatic experiences? *Psychiatric Clinics of North America, 29,* 63–86.

Lyons-Ruth, K., & Jacobvitz, D. (2008). Attachment disorganization: Genetic factors, parenting contexts, and developmental transformation from infancy to adulthood. In J. Cassidy & P. R. Shaver (Eds.), *Handbook of attachment: Theory, research, and clinical applications* (2nd ed. pp. 666–697). New York: Guilford Press.

Main, M. (1990). Parental aversion to infant-initiated contact is correlated with the parent's own rejection during childhood: The effects of experience on signals of security with respect to attachment. In K. E. Barnard & T. B. Brazelton (Eds.), *Touch: The foundation of experience: Full revised and expanded proceedings of Johnson & Johnson Pediatric Round Table X. Clinical infant reports* (pp. 461–495). Madison, CT: International Universities Press.

Main, M., & Hesse, E. (1990). Parents' unresolved traumatic experiences are related to infant disorganized attachment status: Is frightened and/or frightening parental behavior the linking mechanism? In M. T. Greenberg, D. Cicchetti & E. M. Cummings (Eds.), *Attachment in the preschool years: Theory, research, and intervention* (pp. 161–182). Chicago, IL: University of Chicago Press.

Main, M., Hesse, E., & Kaplan, N. (2005). Predictability of attachment behavior and representational processes at 1, 6, and 19 years of age: The Berkeley longitudinal study. In K. E. Grossmann, K. Grossmann & E. Waters (Eds.), *Attachment from infancy to adulthood: The major longitudinal studies* (pp. 245–304). New York: Guilford Press.

Main, M., Kaplan, N., & Cassidy, J. (1985). Security in infancy, childhood, and adulthood: A move to the level of representation. *Monographs of the Society for Research in Child Development, 50*(1–2), 66–104.

Main, M., & Morgan, H. (1996). Disorganization and disorientation in infant strange situation behavior: Phenotypic resemblance to dissociative states. In L. K. Michelson & W. J. Ray (Eds.), *Handbook of dissociation: Theoretical, empirical, and clinical perspectives* (pp. 107–138). New York: Plenum Press.

Main, M., & Solomon, J. (1986). Discovery of an insecure-disorganized/disoriented attachment pattern. In T. B. Brazelton & M. W. Yogman (Eds.), *Affective development in infancy* (pp. 95–124). Norwood, NJ: Ablex Publishing Company.

Main, M., & Solomon, J. (1990). Procedures for identifying infants as disorganized /disoriented during the Ainsworth Strange Situation. In M. T. Greenberg, D. Cicchetti & E. M. Cummings (Eds.), *Attachment in the preschool years: Theory, research, and intervention* (pp. 121–160). Chicago, IL: University of Chicago Press.

Maine, M. (2000). *Body wars: Making peace with women's bodies: An activist's guide.* Carlsbad, CA: Gurze Books.

Malatesta, C. Z., Fiore, M. J., & Messina, J. J. (1987). Affect, personality, and facial expressive characteristics of older people. *Psychology and Aging, 2,* 64–69.

Malkiel, B. G. (2003). *A random walk down Wall Street: The time-tested strategy for successful investing (completely revised and updated).* New York: W. W. Norton.

Marshall, P. J., Reeb, B. C., & Fox, N. A. (2009). Electrophysiological responses to auditory novelty in temperamentally different 9-month-old infants. *Developmental Science, 12,* 568–582.

Matsumoto, D. (2005). Scalar ratings of contempt expressions. *Journal of Nonverbal Behavior, 29,* 91–104.

Matsumoto, D., & Willingham, B. (2006). The thrill of victory and the agony of defeat: Spontaneous expressions of medal winners of the 2004 Athens Olympic games. *Journal of Personality and Social Psychology, 91,* 568–581.

Mattes, K., Spezio, M., Kim, H., Todorov, A., Adolphs, R., & Alvarez, R. M. (2010). Predicting election outcomes from positive and negative trait assessments of candidate images. *Political Psychology, 31,* 41–58.

Maynard, W. B. (2010, September 14). Debating on television: Then and now. *Smithsonian.* Retrieved from http://www.smithsonianmag.com/history-archaeology/Debating-on-Television-Then-and-Now.html.

McDonald, G. (2004). Lying and deceit—the Wizards Project. EurekAlert! Retrieved from http://www.eurekalert.org/pub_releases/2004-10/ama-lad100804.php.

Medin, D. L. (2012). Galton's techniques, not his values, improved science. *Observer, 25,* 4.

Medina, J. (2013, April 30). Jason Collins took personal steps before coming out publicly. *New York Times.* Retrieved from http://www.nytimes.com/2013/05/01/sports/jason-collins-took-personal-steps-before-coming-out-publicly.html?_r=1&.

Medvec, V. H., Madey, S. F., & Gilovich, T. (1995). When less is more: Counterfactual thinking and satisfaction among Olympic medalists. *Journal of Personality and Social Psychology, 69,* 603–610.

Mencken, H. L. (n.d.). H. L. Mencken quotes. Brainy Quote. Retrieved from http://www.brainyquote.com/quotes/quotes/h/hlmencke163179.html.

Mendel, R., Traut-Mattausch, E., Jonas, E., Leucht, S., Kane, J. M., Maino, K., . . . Hamann, J. (2011). Confirmation bias: Why psychiatrists stick to wrong preliminary diagnoses. *Psychological Medicine, 41,* 2651–2659.

Meyer, P. (2010). *Liespotting: Proven techniques to detect deception.* New York: St. Martin's Griffin.

Miller, B. J., & Lundgren, J. D. (2010). An experimental study of the role of weight bias in candidate evaluation. *Obesity, 18,* 712–718.

Miller, Geoffrey. (2000). *The mating mind: How sexual choice shaped the evolution of human nature.* New York: Doubleday.

Miller, Geoffrey. (2009). *Spent: Sex, evolution, and consumer behavior.* New York: Viking.

Miller, Geoffrey. (2012). Galton dissed? *Observer, 25,* 4.

Miller, Greg. (2010). fMRI lie detection fails a legal test. *Science, 328,* 1336–1337.

Miller, Greg. (2012). Stopping Alzheimer's before it starts. *Science, 337,* 790–792.

Minnesota Secretary of State. (2008). 2008 Election results table by precinct. Retrieved from http://www.sos.state.mn.us/index.aspx?page=1405.

Morris, D. (1967). *The naked ape: A zoologist's study of the human animal.* London: Jonathan Cape.

Mueller, U., & Mazur, A. (1996). Facial dominance of West Point cadets as a predictor of later military rank. *Social Forces, 74,* 823–850.

Murphy, N. A. (2007). Appearing smart: The impression management of intelligence, person perception accuracy, and behavior in social interaction. *Personality and Social Psychology Bulletin, 33,* 325–339.

Murphy, N. A., Hall, J. A., & Colvin, C. R. (2003). Accurate intelligence assessments in social interactions: Mediators and gender effects. *Journal of Personality, 71,* 465–493.

Murray, G. R., & Schmitz, J. D. (2011). Caveman politics: Evolutionary leadership preferences and physical stature. *Social Science Quarterly, 92,* 1215–1235.

Myers, D. G. (2000). *The American paradox: Spiritual hunger in an age of plenty.* New Haven, CT: Yale University Press.

Myers, D. G. (2002). *Intuition: Its powers and perils*. New Haven, CT: Yale University Press.

Myers, D. G. (2013). *Psychology* (10th ed.). New York: Worth.

National Center for Health Statistics. (2012). Health, United States, 2011: With special feature on socioeconomic status and health. Centers for Disease Control. Retrieved from http://www.cdc.gov/nchs/fastats/lifexpec.htm.

Naumann, L. P., Vazire, S., Rentfrow, P. J., & Gosling, S. D. (2009). Personality judgments based on physical appearance. *Personality and Social Psychology Bulletin, 35,* 1661–1671.

Naylor, R. W. (2007). Nonverbal cues-based first impressions: Impression formation through exposure to static images. *Market Letters, 18,* 165–179.

Negriff, S., Susman, E. J., & Trickett, P. K. (2011). The developmental pathway from pubertal timing to delinquency and sexual activity from early to late adolescence. *Journal of Youth and Adolescence, 40,* 1343–1356.

Nelson, T. L., Palmer, R. F., Pedersen, N. L., & Miles, T. P. (1999). Psychological and behavioral predictors of body fat distribution: Age and gender effects. *Obesity Research, 7,* 199–207.

New York Times. (1966, August 9). Kansas honors girl who urged Lincoln to grow whiskers. Retrieved from http://select.nytimes.com/gst/abstract.html?res=F40716F73D5D137B93CBA91783D85F428685F9.

New York Times. (1989, February 16). Rock Hudson's lover wins suit. Retrieved from http://www.nytimes.com/1989/02/16/us/rock-hudson-s-lover-wins-suit.html.

Newton, I. (1729). *The mathematical principles of natural philosophy*. London: Benjamin Motte. (Original work published in 1687).

Nir, S. M. (2012, May 16). Rediscovering a shortcut to an hourglass figure. *New York Times.* Retrieved from http://www.nytimes.com/2012/05/16/nyregion/with-fajas-tight-as-corsets-shortcut-to-hourglass-figure-is-rediscovered.html.

Norman, W. T., & Goldberg, L. R. (1966). Raters, ratees, and randomness in personality structure. *Journal of Personality and Social Psychology, 4,* 681–691.

O'Sullivan, M. (2003). The fundamental attribution error in detecting deception: The boy-who-cried-wolf effect. *Personality and Social Psychology Bulletin, 29,* 1316–1327.

O'Sullivan, M. (2007a). The detection of deception by detection "wizards." In B. Cutler (Ed.), *Encyclopedia of Psychology and the Law* (pp. 206–207). Thousand Oaks, CA: Sage.

O'Sullivan, M. (2007b). Unicorns or Tiger Woods: Are lie detection experts myths or rarities? A response to "On lie detection 'wizards'" by Bond and Uysal. *Law and Human Behavior, 31,* 117–123.

O'Sullivan, M. (2008). Home runs and humbugs: Comment on Bond and DePaulo (2008). *Psychological Bulletin, 134,* 493–497.

O'Sullivan, M. (2009a, March 23). Are there any "natural" lie detectors? *Psychology Today.* Retrieved from http://www.psychologytoday.com/blog/deception/200903/are-there-any-natural-lie-detectors.

O'Sullivan, M. (2009b). Why most people parse palters, fibs, lies, whoppers, and other deceptions poorly. In B. Harrington (Ed.), *Deception: From ancient empires to Internet dating* (pp. 74–91). Stanford, CA: Stanford University Press.

O'Sullivan, M., & Ekman, P. (2004). The wizards of deception detection. In P. Granhag & L. Strömwall (Eds.), *The detection of deception in forensic contexts* (pp. 269–286). New York: Cambridge University Press.

O'Sullivan, M., Frank, M. G., Hurley, C. M., & Tiwana, J. (2009). Police lie detection accuracy: The effect of lie scenario. *Law and Human Behavior, 33,* 530–538.

Ogawa, J. R., Sroufe, L. A., Weinfield, N. S., Carlson, E. A., & Egeland, B. (1997). Development and the fragmented self: Longitudinal study of dissociative symptomatology in a nonclinical sample. *Development and Psychopathology, 9,* 855–879.

Olivola, C., & Todorov, A. (2009). The look of a winner: The emerging—and disturbing—science of how candidates' physical appearances influence our choice in leaders. *Scientific American.* Retrieved from http://www.scientificamerican.com/article.cfm?id=the-look-of-a-winner.

Olivola, C. Y., & Todorov, A. (2010). Elected in 100 milliseconds: Appearance-based trait inferences and voting. *Journal of Nonverbal Behavior, 34,* 83–110.

Onion. (2008, September 2). McCain speechwriter trying to write lines that don't lead to creepy smile. Retrieved from http://www.theonion.com/articles/mccain-speechwriter-trying-to-write-lines-that-don,6296/?ref=auto.

Orrell, D. (2007). *The future of everything: The science of prediction.* New York: Thunder's Mouth Press.

Owen, K. (2005, April 25). Overflow crowd welcomes Paul Rusesabagina, hero of *Hotel Rwanda,* to DePauw. DePauw. Retrieved from http://www.depauw.edu/news-media/latest-news/details/15762.

Özener, B. (2012). Facial width-to-height ratio in a Turkish population is not sexually dimorphic and is unrelated to aggressive behavior. *Evolution and Human Behavior, 33,* 169–173.

Papalia, D. E., Feldman, R. D., & Martorell, G. (2012). *Experience human development* (12th ed.). New York: McGraw-Hill.

Papalia, D. E., Olds, S. W., & Feldman, R. D. (2007). *Human development* (10th ed.). New York: McGraw-Hill.

Pasco Fearon, R. M., & Belsky, J. (2011). Infant-mother attachment and the growth of externalizing problems across the primary-school years. *Journal of Child Psychology and Psychiatry, 52,* 782–791.

Pawlowski, B., & Koziel, S. (2002). The impact of traits offered in personal advertisements on response rates. *Evolution and Human Behavior, 23,* 139–149.

Pear, R. (2011, October 9). Recession officially over, US income kept falling. *New York Times.* Retrieved from http://www.nytimes.com/2011/10/10/us/recession-officially-over-us-incomes-kept-falling.html.

Penton-Voak, I. S., Pound, N., Little, A. C., & Perrett, D. I. (2006). Personality judgments from natural and composite facial images: More evidence for a "kernel of truth" in social perception. *Social Cognition, 24,* 607–640.

Pérez-Edgar, K., Roberson-Nay, R., Hardin, M. G., Poeth, K., Guyer, A. E., Nelson, E. E., . . . Ernst, M. (2007). Attention alters neural responses to evocative faces in behaviorally inhibited adolescents. *NeuroImage, 35,* 1538–1546.

Perrett, D. I., May, K. A., & Yoshikawa, S. (1994). Facial shape and judgements of female attractiveness. *Nature, 368,* 239–242.

PEW. (2012). The high cost of corrections in America: Infographic. Public Safety Performance Project. Retrieved from http://www.pewstates.org /research/data-visualizations/the-high-cost-of-corrections-in-america-info graphic-85899397897.

Pierrehumbert, J. B., Bent, T., Munson, B., Bradlow, A. R., & Bailey, J. M. (2004). The influence of sexual orientation on vowel production (L). *Acoustical Society of America Journal, 116,* 1905–1908.

Piff, P. K., Purcell, A., Gruber, J., Hertenstein, M. J., & Keltner, D. (2012). Contact high: Mania proneness and positive perception of emotional touches. *Cognition and Emotion, 26,* 1116–1123.

Pinker, S. (2012). *How the mind works.* New York: W. W. Norton.

Pipher, M. (2009). *Seeking peace: Chronicles of the worst Buddhist in the world.* New York: Riverhead Books.

Platek, S. M., & Singh, D. (2010). Optimal waist-to-hip ratios in women activate neural reward centers in men. *PLoS ONE, 5,* e9042.

Plissner, M. (1999). *The control room: How television calls the shots in presidential elections.* New York: Free Press.

Porter, S., & ten Brinke, L. (2008). Reading between the lies: Identifying concealed and falsified emotions in universal facial expressions. *Psychological Science, 19,* 508–514.

Potok, M. (2010). Anti-gay hate crimes: Doing the math. *Intelligence Report 140.* Southern Poverty Law Center. Retrieved from http://www.splcenter.org/get -informed/intelligence-report/browse-all-issues/2010/winter/anti-gay-hate -crimes-doing-the-math.

Poutvaara, P., Jordahl, H., & Berggren, N. (2009). Faces of politicians: Babyfacedness predicts inferred competence but not electoral success. *Journal of Experimental Social Psychology, 45,* 1132–1135.

Pradel, J., Euler, H. A., & Fetchenhauer, D. (2009). Spotting altruistic dictator game players and mingling with them: The elective assortation of classmates. *Evolution and Human Behavior, 30,* 103–113.

Quattrone, G. A., & Tversky, A. (1988). Contrasting rational and psychological analyses of political choice. *American Political Science Review, 82,* 719–736.

Ranft, A. L., Zinko, R., Ferris, G. R., & Buckley, M. R. (2006). Marketing the image of management: The costs and benefits of CEO reputation. *Organizational Dynamics, 35,* 279–290.

Rasmus, J. (2004). Wages in America: The rich get richer and the rest get less. Kyklos Productions. Retrieved from http://www.kyklosproductions.com/articles /wages.html.

Ray, W. J. (2000). Dissociative identity disorder. In A. E. Kazdin (Ed.), *Encyclopedia of psychology* (Vol. 3, pp. 59–61). Washington, DC: American Psychological Association.

Reichow, B. (2012). Overview of meta-analyses on early intensive behavioral intervention for young children with autism spectrum disorders. *Journal of Autism and Developmental Disorders, 42,* 512–520.

Remedios, J. D., Chasteen, A. L., Rule, N. O., & Plaks, J. E. (2011). Impressions at the intersection of ambiguous and obvious social categories: Does gay + Black = likable? *Journal of Experimental Social Psychology, 47,* 1312–1315.

Renken, B., Egeland, B., Marvinney, D., & Mangelsdorf, S. (1989). Early childhood antecedents of aggression and passive-withdrawal in early elementary school. *Journal of Personality, 57,* 257–281.

Reuter, D. F. (2002). *Gaydar: The ultimate insider guide to the gay sixth sense.* New York: Crown.

Rhodes, G. (2006). The evolutionary psychology of facial beauty. *Annual Review of Psychology, 57,* 199–226.

Rieger, G., Linsenmeier, J. A. W., Gygax, L., Garcia, S., & Bailey, J. M. (2010). Dissecting "gaydar": Accuracy and the role of masculinity-femininity. *Archives of Sexual Behavior, 39,* 124–140.

Riggio, H. R., & Riggio, R. E. (2010). Appearance-based trait inferences and voting: Evolutionary roots and implications for leadership. *Journal of Nonverbal Behavior, 34,* 119–125.

Riggle, E. D., Ottati, V. C., Wyer, R. S., Kuklinski, J., & Schwarz, N. (1992). Bases of political judgments: The role of stereotypic and nonstereotypic information. *Political Behavior, 14,* 67–87.

Rochman, B. (2010, September 17). Moms: Guilty of driving their daughters to early puberty? *Time.* Retrieved from http://healthland.time.com/2010/09/17 /moms-guilty-of-driving-their-daughters-to-early-puberty.

Rodrigues, S. M., Saslow, L. R., Garcia, N., John, O. P., & Keltner, D. (2009). Oxytocin receptor genetic variation relates to empathy and stress reactivity in humans. *Proceedings of the National Academy of Sciences of the United States of America, 106,* 21437–21441.

Roese, N. J., & Vohs, K. D. (2012). Hindsight bias. *Perspectives on Psychological Science, 7,* 411–426.

Rogers, S. J. (2009). What are infant siblings teaching us about autism in infancy? *Autism Research, 2,* 125–137.

Rojstaczer, S., & Healy, C. (2012). Where A is ordinary: The evolution of American college and university grading, 1940–2009. *Teachers College Record, 114,* 1–23.

Romney, L. (2011, July 13). Hate crimes against gay, transgender people rise, report says. *Los Angeles Times.* Retrieved from http://articles.latimes.com/2011 /jul/13/nation/la-na-lgbt-hate-crimes-20110713.

Rose, C. P. (Writer). (2011, November 29). *Charlie Rose: The brain series* [Television broadcast]. New York: PBS.

Rosenberg, S. W., Kahn, S., & Tran, T. (1991). Creating a political image: Shaping appearance and manipulating the vote. *Political Behavior, 13,* 345–367.

Roskin, M. G., Cord, R. L., Medeioros, J. A., & Jones, W. S. (2012). *Political science: An introduction* (12th ed.). Boston, MA: Pearson Longman.

Rule, N. O., & Ambady, N. (2008a). Brief exposures: Male sexual orientation is accurately perceived at 50 ms. *Journal of Experimental Social Psychology, 44*, 1100–1105.

Rule, N. O., & Ambady, N. (2008b). The face of success: Inferences from chief executive officers' appearance predict company profits. *Psychological Science, 19*, 109–111.

Rule, N. O., & Ambady, N. (2008c). *First impressions: Peeking at the neural underpinnings.* New York: Guilford Press.

Rule, N. O., & Ambady, N. (2009). She's got the look: Inferences from female chief executive officers' faces predict their success. *Sex Roles, 61*, 644–652.

Rule, N. O., & Ambady, N. (2011a). Face and fortune: Inferences of personality from managing partners' faces predict their law firms' financial success. *Leadership Quarterly, 22*, 690–696.

Rule, N. O., & Ambady, N. (2011b). Judgments of power from college yearbook photos and later career success. *Social Psychological and Personality Science, 2*, 154–158.

Rule, N. O., Ambady, N., Adams, R. B., Jr., & Macrae, C. N. (2007). Us and them: Memory advantages in perceptually ambiguous groups. *Psychonomic Bulletin and Review, 14*, 687–692.

Rule, N. O., Ambady, N., Adams, R. B., Jr., & Macrae, C. N. (2008). Accuracy and awareness in the perception and categorization of male sexual orientation. *Journal of Personality and Social Psychology, 95*, 1019–1028.

Rule, N. O., Ambady, N., Adams, R. B., Jr., Ozono, H., Nakashima, S., Yoshikawa, S., & Watabe, M. (2010). Polling the face: Prediction and consensus across cultures. *Journal of Personality and Social Psychology, 98*, 1–15.

Rule, N. O., Ambady, N., & Hallett, K. C. (2009). Female sexual orientation is perceived accurately, rapidly, and automatically from the face and its features. *Journal of Experimental Social Psychology, 45*, 1245–1251.

Rule, N. O., Ishii, K., & Ambady, N. (2011). Cross-cultural impressions of leaders' faces: Consensus and predictive validity. *International Journal of Intercultural Relations, 35*, 833–841.

Rule, N. O., Ishii, K., Ambady, N., Rosen, K. S., & Hallett, K. C. (2011). Found in translation: Cross-cultural consensus in the accurate categorization of male sexual orientation. *Personality and Social Psychology Bulletin, 37*, 1499–1507.

Rule, N. O., Moran, J. M., Freeman, J. B., Whitfield-Gabrieli, S., Gabrieli, J. D. E., & Ambady, N. (2011). Face value: Amygdala response reflects the validity of first impressions. *NeuroImage, 54*, 734–741.

Rule, N. O., Rosen, K. S., Slepian, M. L., & Ambady, N. (2011). Mating interest improves women's accuracy in judging male sexual orientation. *Psychological Science, 22*, 881–886.

Santarcangelo, M. (2008). Detecting deception. In D. Canter (Ed.), *Criminal psychology* (pp. 161–175). London: Hodder Education Group.

Schaller, M. (2008). Evolutionary bases of first impressions. In N. Ambady & J. J. Skowronski (Eds.), *First impressions.* New York: Guilford Press.

Schlesinger, S. (2008, September 5). McCain was McCain. *Huffington Post.* Retrieved from http://www.huffingtonpost.com/stephen-schlesinger/mccain-was-mccain_b_124220.html.

Schultz, D. P., & Schultz, S. E. (2004). *A history of modern psychology* (8th ed.). Belmont, CA: Thomson/Wadsworth.

Schwartz, C. E., Kunwar, P. S., Greve, D. N., Moran, L. R., Viner, J. C., Covino, J. M., . . . Wallace, S. R. (2010). Structural differences in adult orbital and ventromedial prefrontal cortex predicted by infant temperament at 4 months of age. *Archives of General Psychiatry, 67,* 78–84.

Schwartz, C. E., Wright, C. I., Shin, L. M., Kagan, J., & Rauch, S. L. (2003). Inhibited and uninhibited infants "grown up": Adult amygdalar response to novelty. *Science, 300,* 1952–1953.

Science Daily. (2003, June 20). Response to new faces varies by temperament, tied to brain activity. Retrieved from http://www.sciencedaily.com/releases/2003/06/030620080750.htm.

Science Daily. (2011, November 15). Is a stranger trustworthy? You'll know in 20 seconds. Retrieved from http://www.sciencedaily.com/releases/2011/11/111115103510.htm.

Seder, J. P., & Oishi, S. (2012). Intensity of smiling in Facebook photos predicts future life satisfaction. *Social Psychological and Personality Science, 3,* 407–413.

Seldin, P. (1999). *Changing practices in evaluating teaching: A practical guide to improved faculty performance and promotion/tenure decisions.* Bolton, MA: Anker Publishing.

Shackelford, T. K., & Larsen, R. J. (1997). Facial asymmetry as an indicator of psychological, emotional, and physiological distress. *Journal of Personality and Social Psychology, 72,* 456–466.

Shakespeare, W. (1922). *As you like it.* J. Samuel Thurber & L. Wetherbee (Eds.). Boston, MA: Allyn & Bacon. (Original work published in 1623).

Shakespeare, W. (1992). *The tragedy of Hamlet, prince of Denmark.* New York: Washington Square Pocket.

Shariff, A. F., & Tracy, J. L. (2011). What are emotion expressions for? *Current Directions in Psychological Science, 20,* 395–399.

Shea, D. M., Connor Green, J., & Smith, C. E. (2011). *Living democracy: National edition 2010 update* (2nd ed.). Boston, MA: Pearson Longman.

Shear, M. D. (2012, March 21). For Romney's trusted adviser, "Etch A Sketch" comment is a rare misstep. *New York Times.* Retrieved from http://www.nytimes.com/2012/03/22/us/politics/etch-a-sketch-remark-a-rare-misstep-for-romney-adviser.html.

Shenkman, R. (2008a, September 7). 5 myths about those civic-minded, deeply informed voters. *Washington Post.* Retrieved from http://www.washingtonpost.com/wp-dyn/content/article/2008/09/05/AR2008090502666.html.

Shenkman, R. (2008b). *Just how stupid are we? Face the truth about the American voter.* New York: Basic Books.

Shermer, M. (2011). *The believing brain: From ghosts and gods to politics and conspiracies—how we construct beliefs and reinforce them as truths.* New York: Holt.

Shields, M. (2010). Two things are important in politics. Creators. Retrieved from http://www.creators.com/opinion/mark-shields/-two-things-are-important -in-politics-quot.html.

Shively, W. P. (2012). *Power and choice: An introduction to political science* (13th ed.). New York: McGraw-Hill.

Shore, Z. (2008). *Blunder: Why smart people make bad decisions.* New York: Bloomsbury.

Short, L. A., Mondloch, C. J., McCormick, C. M., Carré, J. M., Ma, R., Fu, G., & Lee, K. (2012). Detection of propensity for aggression based on facial structure irrespective of face race. *Evolution and Human Behavior, 33,* 121–129.

Silver, N. (2012). *The signal and the noise: Why so many predictions fail—but some don't.* New York: Penguin Press.

Silverman, L. K. (2013). *Giftedness 101.* New York: Springer.

Simpson, J. A., & Belsky, J. (2008). Attachment theory within a modern evolutionary framework. In J. Cassidy & P. R. Shaver (Eds.), *Handbook of attachment: Theory, research, and clinical applications* (2nd ed., pp.131–157). New York: Guilford Press.

Singh, D. (1993). Adaptive significance of female physical attractiveness: Role of waist-to-hip ratio. *Journal of Personality and Social Psychology, 65,* 293–307.

Singh, D., Dixson, B. J., Jessop, T. S., Morgan, B., & Dixson, A. F. (2010). Cross-cultural consensus for waist-hip ratio and women's attractiveness. *Evolution and Human Behavior, 31,* 176–181.

Singh, D., Vidaurri, M., Zambarano, R. J., & Dabbs, J. M., Jr. (1999). Lesbian erotic role identification: Behavioral, morphological, and hormonal correlates. *Journal of Personality and Social Psychology, 76,* 1035–1049.

Slayen, G. (2011, April 8). The scary reality of a real-life Barbie doll. *Huffington Post.* Retrieved from http://www.huffingtonpost.com/galia-slayen/the-scary -reality-of-a-re_b_845239.html.

Slotten, R. A. (2004). *The heretic in Darwin's court: The life of Alfred Russel Wallace.* New York: Columbia University Press.

Smith, D. L. (2005, May 18). Natural born liars. *Scientific American Mind, 16*(2), 16–23. Retrieved from http://www.scientificamerican.com/article .cfm?id=natural-born-liars.

Smith, M. J. L., Perrett, D. I., Jones, B. C., Cornwell, R. E., Moore, F. R., Feinberg, D. R., . . . Hillier, S. G. (2006). Facial appearance is a cue to oestrogen levels in women. *Proceedings of the Royal Society B, 273,* 135–140.

Smith, M. M., Williams, G. C., Powell, L., & Copeland, G. A. (2010). *Campaign finance reform: The political shell game.* Lanham, MD: Lexington Books.

Smyth, R., Jacobs, G., & Rogers, H. (2003). Male voices and perceived sexual orientation: An experimental and theoretical approach. *Language in Society, 32,* 329–350.

Soler, C., Núñez, M., Gutiérrez, R., Núñez, J., Medina, P., Sancho, M., . . . Núñez, A. (2003). Facial attractiveness in men provides clues to semen quality. *Evolution and Human Behavior, 24,* 199–207.

Sommers, P. M. (2002). Is presidential greatness related to height? *College Mathematics Journal, 33,* 14–16.

Sroufe, L. A. (2005). Attachment and development: A prospective, longitudinal study from birth to adulthood. *Attachment and Human Development, 7,* 349–367.

Sroufe, L. A., Egeland, B., Carlson, E. A., & Collins, W. A. (2005). *The development of the person: The Minnesota study of risk and adaptation from birth to adulthood.* New York: Guilford Press.

St. Petersburg—USA Orphanage Research Team. (2008). The effects of early socialemotional and relationship experience on the development of young orphanage children: VIII. Intervention effects on physical growth. *Monographs of the Society for Research in Child Development, 73,* 124–141.

Stanovich, K. E. (2010). *How to think straight about psychology* (9th ed.). Boston, MA: Pearson.

Stanton, F. (2000, September 25). The first debate over presidential debates. *Newsweek, 136,* 11.

Steele, H., Steele, M., & Fonagy, P. (1996). Associations among attachment classifications of mothers, fathers, and their infants. *Child Development, 67,* 541–555.

Steele, V. (2001). *The corset: A cultural history.* New Haven, CT: Yale University Press.

Stern, C., West, T. V., Jost, J. T., & Rule, N. (2012). The politics of gaydar: Ideological differences in the use of gendered cues in categorizing sexual orientation. *Journal of Personality and Social Psychology, 104,* 520–541.

Sternberg, R. J. (2006). *Cognitive psychology* (4th ed.). Belmont, CA: Wadsworth.

Stirrat, M., & Perrett, D. I. (2010). Valid facial cues to cooperation and trust: Male facial width and trustworthiness. *Psychological Science, 21,* 349–354.

Stirrat, M., Stulp, G., & Pollet, T. V. (2012). Male facial width is associated with death by contact violence: Narrow-faced males are more likely to die from contact violence. *Evolution and Human Behavior, 33,* 551–556.

Stoll, C. (1995). *Silicon snake oil: Second thoughts on the information highway.* New York: Doubleday.

Hamptonroads.com. (2008, February 13). Stop that weird smiling! Retrieved from http://hamptonroads.com/2008/02/stop-weird-smiling.

Streeter, L. A., Krauss, R. M., Geller, V., Olson, C., & Apple, W. (1977). Pitch changes during attempted deception. *Journal of Personality and Social Psychology, 35,* 345–350.

Sugiyama, L. S. (2005). Physical attractiveness in adaptationist perspective. In D. M. Buss (Ed.), *The handbook of evolutionary psychology* (pp. 292–343). Hoboken, NJ: John Wiley.

Supreme Court of the United States. (2009). *George W. Bush, et al., petitioners v. Albert Gore, Jr., et al. on writ of certiorari to the Florida Supreme Court.* Florida Supreme Court. Retrieved from http://www.floridasupremecourt.org/pub_info/election/USSCTBushvGore.pdf.

Surowiecki, J. (2004). *The wisdom of crowds: Why the many are smarter than the few and how collective wisdom shapes business, economies, societies and nations.* New York: Doubleday.

Tabak, J. A., & Zayas, V. (2012a). The roles of featural and configural face processing in snap judgments of sexual orientation. *PLoS ONE, 7,* e36671.

Tabak, J. A., & Zayas, V. (2012b, June 1). The science of "gaydar." *New York Times.* Retrieved from http://www.nytimes.com/2012/06/03/opinion/sunday /the-science-of-gaydar.html.

Talbot, M. (1998, May 24). The disconnected; attachment theory: The ultimate experiment. *New York Times.* Retrieved from http://www.nytimes.com/1998/05/24 /magazine/the-disconnected-attachment-theory-the-ultimate-experiment .html?pagewanted=all&src=pm.

Taleb, N. N. (2004). *Fooled by randomness: The hidden role of chance in life and in the markets.* New York: Random House.

Taleb, N. N. (2010). *The black swan: The impact of the highly improbable.* New York: Random House.

Taranto, J. (2005, September 12). How's he doing? *Wall Street Journal.* Retrieved from http://www.jamestaranto.com/average.htm.

Taylor, J. (2011, May 23). Politics: Please fire the pundits! *Psychology Today.* The Power of Prime [blog]. Retrieved from http://www.psychologytoday.com /blog/the-power-prime/201105/politics-please-fire-the-pundits.

Taylor, J. B. (2009, April 30). Paul Ekman. *Time.* Retrieved from http://www.time .com/time/specials/packages/article/0,28804,1894410_1893209_1893475,00 .html.

Temple-Raston, D. (2007). Lies as plain as the nose on your face? National Public Radio. Retrieved from http://www.npr.org/templates/story/story.php?story Id=15791790.

Terrill, M. J. (2012, June 23). Smell our way to love? One matchmaker pairs singles scents. *USA Today.* Retrieved from http://www.usatoday.com/news/health /story/2012-06-23/pheromone-party-dating/55782504/1.

Tetlock, P. E. (2005). *Expert political judgment: How good is it? How can we know?* Princeton, NJ: Princeton University Press.

Thompson, R. A. (2008). Early attachment and later development: Familiar questions, new answers. In J. Cassidy & P. R. Shaver (Eds.), *Handbook of attachment: Theory, research, and clinical applications* (2nd ed., pp. 348–365). New York: Guilford Press.

Thornhill, R., & Gangestad, S. W. (2006). Facial sexual dimorphism, developmental stability, and susceptibility to disease in men and women. *Evolution and Human Behavior, 27,* 131–144.

Thornhill, R., Gangestad, S. W., Miller, R., Scheyd, G., McCollough, J. K., & Franklin, M. (2003). Major histocompatibility complex genes, symmetry, and body scent attractiveness in men and women. *Behavioral Ecology, 14,* 668–678.

Tigue, C. C., Borak, D. J., O'Connor, J. J. M., Schandl, C., & Feinberg, D. R. (2012). Voice pitch influences voting behavior. *Evolution and Human Behavior, 33,* 210–216.

Todorov, A., Mandisodza, A. N., Goren, A., & Hall, C. C. (2005). Inferences of competence from faces predict election outcomes. *Science, 308,* 1623–1626.

Todorov, A., Pakrashi, M., & Oosterhof, N. N. (2009). Evaluating faces on trustworthiness after minimal time exposure. *Social Cognition, 27,* 813–833.

Todorov, A., Said, C. P., Engel, A. D., & Oosterhof, N. N. (2008). Understanding evaluation of faces on social dimensions. *Trends in Cognitive Sciences, 12,* 455–460.

Todorov, A., Said, C. P., & Verosky, S. C. (2011). Personality impressions from facial appearance. In A. J. Calder, G. Rhodes, M. H. Johnson & J. V. Haxby (Eds.), *The Oxford handbook of face perception* (pp. 631–651). Oxford: Oxford University Press.

Tops, M., Wijers, A. A., van Staveren, A. S. J., Bruin, K. J., Den Boer, J. A., Meijman, T. F., & Korf, J. (2005). Acute cortisol administration modulates EEG alpha asymmetry in volunteers: Relevance to depression. *Biological Psychology, 69,* 181–193.

Tosi, H. L., Misangyi, V. F., Fanelli, A., Waldman, D. A., & Yammarino, F. J. (2004). CEO charisma, compensation, and firm performance. *Leadership Quarterly, 15,* 405–420.

Tost, H., Kolachana, B., Hakimi, S., Lemaitre, H., Verchinski, B. A., Mattay, V. S., . . . Meyer-Lindenberg, A. (2010). A common allele in the oxytocin receptor gene (OXTR) impacts prosocial temperament and human hypothalamic-limbic structure and function. *Proceedings of the National Academy of Sciences of the United States of America, 107,* 13936–13941.

Trivers, R. (2011). *The folly of fools: The logic of deceit and self-deception in human life.* New York: Basic Books.

Troy, M., & Sroufe, L. A. (1987). Victimization among preschoolers: Role of attachment relationship history. *Journal of the American Academy of Child and Adolescent Psychiatry, 26,* 166–172.

Trump, F. (1977). *Lincoln's little girl.* Honesdale, PA: Boyds Mills Press.

Twain, M. (1885). *On the decay of the art of lying.* The Literature Network. Retrieved from http://www.online-literature.com/wilde/1320.

United States Government. 10 U. S. C. § 654. Policy concerning homosexuality in the armed forces. Cornell University Law School. Retrieved from http://www.law.cornell.edu/uscode/text/10/654#b.

University of Iowa Tippie College of Business. (2012). Current IEM quotes. Retrieved from http://tippie.uiowa.edu/iem/quotes.cfm.

Valentova, J., Rieger, G., Havlicek, J., Linsenmeier, J. A. W., & Bailey, J. M. (2011). Judgments of sexual orientation and masculinity-femininity based on thin slices of behavior: A cross-cultural comparison. *Archives of Sexual Behavior, 40,* 1145–1152.

Valla, J. M., Ceci, S. J., & Williams, W. M. (2011). The accuracy of inferences about criminality based on facial appearance. *Journal of Social, Evolutionary, and Cultural Psychology, 5,* 66–91.

van den Boom, D. C. (1990). Preventive intervention and the quality of mother-infant interaction and infant exploration in irritable infants. In W. Koops, H. J. G. Soppe, O. C. M. van der Linden, J. Molenaar & J. F. Schroots (Eds.), *Developmental psychology behind the dikes* (pp. 249–270). Delft, Netherlands: Eburon.

van den Boom, D. C. (1994). The influence of temperament and mothering on attachment and exploration: An experimental manipulation of sensitive responsiveness among lower-class mothers with irritable infants. *Child Development, 65,* 1457–1477.

Van Hecke, M. L. (2007). *Blind spots: Why smart people do dumb things*. New York: Prometheus Books.

van Hooff, M. H. A., Voorhorst, F. J., Kaptein, M. B. H., Hirasing, R. A., Koppenaal, C., & Schoemaker, J. (2000). Insulin, androgen, and gonadotropin concentrations, body mass index, and waist-to-hip ratio in the first years after menarche in girls with regular menstrual cycles, irregular menstrual cycles, or oligomenorrhea. *Journal of Clinical Endocrinology and Metabolism, 85,* 1394–1400.

van IJzendoorn, M. H. (1995). Adult attachment representations, parental responsiveness, and infant attachment: A meta-analysis on the predictive validity of the Adult Attachment Interview. *Psychological Bulletin, 117,* 387–403.

van IJzendoorn, M. H., & Bakermans-Kranenburg, M. J. (2009). Attachment security and disorganization in maltreating families and orphanages. In R. E. Tremblay, M. Boivin & R. D. Peters (Eds.), *Encyclopedia on early childhood development* (pp. 1–7). Retrieved from http://www.child-encyclopedia .com/documents/van_IJzendoorn-Bakermans-KranenburgANGxp-Attach ment.pdf.

van IJzendoorn, M. H., & Sagi-Schwartz, A. (2008). Cross-cultural patterns of attachment: Universal and contextual dimensions. In J. Cassidy & P. R. Shaver (Eds.), *Handbook of attachment: Theory, research, and clinical applications* (2nd ed., pp. 880–905). New York: Guilford Press.

van IJzendoorn, M. H., Schuengel, C., & Bakermans-Kranenburg, M. J. (1999). Disorganized attachment in early childhood: Meta-analysis of precursors, concomitants, and sequelae. *Development and Psychopathology, 11,* 225–249.

Van Ryzin, M. J., Carlson, E. A., & Sroufe, L. A. (2011). Attachment discontinuity in a high-risk sample. *Attachment and Human Development, 13,* 381–401.

Vancil, D. L., & Pendell, S. D. (1987). The myth of viewer-listener disagreement in the first Kennedy-Nixon debate. *Central States Speech Journal, 38,* 16–27.

Verdonck, A., Gaethofs, M., Carels, C., & de Zegher, F. (1999). Effect of low-dose testosterone treatment on craniofacial growth in boys with delayed puberty. *European Journal of Orthodontics, 21,* 137–143.

Verplaetse, J., Vanneste, S., & Braeckman, J. (2007). You can judge a book by its cover: The sequel. A kernel of truth in predictive cheating detection. *Evolution and Human Behavior, 28,* 260–271.

Vrij, A. (2004). Guidelines to catch a liar. In P. Granhag & L. Strömwall (Eds.), *The detection of deception in forensic contexts* (pp. 287–314). New York: Cambridge University Press.

Vrij, A. (2008). *Detecting lies and deceit: Pitfalls and opportunities* (2nd ed.). New York: John Wiley.

Vrij, A., Granhag, P. A., & Porter, S. (2010). Pitfalls and opportunities in nonverbal and verbal lie detection. *Psychological Science in the Public Interest, 11,* 89–121.

Walker, C. (1977). Some variations in marital satisfaction. In R. Chester & J. Peel (Eds.), *Equalities and inequalities in family life* (pp. 127–139). London: Academic Press.

Warren, S. L., Huston, L., Egeland, B., & Sroufe, L. A. (1997). Child and adolescent anxiety disorders and early attachment. *Journal of the American Academy of Child and Adolescent Psychiatry, 36,* 637–644.

Wass, P., Waldenström, U., Rössner, S., & Hellberg, D. (1997). An android body fat distribution in females impairs the pregnancy rate of in-vitro fertilization-embryo transfer. *Human Reproduction, 12,* 2057–2060.

Wasserman, G. (2011). *The basics of American politics* (14th ed.). Boston, MA: Pearson Longman.

Wayne, S. J. (2011). *Is this any way to run a democratic election?* Washington, DC: CQ Press.

Weinberg, B. A., Hashimoto, M., & Fleisher, B. M. (2009). Evaluating teaching in higher education. *Journal of Economic Education, 40,* 227–261.

Weinfield, N. S., Sroufe, L. A., Egeland, B., & Carlson, E. (2008). Individual differences in infant-caregiver attachment: Conceptual and empirical aspects of security. In J. Cassidy & P. R. Shaver (Eds.), *Handbook of attachment: Theory, research, and clinical applications* (2nd ed., pp. 78–101). New York: Guilford Press.

Wells, C. (n.d.). Carolyn Wells quotes. Quotations Page. Retrieved from http://www.quotationspage.com/quote/1172.html.

Weston, E. M., Friday, A. E., & Liò, P. (2007). Biometric evidence that sexual selection has shaped the hominin face. *PLoS ONE, 2,* e710.

Wikipedia. (n.d.). Heights of presidents and presidential candidates of the United States. Retrieved from http://en.wikipedia.org/wiki/Heights_of_presidents_and_presidential_candidates_of_the_United_States.

Wilde, O. (1988). *The picture of Dorian Gray.* In D. L. Lawler (Ed.), *The picture of Dorian Gray by Oscar Wilde* (pp. 23). New York: W. W. Norton.

Williams, W. M., & Ceci, S. J. (1997). "How'm I doing?" Problems with student ratings of instructors and courses. *Change, 29,* 12–23.

Wilson, R. (1998). New research casts doubt on value of student evaluations of professors. *Chronicle of Higher Education, 44,* A12–A14.

Wilson, T. D. (2012, July 12). Stop bullying the "soft" sciences. *Los Angeles Times.* Retrieved from http://articles.latimes.com/2012/jul/12/opinion/la-oe-wilson-social-sciences-20120712.

Wittling, W., & Pflüger, M. (1990). Neuroendocrine hemisphere asymmetries: Salivary cortisol secretion during lateralized viewing of emotion-related and neutral films. *Brain and Cognition, 14,* 243–265.

Wolff, J. J., Gu, H., Gerig, G., Elison, J. T., Styner, M., Gouttard, S., . . . IBIS Network. (2012). Differences in white matter fiber tract development present from 6 to 24 months in infants with autism. *American Journal of Psychiatry, 169,* 589–600.

Wong, E. M., Ormiston, M. E., & Haselhuhn, M. P. (2011). A face only an investor could love: CEOs' facial structure predicts their firms' financial performance. *Psychological Science, 22,* 1478–1483.

Woolery, L. M. (2007). Gaydar: A social-cognitive analysis. *Journal of Homosexuality, 53,* 9–17.

World Health Organization. (2008). *Waist circumference and waist-hip ratio: Report of WHO organization consultation.* Geneva: World Health Organization.

Yirmiya, N., & Ozonoff, S. (2007). The very early autism phenotype. *Journal of Autism and Developmental Disorders, 37,* 1–11.

Zaadstra, B. M., Seidell, J. C., Van Noord, P. A. H., Velde, E. R. T., Habbema, J. D. F., Vrieswijk, B., & Karbaat, J. (1993). Fat and female fecundity: Prospective study of effect of body fat distribution on conception rates. *BMJ: British Medical Journal, 306,* 484–487.

Zaino, J. (2012). *Core concepts in American government: What everyone should know.* Boston, MA: Pearson.

Zajonc, R. B., Adelmann, P. K., Murphy, S. T., & Niedenthal, P. M. (1987). Convergence in the physical appearance of spouses. *Motivation and Emotion, 11,* 335–346.

Zeanah, C. H., Smyke, A. T., Koga, S. F., & Carlson, E. (2005). Attachment in institutionalized and community children in Romania. *Child Development, 76,* 1015–1028.

Zebrowitz, L. A. (1997). *Reading faces: Window to the soul?* Boulder, CO: Westview Press.

Zebrowitz, L. A., Andreoletti, C., Collins, M. A., Lee, S. Y., & Blumenthal, J. (1998). Bright, bad, babyfaced boys: Appearance stereotypes do not always yield self-fulfilling prophecy effects. *Journal of Personality and Social Psychology, 75,* 1300–1320.

Zebrowitz, L. A., Collins, M. A., & Dutta, R. (1998). The relationship between appearance and personality across the life span. *Personality and Social Psychology Bulletin, 24,* 736–749.

Zebrowitz, L. A., Hall, J. A., Murphy, N. A., & Rhodes, G. (2002). Looking smart and looking good: Facial cues to intelligence and their origins. *Personality and Social Psychology Bulletin, 28,* 238–249.

Zebrowitz, L. A., & McDonald, S. M. (1991). The impact of litigants' baby-facedness and attractiveness on adjudications in small claims courts. *Law and Human Behavior, 15,* 603–623.

Zebrowitz, L. A., & Montepare, J. M. (2008). First impressions from facial appearance cues. In N. Ambady & J. J. Skowronski (Eds.), *First impressions* (pp. 171–204). New York: Guilford Press.

Zebrowitz, L. A., & Rhodes, G. (2004). Sensitivity to "bad genes" and the anomalous face overgeneralization effect: Cue validity, cue utilization, and accuracy in judging intelligence and health. *Journal of Nonverbal Behavior, 28,* 167–185.

Zebrowitz, L. A., Tenenbaum, D. R., & Goldstein, L. H. (1991). The impact of job applicants' facial maturity, gender, and academic achievement on hiring recommendations. *Journal of Applied Social Psychology, 21,* 525–548.

Zwaigenbaum, L., Bryson, S., Lord, C., Rogers, S., Carter, A., Carver, L., . . . Yirmiya, N. (2009). Clinical assessment and management of toddlers with suspected autism spectrum disorder: Insights from studies of high-risk infants. *Pediatrics, 123,* 1383–1391.

CREDITS

58   Photo courtesy of DePauw University Communications Office.

61   Figure from Carré, J. M., McCormick, C. M., & Mondloch, C. J., *Psychological Science*, (Vol. 20, Issue 10), pp. 1194–1198 copyright © 2009. Reprinted by permission of Sage Publications.

64   Photo by Amber Bowers Photography.

88   Photo by Larry Liggett, DePauw University.

95   Reprinted from *Evolution and Human Behavior*, Vol. 33, Issue 2, Kościński, D., Mere visual experience impacts preference for body shape: Evidence from male competitive swimmers, Pages No. 137–146, Copyright © 2012, with permission from Elsevier.

99   Reproduced with permission from Galia Slayen.

104   Photo by Larry Liggett, DePauw University.

108   Willie Mays: By *New York World–Telegram and the Sun* staff photographer William C. Greene, [public domain] via Wikimedia Commons.

108   Eddie Mathews: Permission to reprint granted by © Bettmann/CORBIS.

114   By Enrico Mazzanti (1852–1910), [public domain] via Wikimedia Commons.

131   Photo by Larry Liggett, DePauw University.

145   Reprinted from *NeuroImage*, Vol. 54, Issue 1, Rule, N. O., Moran, J. M., Freeman, J. B., Whitfield-Gabrieli, S., Gabrieli, J. D. E., & Ambady, N., Face value: Amygdala response reflects the validity of first impressions, Pages No. 734–741, Copyright © 2011, with permission from Elsevier.

157   By T. P. Pearson, Macomb, Illinois, [public domain] via Wikimedia Commons.

159   Alexander Gardner, [public domain] via Wikimedia Commons.

160   By National Park Service, [public domain] via Wikimedia Commons.

163   Figure from Todorov, A., Mandisodza, A. N., Goren, A., & Hall, C. C. (2005). Inferences of competence from faces predict election outcomes. *Science, 308,* 1623–1626. Reprinted by permission of the American Association for the Advancement of Science.

INDEX